Taylor ·

M000267148

Vol. 2 *The Keys*	1865	English Nobleman, John Francis Taylor, surrenders to the Lordship of Jesus Christ. Travels to the Orient.
	1866	John Francis Taylor marries Mary Elizabeth Van Zandt John Francis Taylor's young wife dies. Infant son adopted by sister – the Paul Wheaton family. Son takes the name of John Edward Wheaton.
Vol. 3 *The Crucible*		
	1868	John F. Taylor sets out to become a traveling preacher. Under threats and disillusionment, John flees to Europe to evangelize, settling in Portugal.
Vol. 4 *The Tent Maker*		John preaches, teaches and evangelizes while supporting himself as a tent maker and sail master. He becomes known as the *Tent Maker* among his friends and followers.

1878   John Taylor is commissioned by Queen Victoria as sail master and evangelist for a church-planting voyage to the Pacific.

1879   Missionary voyage sets sail for Pacific.

1880   John and crew arrive at the volcanic island (first visit).

1885   Island successfully evangelized.

1886   Arrives back in England. John F. Taylor is knighted by Queen Victoria for heroics and for the success of their mission.

1894   John Francis Taylor appointed as *Ambassador to the Philippines* as Sir John Francis Taylor.

1895   Sir John F. Taylor sets sail for the Philippines as Ambassador.

1896   Diplomatic trip diverted to New Guinea for a six-month stay.

1897   Ambassadorial entourage arrives at evangelized island for a second visit in great ceremony and friendship.

1898   John Paul "Papa" Wheaton born to John Edward Wheaton.

1901   John Edward Wheaton emigrates to the U.S. with his young family.

1902   Sir John (whose island name is "Monteau") marries Kalana. His second son, Paiyan, is born.

1910   Sir John dies by a shipwreck.

1912   After John's death, most Islanders begin a slow but steady falling away from the One True God, leaving a remnant of true believers who band together to remain strong.

1920   John Wheaton Jr. born—Papa Wheaton's firstborn son.

Continued on the back inside cover

His Story *as told by Grace Chloe Wheaton*

The Keys

for John Francis Taylor

END TIME HEROES LIVING FIRST CENTURY FAITH

By David E. McFadden

Publisher—About My Father's Business, Inc.
Interior formatting by David E. McFadden
(Interior renderings from public domain)
Cover Design by Wendy K. Walters / Palm Tree Productions
www.palmtreeproductions.net

ISBN-13: 978-0692338766
ISBN-10: 0692338764

Printed in the USA.

For more information:

www.DeeperLifeSeries.com

What Others Are Saying

"David E. McFadden has once again created a compelling read in this latest novel, *The Keys for John Francis Taylor*—an intertwining tale of crime, murder, mystery and romance. The story begins in Victorian-era England where John F. Taylor is transformed by God's amazing grace. Once an arrogant, self-absorbed aristocrat, John begins a new life guided by *the keys* of life. McFadden has knit together a cast of characters who experience God in their daily life as He brings them into relationship with Him. I eagerly await the next book in this series of chronicles."   —Diane Blose

---

"McFadden's novel, *The Keys,* is a well-written historical narrative with a delightfully interesting and suspenseful plot. Over the years, I have enjoyed David's scripturally accurate books and now welcome his latest dramatic novel. I was impressed with the care taken to feed us important Biblical truths as he entertains the reader. I am certain we will hear more from David McFadden." —Tom Hoskins

---

"*The Keys* eloquently weaves the story of young John Francis Taylor, whose life is relentlessly threatened while coming to Saving grace. His new life is transformed by a Love that captures his heart and brings a family together. As I read the book, my curiosity kept me riveted—anxious to see how the story will continue in the upcoming volume."   —*Betty Bostrom*

"*The Keys* is a historical perspective delicately woven with intrigue as David creatively guides the reader on a powerful journey of pursuit and mission.   —Pat Gerard

"I have read many historical novels and Christian-themed books, but I cannot recall a book that combines both history and a Christian love story intertwined in the same book as does *The Keys* by David McFadden. It was so interesting to see the progression of John Francis Taylor's life and the experiences that led to his acceptance of Christ. The characters were so believable to me, and the setting of Victorian era England is a timeframe that has always piqued my interest. Nineteenth century England was a time of great change as the Gospel was being spread to other cultures. The historical significance made by the different characters was very compelling to read and kept me wanting to know what would happen next. I look forward to the sequel to come out and to be able to see what else happens to these people I feel I know."   —Jackie Jones

---

"The test of any literary work's power lies in its ability to invade our random thoughts, pulling us into the author's fictional world as if it really exists. David McFadden's *The Keys* is indeed such a work, and after completing this novel, I have found myself thinking about his fictional characters as I might think about actual people. David's commitment to honor Christ and to create a compelling story shines beautifully in this exciting novel. I highly recommend *The Keys.*"
     —Rita Wisdom

"The Keys grabs your attention as scenes, set in nineteenth century England, quickly unfold in this historical chronicle. I now have a deeper appreciation for the price that previous generations have paid for the Gospel message. Because of these sacrifices, my generation can know the priceless truths of *the keys of the Kingdom of heaven."*
     —Terrie Bostrom

The
Keys

for John Francis Taylor

His Story as told by Grace Chloe Wheaton

End Time Heroes
Living First Century Faith

A Novel by

David E. McFadden

Acknowledgements

To my wife, Cathy, who inspires me
with her relentless pursuit of God.

To my friends and family, thank you. You have encouraged me in my efforts to glorify God through my writing.

Thanks to my reviewers many of who edited for me: Cathy McFadden, Tony Gentry, Barbara and Ashley Clawson, Mike Morris, Larry Angel, Veronica Guerriero, Jackie Jones, Joy Yeats, Jim Morrison, Diane Blose, Terrie and Betty Bostrom, Tom Hoskins, Rita Wisdom, Pat Gerard and Nicki Ziegler.

Matthew 16:19

*And I will give unto thee the keys
of the kingdom of heaven.* (NLT)

— **Jesus**

1865 London, England

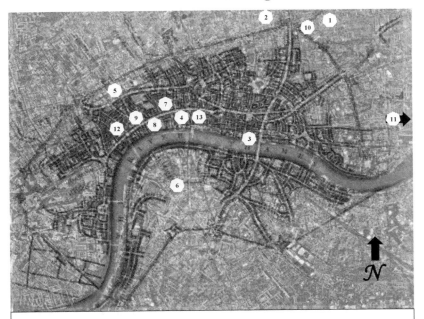

Legend

1) Riding Club and Stables
2) The Taylor Estate
3) China Tea's Moorings
4) Bank of England
5) The Van Zandt Home
6) Metropolitan Tabernacle
7) Mitre Restaurant
8) The Murray's Downtown Residence
9) The Van Zandt Printing Co.
10) Dr. Andrew Murray's Country Home and Office
11) Paul and Veronica Wheaton's Estate (off map)
12) De Beers Jewellery
13) Precinct Police Station

TABLE of CONTENTS

Historical Notes and Disclaimers
Preface
Introduction - Bridge from Volume One—*The Journals*

1. The Foxhunt
2. The Country Doctor
3. Wounded Ego
4. A Sad Farewell
5. Empire Lost
6. Fading Hopes
7. A Matter of Honor
8. Confidentiality and the Key
9. Arresting Suspicion
10. Pilfered
11. The Promise
12. Unanticipated Transformation
13. The Two Shall Become One.
14. One Sows and Another Reaps
15. Taking Care of Business
16. With God's Help
17. Unto the Least of These
18. Overwhelming Sense of Wellbeing
19. Casting a Broader Net
20. "Come and See…"
21. London's Finest
22. "Watering Others…"
23. The Pocket Watch
24. Victorian Courtship
25. The Cottage
26. The English Patient
27. What Must I Do?
28. See for Yourself
29. Sister Veronica
30. Web of Treachery
31. The Vigilante
32. Captivating Love
33. Mary's Answer
34. The Tentmaker
35. The Execution
36. Testing of God's Will
37. Ship Shape
38. Corroborating Testimony
39. Ports of Call
40. The Evangelist

Historical Notes and Disclaimer

In this story, all characters are fictional except for Charles Spurgeon and Dr. David Livingstone. The participation of these historical figures is based on actual events. The references to Charles Spurgeon are based upon research, and all quotes attributed to him are from his actual sermons. The references to Dr. David Livingstone are based on actual events. However, the quotes attributed to him are fictional, but are highly in line with how he felt, based upon research. Additionally, there are many factual notes of interest, such as sailing with the tides, the outlawing of duels, the introduction of Phenol as a wound dressing and Victorian standards for courtship. However, many of the other events and happenings are purely fictional.

PREFACE

They say that people's lives are often more interesting than fiction. I found this to be true while researching the incredible men and women who are my ancestors. All of us have heroes in our family tree. That is why I feel so blessed to bring John F. Taylor's story to you. The privilege of writing this narrative, as well as documenting his continuing legacy could very well be my life's work.

This volume reveals John's early years from 1865 to 1866 when his life takes a dramatic turn that eventually led him to discover Salvation in the Lord Jesus. It is here in this timeframe that we witness how God used events and circumstances to prepare John to meet Him. In the ensuing months and years of his life, it became evident that God was equipping John for an extraordinary life where he would be consumed for His purposes.

While researching this story, I literally felt as if I had stepped back into the pages of history to be there with my great-great grandfather. I was fascinated by how the details came together, as I unraveled my ancestors' historical past. I accomplished this connection by going through old newspaper articles, public records and two extensive diaries purchased at an estate sale. My father came across these remarkable diaries in post-war Europe while he was stationed there—a story I hope to tell at a later date.

An immensely detailed diary written by Ruth Murray provided much of the detail concerning John's life up to the time he boarded the ship. John's story aboard the *Anastasis* was taken from the ship's log, as well as from his own writings. John did not begin his daily journaling until his first visit to Cape Town S.A. Apparently, he bought a locally made journal and became inspired to start recording his life story.

His first journal entries were predated to corroborate much of what Ruth Murray had recorded plus his own personal perspectives, especially his more intimate encounters with Mary Van Zandt.

A note concerning the narrative: The language and spoken discourse during this time in history were formal and respectful in nature, especially in Victorian England. In telling this story, I have attempted to recreate this air of dignity.

This book begins with my flight home from New Guinea. To provide you with a backstory and context, I have used my personal journaling to form a bridge from the first volume, the story detailing the discovery of John F. Taylor's journals. The story in this volume tells how my great, great, grandfather began his new life in Christ. Please enjoy this remarkable account of God's goodness.

In His Service,
Grace Chloe Wheaton

Bridge from Volume One
The Journals
of John Francis Taylor

September 14, 1987 —As I leave New Guinea, the drone of the airplane engines is a comforting sound...it means that I am finally going home. My world has been turned upside down, but I know the dramatic shifts that my life has taken will ultimately determine my destiny. Finding my great-great- grandfather's journals in the interior jungles of New Guinea is beyond belief.

The days following Frank's murder were mind numbing. In the same tragic event, my great-uncle Paiyan and I sustained fairly serious injuries. These injuries landed me in the hospital in Port Moresby, three hundred miles away from the others. In our time of grieving, and before I left in the ambulance for the hospital, we all agreed to take our time with Frank's memorial, staying in New Guinea until it felt right to leave.

After I left the hospital in Port Moresby, which culminated in a three-day stay, I returned to Lae where Frank's body was being held in cold storage. Uncle Paiyan and Konii drove up from the valley village to pick me up, along with Frank's body.

One of the benefits that emerged from the delay of Frank's burial was that his parents were able to fly in from the States to be a part of his home-going celebration. This turned out to be a miraculous time of spiritual renewal for both of them.

Frank had left a carefully placed note in his personal journal where he kept his emergency information. He had penned a poignant message, telling of his life-changing encounter with God as a reminder to himself, as well as anyone who might need his critical information. With his parent's approval, we decided to engrave his headstone with this touching epitaph:

"His heart is in New Guinea
because his Lord led him here"

Concerning the others: Dad is on the plane, as well as Frank's parents. Uncle Paiyan has chosen to stay behind in New Guinea for an indefinite time. He has expressed a desire to join in with the hidden church that he discovered while searching for lost friends and family members. I am sure there will be more discoveries, possibly some that will help me unravel our common past.

Once stateside, I plan to take deliberate actions to order my life around writing the story of my family heritage. In His Service.— G.C.W.

September 18—It feels good to be back home in Seattle. The reception at the airport was wonderful and heartwarming, but truthfully, I was surprised how many people came to greet us. Once back at my dad's house, a dozen red roses arrived from Dr. Richard Hamas. His note was quite endearing. I have had time to think about our trip together and do hope I can see him again in a more personal setting.

September 21—In a complete surprise announcement, my dad informed me that when he was in the service, while stationed in England, he did extensive research into our ancestry. He promised to locate his collection of articles, notes and findings for me to use when I get started with writing the chronicle of our family heritage.

September 23—I found the perfect apartment today, one block from the library. This will allow me to do the extensive research that will be necessary to corroborate the journaling that g.g.gfather did. I think that by immersing myself in the times in which he lived will help me understand his story—sometimes the details will make the difference.

September 25—Just finished moving my old dorm room furniture, at least the pieces I wanted to bring with me. Looks a little sparse, but that's O.K. for now. Richard stopped by with a nice floral arrangement as a housewarming gift—he is quite the gentleman. I think I could get used to him.

September 26—Dad stopped by this morning with another surprise. In a meeting with the M.I. board of directors, an announcement was made that an anonymous donor wanted to purchase several Macintosh computers for the ministry, one of which was to be given to me for my writing project.

He brought it by, and we set it up in the guest bedroom. Things are falling into place...P.T.L.

October 1—This is the day I begin... my nest has been made. Dad brought several boxes over that were brimming with newspaper clippings, Xerox copies of public records, as well as two diaries he bought at an estate auction. He spent over two hours recounting how he became interested in tracing our ancestry while stationed in England after the war ended. His efforts to find out about John Edward Wheaton led to a split in our family tree. To his utter surprise and amazement, he discovered a poignant twist of fate that led him directly to John Francis Taylor instead of John Edward Wheaton. The intrigue has already begun with this mystery.

October 2—After dad left last evening, I re-read an obscure article that he was especially proud of finding in his search. A bulletin published by a prominent equestrian club detailed a riding mishap that occurred during a foxhunt. The rider was an aristocrat that was none other than John Francis Taylor. It looks like this will be the time-period where I will begin telling his story. This genesis seems fitting because the foxhunt is so iconic to the British culture.

— Grace Chloe Wheaton

Chapter One
The Foxhunt

English Countryside
Saturday, May 27, 1865

"Splendid jump, John," yelled Bradley as the two riders galloped beyond a too-narrow stone gate. John was forced to jump the low stone wall as Bradley stole the gate's center. Nevertheless, John took the advantage. His challenging jump placed him in a better position to take a sharp turn demanded by the howling hounds.

Bradley heeled his steed, lying low in the saddle, trying to catch John before the narrow lane turned toward a wooded area. As best friends and co-conspirators for fun and frivolity, the challenge of the foxhunt gave way to a more immediate competition. The hunt mystically shifted to a horse race and the matter of defeating a cohort's ego. Putting down the fox would have to wait.

As they reached the wood in a fiercely fought tie, the low hanging boughs began tearing at the reckless pair. One of the riders must relent or be ripped from his mount, lending the fox a momentary but unsure win. Bradley was taking the worst of the beatings, but it was John who took flight. Just at the last opportunity, and only ten yards from entering an open meadow. John brutally hit the ground.

Flipping backward, John first landed on his hands and knees. He then collapsed to a severe chest-pounding flop. His senses were overwhelmed as time stood still. The world began to throb around him as he remained face down, trying to recover from his blinding retracement. John fought to catch his breath as he struggled to push himself over onto his back to ease his labored breathing.

Having witnessed the spine-chilling episode, Bradley ruthlessly pulled back on his reins, risking injury to his horse. His charger revolted, standing on its hind legs, straining to meet Bradley's unexpected and callous command. Bradley made a breathtaking dismount, displaying his accomplished riding skills. Out of the saddle, he rode the stirrup the last ten yards, launching him at full stride toward his fallen friend. With fearful dread, Bradley carefully surveyed John, who now lay face up and motionless with his eyes closed.

After only the slightest few moments had passed, John smiled up at Bradley and quipped, "I kept my face up old chap... see... not a scratch. You know the ladies wouldn't appreciate me spoiling this handsome mug." Ignoring Bradley's offer to lend a hand, John jumped to his feet as further proof of his proud vanity.

Bradley was accustomed to John's often startling antics. He wondered if John's acrobatic dismount had been staged for comedic effect. Not yet certain, Bradley quipped his angst, "You could have been killed, you bloody fool!"

The ever jovial John was feeling pleased with his apparent recovery from his careless horsemanship when he suddenly paled and passed out. Bradley was completely caught off guard. He made a valiant effort to catch John as he fell, but missed him completely. John hit hard as he fell face first onto the fallow ground. *Unrealized by the mortal world, John's ghastly fall was a prophetically scripted metaphor.* John's sudden relapse jolted Bradley back to his former dread, ceding to momentary helplessness. This time, John's often-mused vanity would give way to sizable gashes on his chin and forehead.

> *This time, John's often mused vanity would give way to sizable gashes on his chin and forehead.*

If John was flawlessly good-looking, then Bradley was ruggedly handsome. He was six-foot-tall with wavy red hair and sported a ruddy freckled complexion that complemented his bold protruding chin. Bradley had been disciplined and hewn through cadet training at the military academy, but John was somewhat pampered and isolated from the cruelties that life can often mete out. Nannies, housekeepers, cooks and maids provided a shield of protection for John, sparing him the unpleasant necessity of having to grow up and face the realities of life. To this brash young aristocrat, embracing the pleasure of the moment was considered more of an entitlement than a privilege.

Once again, the barking hounds could be heard coming from the direction of the low creek bottom that cut its way through the adjacent pasture. Just a half furlong beyond the hedgerow, the ruckus was growing ever louder as the mounted hunters rode in the direction of the stranded and injured duo.

Adrenaline and alarm coursed through Bradley with a heart-pounding throb. With little calm, he remembered one thing from his military training: if at all possible, he should not move John from where he lay. Breaking through his panic, Bradley began to follow some heaven-sent inclinations, guiding him to help alleviate John's silent suffering.

The ever-approaching sound of squawking dogs prompted Bradley to move decisively. He quickly tied up the horses and then removed his riding jacket. He folded the red obligatory garment and placed it under John's head. He then made a mad dash toward the sound of advancing hoofs.

Riders are often involuntarily dismounted in the chase, which meant that Bradley's flailing arms would be routinely ignored. After all, it was a competition and the unfortunate fate of a contender should not betray the genuine needs of a worthy challenger.

It must have been Bradley's screams of desperation that halted the lone, wary straggler. Subconsciously, the "good

Samaritan" (Peter Mann) had already contemplated giving up the chase, so Bradley's cries for help offered him a redeeming cause. Even so, the sureness of the male ego would not allow Peter to reveal his lost heart. In an irritated scold, Peter demanded, "What's your problem, man? Can't you see I'm in the hunt?"

Bradley was breathless and speechless as he grabbed Peter's bootstraps—the still mounted rescuer. Bradley was intent on retaining him until he could catch his breath enough to speak. "John Taylor is down... he needs help. Ride to the stables and secure the wagon. Quick! Bring it man!" Before releasing Peter, Bradley pointed across the meadow to a grove of trees where the horses could scarcely be seen tied to the low hanging branches. Still short of breath, Bradley pleaded, "He's there... bring the wagon there... hurry and Godspeed!"

Peter found the riding club mostly deserted except for a few early casualties related to minor mishaps. Every foxhunt will have its share of halfhearted attempts, producing the usual broken strap or saddle, loose shoe, or in some cases, a desperate hangover from an untimely celebration.

Roger was the stable hand who saw Peter Mann approach at full gallop. You could ask anything of Roger, who possessed a calm temperament and known to be reliable and steady, but today he was caught off guard. "Roger, ready the wagon! John Taylor is injured. He's down at the wood where it opens into the north pasture. Get to it, man! Don't just stand there gaping!"

Still mounted, Peter Mann hurriedly galloped on to the stable area. He never stopped moving while making a running dismount, rushing to get blankets from the tack room near the stables. The wagon was comfortable when seated, but Peter knew that John would be lying prone and the cushioning of blankets would help prevent further injuries. By the time Peter returned, Roger had the wagon ready to go to John's rescue.

Peter and Roger hurried the wagon over the uneven field as they navigated out to the north pasture where Bradley kept watch over John. In what seemed to be a maddening rush, Peter and Bradley loaded John into the improvised ambulance, while Roger tied their two horses to the back of the wagon. Even with the cushioning of blankets, it would turn out to be a brutally jarring ride to the local parish doctor.

Chapter Two
The Country Doctor

Dr. Andrew Murray was the parish physician who lived roughly a one-half mile down the lane from the riding club. Dr. Murray was considered a "country doctor," an unfortunate and somewhat demeaning class distinction. The aristocratic elite, as well as any wealthy city dweller, would often shun a country doctor no matter his qualifications. Seeking the advice of a country doctor or, God forbid, being in his care might place one's social status at risk. Social standing was very important, and for some, maintaining it was often a full-time enterprise. Even so, John was in trouble and such distinctions seemed unimportant, at least for the moment.

Anyone can be humbled when faced with a cruel illness even the prideful upper class—hypocrisy will always have its day. Stripped of vanity, a well-heeled patient might discreetly seek out a country doctor of exceptional talent. And so it was with Dr. Andrew Murray. This amiable and talented doctor often received cloaked after-hours visitors at his back door. He was known as a highly skilled country doctor who possessed a favorable bedside manner often found lacking in a city doctor.

Roger, who cared little for such social peculiarities, drove the horses while Bradley rode with John in the rear of the wagon. Peter galloped ahead on horseback to alert the doctor of John's arrival.

The trio of men carefully carried the young injured nobleman through the back door of Dr. Murray's unpretentious home and office. The rear entrance opened to a large multi-purpose exam room where he often received critically ill patients.

Once inside, it was easy to see that there was more to Dr. Murray than a casual observer would have thought. A look around the large but congested "emergency room" revealed a fully functioning laboratory where examinations and surgical procedures were routinely performed. On one side of the room, there was an awe-inspiring wall of books and journals, suggesting a lifetime of study. Unknown to most, Dr. Murray's own research could be referenced in several of the published medical journals in his library. The opposite side of the room revealed a large glass-enclosed armoire fully stocked with bottles and tins containing formularies, elixirs, medicines, tonics, compounds, as well as various remedies. The doctor even possessed a foot-peddle lathe that would allow him to fashion a wooden arm or leg when needed.

Bradley and Peter hoisted John, still wrapped in horse blankets, onto Dr. Murray's handcrafted operating table. While Bradley explained John's calamity to Dr. Murray, Roger went about preparing to stall John's horse in Dr. Murray's stable.

Bradley noticed Roger readying the horse. "Roger, would you please stall my horse as well? I'm going to stay to help the doctor." After complying with Bradley's request, Roger returned with Peter Mann to the riding club.

Unfortunately, John had not received the benefit of any attempt at first aid in the hour since the accident. By now, the blood had dried, creating a mask on his face and neck. He looked as if he could be dead, only defying the need for a morgue by an occasional moan or jerk. In addition, most regrettable to John's vanity, the gashes on his face had swollen, transforming them into puffy gaping wounds.

Dr. Murray immediately began the difficult task of restoring a broken life. Even though he could see that John's nose was broken, his cuts needed to be cleaned and sutured first. With great care, Dr. Murray expertly crafted fifty-three extra-fine stitches that any good city doctor would certainly require for the handsome face of an aristocrat.

After putting in many hours of tedious work, Dr. Murray accomplished the most critical tasks by late evening. Beyond the lacerations, bruises and four broken ribs, his examination left him troubled. He felt strongly that John was suffering the effects of a bruised heart muscle. John's chest-pounding fall from his horse fractured his ribcage, which allowed the crushing blow to his heart.

With John's immediate wounds assessed and treated, the doctor needed to move him to a more comfortable bed in the adjacent room. Dr. Murray used smelling salts to partially revive him, hoping to coax John into at least a small amount of self-mobility. John was very feeble, but with Bradley's help, the three men made it to the next room. Once John began sleeping peacefully, Bradley took the opportunity to end his late-night vigil.

Alone with John, Dr. Murray spent the remainder of the night preparing and constructing a body cast for John's midsection. As the doctor worked through the night, he would take breaks to look through his medical journals, hoping to confirm his earlier diagnosis for John's irregular heartbeat. After considerable thought and research, Dr. Murray concluded that he was right about John's bruised heart. With deepening concern, it was now clear that John's multiple injuries would need a minimum of several days of intense care.

John awoke early Sunday morning with a heart-wrenching ache accompanied by throbbing pain in his midsection. The unfamiliar surroundings could only hold his blurry attention for so long before he called out in agony. "Help me, *please...* do something for this bloody ache."

> *"Help me, please... do something for this bloody ache."*

To ease the pain, Dr. Murray's limited choices included putting John back under with chloroform or to administer morphine. After careful consideration, he concluded that with a bruised heart muscle, either therapy might cause his heart to stop beating. To be safe, Dr. Murray decided to treat John's pain with a more primitive therapy—evenly spaced doses of whiskey. As the hours wore on, the severity of John's injuries became more evident, fitting the body cast would have to wait for another day.

Thursday marked John's fifth day under Dr. Murray's care. John was now fitted with a body cast and able to walk with limited mobility. Since the accident, he had been too incoherent for conversation beyond the typical patient-doctor talk, but today would be different. Dr. Murray had several matters he needed to discuss that were certain to affect John's future. Dr. Murray had spent the last several days rehearsing how he would broach the difficult topics. Little did John know that the privileged life he had always known was in the throes of drastic change.

It was late morning and both men were seated at the small kitchen table. Dr. Murray began his reluctant discourse with small talk. "John, I think you're ready to leave provided that you will go easy. Even so, ole chap, you'll need to come see me next week so I can check your progress."

John replied in a rather arrogant high-minded way. "Dr. Murray, I will bother you no further, as I will continue my rehabilitation with Dr. Weathersby Hodgins, my in-town physician." Not entirely appreciating how Dr. Murray had cared for him day and night for the past week, he continued with a somewhat haughty tone. "Doctor, you've taken good care of me, and of course, I'll reward you handsomely. Even so, my family doctor will be most available to look after me."

Dr. Murray was disheartened. His unease was not because of John's arrogance, or his unwillingness to return. His sadness was for having to broach unwanted news. "John… your family is bankrupt. You—"

John rudely interrupted Dr. Murray with a brash rebuke while feebly attempting to stand. "How dare you, sir!" His emotional outburst caused severe pain, preventing him from standing erect. After struggling to upright himself, he paused to take several deep breaths. Still angered, he hobbled over to retrieve his hat and coat from the ornate coat rack by the back door; the same door he entered only days earlier while in grave distress.

Dr. Murray tried to remain calm as he spoke to John, who had his back to the doctor. "Your mum has been seeing me for months. Her in-town doctor turned her away because she was behind in her account with him. She couldn't continue to pay his high fees."

John was unaware that his mother was sick and seeing a doctor. In a contemptuous and immature response, John partially turned as he blurted out, "For what reason could my mum possibly need to see you? You're nothing more than a country doctor."

Dr. Murray was expecting John's thoughtless response, but his tactless demeanor was tiring. Growing weary of John's complete lack of respect, the doctor lashed out. "My god, man, are you the only one you care about? Don't you know your mum is dying? You must be the only person in London who doesn't care enough to know!"

John had been living in a charmed world, replete with selfish arrogance and vanity. The last few years he rarely bothered to show any genuine interest in the welfare of his mother, or the affairs of his late father.

As if to avoid facing the truth, John continued staring into the hat rack with his back to the doctor. His mind was trying to process the information about his mother, as well as face his own dilemma of being extremely self-absorbed. After several long moments, he slowly turned to face Dr. Murray. In a somber and more humbled tone, John asked, "What's wrong with my mum?"

"I'm sorry that I had to be the one to tell you. I was hoping you already knew. Your mum has been suffering from the symptoms of a bad heart for years—she just never let on to anyone. About a year ago, she had a mild heart attack, fortunately with little noticeable damage to her health. Even so, she has been getting weaker by the month. John, she won't last much longer. You should go to her."

John's world was in turmoil and seemed to be crumbling around him, as he grasped the harsh realities confronting him. He felt an odd crush on his emotions, something that was quite unfamiliar to his living-large persona. Broken in body and spirit, he was blindsided with regret for his arrogant attitude and disrespect toward Dr. Murray. With genuine brokenness apparent in his words, he lamented, "Dr. Murray, please forgive me for the way I have spoken to you. You saved my life, and in return for your compassion, I have treated you badly. How can I make it up to you?"

Dr. Murray was duly impressed by John's remorseful bearing. "John, go to your mum and spend as much time with her as possible. I'm confident the two of you will have much to talk about. This may be your last chance to make things right with her. Come see me next Thursday so I can check on your progress. We can talk then about how to settle your debts with me. I may even have a way that you can work off what you owe."

The term "work" was a foreign word for John, and he took the sound of it with an inward grimace. "Dr. Murray, thanks for your help. I will make arrangements to see that you are paid everything owed to you."

Dr. Murray possessed an insightfulness that John did not. With compassionate understanding, the fatherly doctor offered, "Just the same, John, I want you here on Thursday."

Chapter Three
Wounded Ego

Dr. Murray kept John steady as they walked out to the stable to saddle his horse. With the doctor's help, he was on his way home. However, it was not long before John was suffering severe pain. He decided that he must return to the riding club and rent a carriage for the week. Riding in a carriage would be much more comfortable, and he could board his horse until he could return it.

Roger was out in the corral working a horse when John rode up to the fence rail. "John, you look awful. Are you going to be all right?"

The relentless pain had left John with little capacity to be civil, much less for small talk. John bluntly responded, "Roger, I need to rent a carriage for a week. Get it ready for me."

In a matter-of-fact way Roger countered, "Yeah, but you'll need to pay up front—Mr. Jenkins says so."

In the deepest level of his intellect, John had refused Dr. Murray's warning about being bankrupt. It's not that he was in denial—he couldn't be because he had not chosen to process the thought of being penniless. With an equal measure of pain and arrogance, John loudly retorted, "Good lord, man, who do you think you are speaking to? Now get on with it. Can't you see I'm in pain?"

Roger was a little wide-eyed, being caught in the middle of an apparent standoff. Taking steps backward, to distance himself from John's scolding, Roger stammered. "I'll get Mr. Jenkins.... You can talk to him."

Mr. Jenkins was a country gentleman with a solid, no-nonsense approach to his business. He would never allow himself to be intimidated by a young aristocrat intent on throwing his weight around.

John managed to dismount his horse, but was pale-faced from his efforts, holding on to the stirrup to keep from falling. As Mr. Jenkins approached John, he was about to give him a lecture on finances when he realized John was ready to pass out. Instead, he offered to help John into the office to discuss his dilemma.

With a more measured level of disdain for John's reckless arrogance, Mr. Jenkins explained, "John, your mum has only paid a small pittance toward the family debt this year. There is too much owed for me to extend any more credit... sorry lad. Perhaps when you are well, you might consider working here at the riding club. You could pay off what you owe."

There was that phrase again: *work off what you owe.* It had such an awful sound, possessing a gritty, woefully mocking tone that was seemingly laced with ridicule. John was just beginning to consider his predicament, but it wasn't helping his situation. Once again, John was being forced into a humble state of mind. "Can we find a way to do business with the carriage rental? I'll do my best to see that the family account is paid."

Mr. Jenkins could sense John's sincerity, as well as his legitimate need for the carriage. "John, here's what I'll do. If you will promise me that you are earnest about taking care of your obligations, then I think we can do business."

John relented, "Sir, you have my word."

As John slowly stood to leave, Mr. Jenkins added, "Oh, John, I'll need for you to leave your pocket watch with me, as collateral, until you come back."

In all of John's life, he had never had to endure this kind of humiliation. If his circumstances weren't so dire, he would have not taken Mr. Jenkins' demand without a surly protest.

Roger readied the carriage, and just as John slowly climbed in, Bradley rode into the stable-yard at full gallop. Seeing Bradley caused John's confidence to soar, as if redemption was at hand. With Bradley's apparent kindred spirit to back him, John could feel life flowing into his depressed state. It would be short-lived, as Bradley's miraculous arrival was not meant to rescue John's wounded pride. It was far more serious. "John, you need to come right away. It's your mum!"

John was dismayed by Bradley's urgent message. How could his world change so drastically in the span of a week? Even now, John's first thoughts were about himself and his own plight. He struggled to compose himself and emerge from his self-pity to ask about his mother, "What is it, Bradley? What's happening with my mum?"

Bradley jumped from his horse and tied the reins to the rear of the carriage. "Hang on, John, we need to be on our way." With those words, Bradley whipped the carriage around and sped off down the lane toward the Taylor estate. John was mercilessly tossed about as he hung on for his life.

Bradley tried to speak loud enough to be heard over the sound of hooves and rattles from the protesting carriage. "Your mum's sick. John, she has had another heart attack. The doctor doesn't think she's going to make it much longer. She's been asking to see you." In the midst of his present trauma and tumult, John was wondering if he would make it much longer either. The rented carriage pulled up to the massive Taylor estate just as John was on the verge of passing out.

Chapter Four

A Sad Farewell

It should have been beyond anyone's capabilities to climb the massive staircase in John's condition. Bradley did the best he could to help John negotiate the steps so he could reach his mother's bedside. It was just as Bradley explained; Madeline

Taylor was indeed in her final hours. Even so, she was invigorated to see her son as she reached out to him.

As John approached her bed, the contents of his mother's heart could not be constrained, as tears of joy moistened her cheeks. Even in her gladness, she began to softly speak of her regrets. Her unfortunate secrets had taken their toll, carrying the weight had been unbearable.

In most ways, only known to a mother's heart, Madeline had endeavored to protect John from the harshness of life. "John, I'm so sorry for leaving you with such a mess." John tried to interrupt her, but she shushed him and then continued. "When your father died, I felt that Romney would run the business fairly and equitably—I wanted to trust him. When I found out differently, it was too late. It seemed as if we owed everybody with no chance of recovery. John, even our estate and grounds don't belong to the family any longer. As a favor to your father, the new owners are allowing me to die here peacefully."

John's mother beckoned him to come close as she continued, "John, I have stashed away enough money to get you by for a while, if you live meagerly and make it last. The money is in a lockbox at the bank." She paused to define her words, "My dear son, listen carefully because I have placed stipulations on the money. Promise me you'll abide by my request in dealing with the money that I have left you."

Although Bradley was not within hearing range of John's soft-spoken conversation with his mother, John felt he needed to be alone with her. With a measure of embarrassment, John pleaded to Bradley, "My dearest friend, could you find it in your heart to leave us for a few minutes?"

Deeply unsettled and with mixed emotions, John returned to his mother's bedside to continue their troubling conversation. Under normal or proper circumstances, the final moments with one's mother should be a time for heartfelt sentiments and expressed love. Nevertheless, the family's state of affairs weren't normal or proper, so he had no choice but to bend with them or be broken by them. Minute by minute, John's resolve was being forced to grow from selfish immaturity to a more manly conviction. He reached deep within to assure his mother of her dying wishes. "Mum, I'll do as you say."

"John, listen very carefully; this is of utmost importance. The sale of our property has helped with some of our personal debts. However, you must seek out those who have not been paid and settle the remaining family obligations. You must restore our good name at all costs. I know it may take time, but promise me you will eventually do it."

Madeline Taylor's grave and austere words were ripping at her son's spoiled nature. As she spoke, John was envisioning himself being thrown from a pinnacle of social standing to the lowest realms of servitude and pittance. He was being humbled to a level he would never have dreamed possible, or dared to imagine. With moistened eyes that displayed a broken heart and a hijacked will, John assured his mother that he would clear the family name. "Yes, mum, even if it takes me the rest of my life, I will make it right with those who trusted us."

The relief to John's mother was tangible—she was actually breathing easier from the apparent sincerity of John's affirmation. After pausing for several minutes, she continued with the most difficult part of her instructions to John. "Take half of the money that you will find in the lockbox and give the staff their back pay, plus a small severance. I will not allow them to be hurt in all of this. They trusted me completely, and I will not let their confidence be in vain. Will you do this John?"

> *John was reeling from the implications of his mother's final requests.*

John was reeling from the implications of his mother's final requests. Questions were flooding his mind. What did all of these things mean?... meagerly living?... give half away?... pay the family debts? John felt as if any future he may have had was being taken away. Reaching beyond himself, he gathered enough composure to submit to his mother's wishes. "Yes, mum, I will do as you have requested."

Silence filled the room as Madeline rested and John contemplated. She lay exhausted from the emotions she had expended over the last half hour of instructing her son. There had been much on Madeline's mind, and being able to spend her last hours with John gave her a measure of relief that soothed her soul.

After a long respite, John's mother resumed her instructions, centering on her husband's business partner. "John, I made Romney promise to give you a position with the company. He assured me that he would provide you with a good job… but you must do well. I do not expect him to give you charity." In all of John's sheltered life, he had never agreed to bear such forceful expectations of responsibility. Furthermore, he had not been raised to be dependent on another person, or to receive charity from anyone.

Looking straight into John's eyes, wanting to emphasize her last yet most important charge, she said, "Romney has the key to the lockbox with money in it. When you see him, ask for the key to the lockbox."

With her anxious burdens released, John's mother seemed much better. Her countenance was calm, displaying genuine peace, freed from the cares that had almost swallowed her up. As she dozed in and out of sleep, John sat at her side, lingering in thought about what life held for him, especially as he contemplated all the instructions given to him over the last hour.

Madeline Taylor seemed to be much better as she began to sleep rather soundly and peacefully. Her health appeared returned to her even if it was for the moment. With her condition stabilized, John decided he could leave her for a few minutes to check on Bradley. When John rose to leave her bedside, Madeline spoke to him. In an eerie sort of way she said, *"John, you must get the key from Romney, your future depends on it."*

John froze in his steps when he realized that his mother was not awake, but speaking to him from her sleep. Her message to him seemed paramount, but it was *how* she spoke to him that sent a chill up his spine. It was definitely time to seriously consider what his mother had spoken to him about the lockbox, as well as the promises he made to her.

There wasn't anything that could be done to forestall Madeline's fate. Her heart was simply weak and getting weaker by the hour. As the next few days wore on, family and friends would indeed have their heartfelt moments with Madeline Taylor. Then in bittersweet finality, she slipped from this world to the next, ending a once noble dynasty.

Chapter Five

Empire Lost

The China Tea Trading Company was one of London's largest seagoing shipping lines to the Orient. John Wilson Taylor (J. W.) and partner Romney Longfellow had built the shipping line from a few retired frigates to a fleet of thirteen schooners and seventeen fast clipper ships. Their troubles began several years earlier when the shipping industry began shifting and drifting toward the relatively new steamer ships. China Tea's clippers could outrun and outdistance a steamship on any given day. Even so, the steamship was slowly proving to be a reliable alternative, especially with their more predictable schedules. Rather than bend and adapt to modern times, the two partners held out too long and began to lose some of their exclusive contracts with valuable customers.

The company was still a bustling enterprise. Even so, the profit margins were slowly falling. Gross "shipped" tonnage had slipped over the last few years, but the real damage was from being unable to increase tonnage rates to offset increased expenses. Eventually, razor-thin margins began to make it difficult to make payroll and to pay bank notes. Romney was the cunning partner who would often bend the rules and rationalize decisions made with shades of grey. When all else failed, he began altering the bookkeeping entries to satisfy the banks, enabling him to borrow more money. Keeping ahead of the bank auditors became a full-time job for Romney.

With net profits slowly yet steadily headed down, both J. W. and Romney began taking a hit to their personal incomes as well. As a direct result, their private debts began to escalate. Fearing the loss of prestige and status, the two partners unduly used funds to prop up their social standing. From a bank examiner's point of view, their actions would certainly border on embezzlement.

One year after the indiscretions began, evidence of financial turmoil was becoming evident to those who were connected with the company. That was when the unthinkable happened. Under a cloud of suspicion, John W. Taylor was involved in an unfortunate accident that claimed his life. He was in charge of the operational end of the shipping line and was on the dock overseeing the loading of a shipment when he was killed. The crane was extending a netted load when the net broke and spilled its massive contents. The wooden crates exploded on impact with the pier, sending wooden spears of shrapnel out in all directions. J. W. was impaled in the chest by a large flying sliver of wood, killing him instantly.

J. W. Taylor was well-loved and respected even among the rough and tumble, often rowdy, dockworkers and ship's crew, making the loss a shock to everyone. J.W. was a man's man and well connected with his employees, so it was not surprising that several loyal employees sought reprisal for his death. According to some of the workers, the nature of the torn netting was suspicious, so behind the scenes, the loading crew was thoroughly questioned to find out if the falling cargo was truly an accident.

In nineteenth century fashion, the loyal and overzealous dockhands carried out several secret and often brutal interrogations. The crane operator, as well as several of the men responsible for netting the cargo, bore black eyes and bruises that resulted from the "intense" questioning.

In the end, all fingers seemed to point to one worker who appeared to have been solely responsible for the mishap. Whether he was a pawn, a conspirator or just negligent will never be known. He was never seen again after his impromptu vigilante trial.

John Wilson Taylor's funeral was a regional affair. Hundreds of people who knew and loved him for his personage, as well as a genuine appreciation for his life, came desiring to pay tribute. The many spoken accolades attributed to him were well deserved.

As a standard business practice, the Bank of England necessitated that China Tea Trading Company's charter require life insurance policies on John Wilson Taylor and Romney Longfellow, as principals. Any business partnership is doomed without the financial underpinning provided by an insured partner. The premise was that if either partner were to die, then the insurance proceeds would help assuage the loss, thereby helping to ensure the survival of the company. Standard terms of the policy expressly forbade diverting a cash settlement for any other purpose.

The insurance company questioned John W. Taylor's accidental death. That was because China Tea's leveraged debt would give "probable cause" for homicide. Fortunately, for Romney, the real debt picture was never revealed. John Taylor's reputation was above reproach, so the dual accounting practices by Romney were never suspected.

Even so, the insurance investigation was a long drawn out affair, forcing Romney to liquidate assets in an effort to salvage the troubled shipping company. By the time the intervening scrutiny was completed, he had sold off thirteen ships. Most transactions were settled at fire-sale prices, often netting only a few hundred pounds sterling after completing each sale. To his credit, Romney deftly managed to retain the most profitable ships, crews and routes. China Tea's bottom line actually got a boost in its overall operating margins by eliminating the assets that were least profitable.

With China Tea's finances stabilized, Romney was able to allocate a small amount of funds to help J. W. Taylor's widow, Madeline. Romney gave her enough money to maintain her household and estate at a minimum level. Even so, her debts continued until she learned how to reduce her expenditures.

In Madeline Taylor's defense, much of the family's financial misfortune was beyond her control. She had to balance the wishes of her husband with the resources given to her. She was responsible for high society events and the sizable staff needed to carry on the massive estate.

> *That is when she decided to start hiding cash to insure against some future financial devastation.*

For many years, the opulent lifestyle fostered by the family's shipping empire secured the Taylors high society standing among the aristocratic and social elite. For Madeline, money had never been a concern until about three years earlier. Then one day, things began to change for the worse. J.W. complained about the cost of an overly extravagant social event. After that, she started to pick up regular hints that things were not as they should be with China Tea. That is when she decided to start hiding money to insure against some future financial devastation.

In the households of nineteenth-century Victorian England, business decisions or company matters were rarely discussed between husband and wife, so Madeline was not fully aware of her husband's declining business. Even so, her intuition prevailed and she began to secretly put away cash. Early on, the hidden money was not missed because it was only a small percentage of the household income. However, after J.W.'s death, it became a sacrifice to stash money away, often letting accounts go delinquent.

In a moment of introspection, Madeline realized that her late husband's miscue with a single business decision, eventually led to the current financial predicament. With newfound clarity, she reached deep within, resolving to make everything right with those who had trusted her and her husband. Madeline Taylor's dying wish was to redeem the family honor, and she would. Once she envisioned how she would do it, she was able to forgive herself. She also realized that she had given her best effort, and that is all anyone could have asked.

Unfortunately, Romney was a financial expert and quickly deduced that Madeline was not spending all the money she was receiving from him. With those suspicions on his mind, the always cash-strapped Romney began to probe into Madeline's spending habits. After a minimum amount of investigation, he uncovered Madeline's confidential plans to secure her future financial survival. With complete self-interest in mind, Romney continued to give her an allowance, which allowed her to continue her practice of hoarding money.

In finality of his deceitfulness, he simply took the secretly stashed money upon her death. To cover his tracks, Romney paid a bank employee to expunge the records pertaining to Madeline Taylor's safe deposit box. When he took the money, he also rifled through the other contents of her lockbox, taking an heirloom jeweled brooch and a pearl necklace, while leaving a few less valuable pieces of jewelry. Equally important, he took a small personal passbook that supported the dated entries of accumulated cash. Romney had descended into the realm of blind duplicity. Morally bankrupt, he assured himself that he was not wrong in what he did, as he left the few other valuables intact.

Madeline Taylor's funeral was a subdued affair. The lack of reverence given her was seen as most inequitable to anyone who had knowledge of her, and the overall circumstances surrounding the end of her life. Sadly, because of the unmanageable financial debacle left to her, she carried most of the blame for ending a once noble estate. Of course, the era in which she lived contributed to the hushed restraint that, to some, vilified her. Nonetheless, it was shamefully obvious how prideful social status prevented her from being properly acknowledged for the valiant person she was.

Chapter Six

Fading Hopes

In the incredibly short span of ten days since his riding accident, the younger John Taylor had endured overwhelming heartbreak, demoralizing financial ruin and a devastating crush to his ingrained prideful nature. In the wake of these realities, John was soon to be homeless and poor as he called the house staff and grounds keepers to a lunchtime meeting. Slowly, the employees gathered in the large Victorian era estate kitchen, the one place they regularly congregated at meal times.

Still very much bruised and somewhat frail, John addressed the staff with waning confidence and a saddened heart. "I want to thank you for your loyalty and trust displayed during my mum's illness. Mum was quite passionate with her appreciation for your faithful service." John hesitated as he changed the subject. "What I have to say may seem disappointing news for many of you." Speaking the words aloud for the first time caused a shuddering pause, not meant for its effect. Looking down in embarrassment, John gathered his thoughts. "Unknown to me, my mum has lost the estate to debtors." There was a sudden gasp by several of the workers who fully intended to remain on as employees. With his fragile emotions barely under control, John continued, "My mum's dying wish was to see that each of you receive what is owed to you and that no one would be harmed by these unfortunate events that will affect us all."

The tension among the crowd was palpable. One of the yardmen quipped, "That's easy for you to say. You'll go on livin' the high life."

John didn't feel like defending himself. It wouldn't solve anything to argue and plead for sympathy. John raised his hands to try to quiet the rumble of talk and whispers spoken beneath audible hearing. "It may not be as grave as you think. Mum has left a small amount of money to pay the wages owed to you, as well as a small severance for those who desire it. Hopefully, the extra money will get you through until you can find other employment."

The crowd exploded with questions, but with nothing left to say, John held his hands up for the last time. "I will go to the bank tomorrow and retrieve the funds. I do not know how much money there will be. Mum simply asked that I be fair with you for your loyalty, as well as the trust you placed in her. I know nothing more. I have no answers to your questions. I'm sorry. I will see you here, this time, tomorrow."

John rose early on Tuesday morning to a new chapter in his life. He was taking upon himself the concerns of others. His new responsibilities were almost overwhelming, but somehow he felt up to the challenge.

Before going to the bank to retrieve the money that his mother had so fortuitously put away, his first order of business was to meet with Romney Longfellow. He held the all-important key that would give him access to the safety deposit box where the money was being secretly and safely held. At some point during his meeting, John also wanted to broach the subject concerning the job Romney held for him—a very important part of his immediate future.

John was curious to learn about his promised position with China Tea. He had never been employed before, so it was hard to imagine what it would be like. His thoughts were a little naïve, so in a humorous sort of way, he allowed his imagination to run away with him. He envisioned being a supervisor over the office staff or possibly the manager in charge of procuring supplies. Better yet, he could see himself calling on important clients, which would help him retain some vestige of social status. John was especially intrigued by the possibilities of his last musings—it was the best fit. Good employment, as he imagined, would allow him a better opportunity to fulfill his mother's dying requests.

Suddenly things didn't seem so harsh. He imagined that he could eventually rise again by becoming his own man. With his challenges framed in a more respectable manner, he came to a profoundly mature thought that was completely contrary to whom he *had* been a few days earlier. He mused that a meaningful place in society *should be earned* and not just handed over to an undeserving young man. As insightful as his revelations were, understanding the dramatic shifts taking place in his life were still beyond his grasp.

The China Tea's headquarters were housed in a large glass enclosed tower that oversaw all the dockside operations that were being conducted below. John slowly and arduously climbed the three-story set of stairs that rose above the loading dock. Still in an optimistic mood, each step that John took toward the top struck a symbolic chord, adding inspiration to the moment. As he climbed, his vantage point provided an ever-widening view of the earth's horizon, offering an unexpected sense of well-being. John was being stirred to think big—his personal horizons were expanding as well.

The massive exterior staircase ended just beneath the lighthouse-inspired tower where an entrance to China Tea's offices were located. As John ended his slow climb, he stood on an oversized landing just outside the main office door. He paused a moment to catch his breath, and then guardedly entered the small somewhat austere reception area that one would expect to find in the rough-and-tumble shipping industry.

It was John's implicit understanding that he had no known legal, or obligatory connection to the China Tea Trading Company, so at 8:00 a.m. sharp, he approached the receptionist desk with hat in hand, literally, as well as figuratively. For the moment, John's future was in Romney's hands. Not only did he possess the lockbox key, but he had also promised Madeline Taylor that he would give John a position in the company. With a newly discovered sense of humility, John stood before the receptionist's desk. "I'm here to see Romney Longfellow. Is he in?"

The secretary peered over her spectacles without fully engaging the inquiring visitor. "We're not hiring, young man."

John was being jolted once again by the quickly emerging realities associated with his new life, experiencing a world foreign to his former sensibilities. Is this how the rest of the world lives—at the end of a sharp tongue? Three weeks earlier, he could have had this woman fired with only a word—or could he? His last thought sunk in deep when he realized that he had been living a lie for who-knows-how-long. John subdued his private musings to respond in a civil manner, "My meeting with Mr. Longfellow involves a personal matter. He'll be expecting me."

The secretary was doubtful. She wasn't aware of a scheduled meeting. "He's with someone right now. Sit over there while I check with him and discuss his schedule."

John was happy for her accommodation, so he agreed to wait. He took a seat on a dusty wooden bench and rehearsed what he might say to Mr. Longfellow.

Romney's secretary was intensely protective of her boss. She knew it was a lie when she relayed Romney's message to John. "Mr. Longfellow doesn't recall agreeing to meet with you. He is with someone; however, he said he might be able to briefly see you after his meeting."

Hour after hour went by and as the morning dragged on, John still remained hopeful that he could make his two appointments in time for his noon hour meeting with the estate workers.

Romney Longfellow never had much to do with the young John Taylor, and why should he? John had been nothing more than the spoiled and selfish son of an aristocrat. Even so, deep in the recesses of his mind, Romney knew this day of reckoning would come. He would have to answer for the more than fifteen-hundred pounds sterling that he stole from his partner's widow. Romney knew that today was not the time he could right his wrongs. Sure, the company had had a few bright moments over the last several months, but overall China Tea Trading Company was barely paying the bills.

Not seeing himself as an evil man, Romney just wasn't overly sympathetic to what he saw as a lost cause. His callousness bore the truth. He had been in survival mode for so long that he was numb to the mores of right and wrong. The lines had been blurred long ago. The sad truth is that someday Romney would have to give an account for the many people he had similarly wronged.

The charade that Romney perpetrated on Madeline Taylor was one of his worst moments, giving with one hand and then taking it back with the other in shameless deceit. In the moment of his indiscretion, he justified his duplicity just as we all have done at some point in time. To his way of thinking, he figured that he was only obligated to keep her from starving. When he discovered she was stashing much of the money he had given to her, he felt like it must be extra that she didn't need. Romney had no understanding of Madeline's need to provide for her future. She knew that she could not survive in a man's world without her husband to provide for her.

> Madeline knew that she could not survive in a man's world without her husband to provide for her.

Romney skipped the formal routine of having his secretary escort his guest into his office. At eleven thirty, he opened his office door and coldly beckoned John to come in. "John, I only have a few minutes. What do you want?" His brash demeanor was even more boorish than normal, proving his unconscious need to cover his guilt.

"Sir, I'm here on behalf of my mum's estate—"

John was cut off before he could finish his first sentence. "Look, John, I have no obligations to you, your mum or her estate. What's done is done. I'm sorry for the position you're in, but I can't help."

John was shocked at Romney's callous attitude toward him. The truth is that John was experiencing the irritation that others had always felt toward him, but were never in a position to voice. In a rather bold and desperate attempt, John raised the ante. "Mr. Longfellow, we have business to conduct and you know it. I will not be brushed off, especially with such an uncivil rebuke."

Romney furled his brow as he studied John for a few moments. It suddenly occurred to him that John looked completely different. John's still-bruised face bore the unhealed scars of his terrible accident, wiping away his once prideful arrogance. Without speaking, as if gathering his thoughts, Romney turned to look out the wall of windows that overlooked the pier.

With a grumbling gasp, Romney lurched toward the window to get a better look at what he thought he was witnessing. There was a full-blown riot in progress. As Romney bolted for the door, he yelled in John's direction. "John, be here at 8:00 a.m. tomorrow, and we'll have our talk."

In desperation, John cried out, "Mr. Longfellow! Wait!" John's shout only slowed Romney for a moment. "Not now, dammit! What's going on down there is more important. Come back tomorrow."

As Romney quickly took the steps down to the loading docks, John could only watch from the elevated vantage point of the outdoor landing. The lingering effects of John's injuries would prevent him from catching up to Romney. His earlier three-story climb, the agonizingly long wait coupled with the short but tense meeting left John depleted. As he looked on, Romney hurriedly made his way to the furthermost clipper ship docked at the end of pier one. Romney was apparently going to try to break up a mob of men who were in the throes of a brawl.

After several suspenseful moments, and without thinking logically, John felt compelled to go help. Considering his physical condition, even if he could make it to the pier in time, what could John possibly do to help Romney?

John's meager chase was an exhausting effort, but he eventually pushed through the gathered crowd of dockworkers. By the time John got to the embroiled standoff, Romney had managed to insert himself in the middle of the brawl, somehow pulling off a tenuous truce of sorts.

Apparently, there was a faceoff between the dockworkers and a soon departing ship's crew. One of the ships that Romney sold off was making ready to leave port when the fight broke out. Angry words were exchanged over what the former crew saw as mean-spirited treatment from Romney and China Tea. In another one of Romney's moral lapses, he negotiated the issue of back pay into the overall deal to sell the ship. He knew that the new owners would be hard pressed to meet their inherited obligation to the workers. Again, from his perspective, Romney felt he had no choice as he made the best deal he could for his company. It was now becoming apparent that the former China Tea workers felt they were being cheated out of promised back pay.

Unfortunately, the raw sentiments began to spread among China Tea's current employees who had been drawn into the name-calling. If the allegations were true, then they could envision themselves in peril at Romney's whim as well. There was grumbling and whispering among the men gathered around the besieged company owner as their angry emotions created an ebb and flow to the powder-keg tensions. One moment the noise would subside, giving pause, only to rise again to a clamor as someone would shout an obscenity. The anxious crowd looked as if they would clash at the slightest provocation with seemingly no escape for Romney.

At the most tenuous moment, John pushed himself into the fray and limped toward Romney. "Get outta' here lad!" screamed Romney. For a few seconds, the crowd's attention shifted to John, who stood bandaged and broken before them. Then without warning, the momentary stalemate was broken when someone threw a brick, hitting Romney in his midsection. He recoiled, falling forward while grasping his stomach. By then John was only one step away, close enough to Romney to do the only thing within his power. He fell over the crumpled and besieged leader, shielding him the best he could.

Fortunately, John was still wearing what was left of the body cast that Dr. Murray had fitted to him. After the pair received a brief flurry of random kicks and blows from nightsticks, the flaring tempers and tumult unexpectedly dissipated. John's oddly sacrificial act was enough of a distraction to defuse the hair-trigger hostility. With their anger vented, and the strain lessened, the men began to back off and slowly disperse. There were perceptible signs of relief as if total mayhem had been averted.

No longer on the brink of bedlam, a few still-loyal workers helped Romney and John to their feet. However, there was a sense that there was no love lost between the workers and their boss. As the stand-down reached an appropriate moment, the much subdued and humbled Romney yelled out, "Alright, men, it's over. Now let's get back to work."

Not sure how to address John for his remarkable show of courage and compassion, Romney felt compelled to extend an offer of conciliation. "John, I'm impressed by your show of grit. I'm grateful for what you did, as you quite possibly saved my life."

The truth is that John was surprised at himself. He didn't know how or why he reacted the way he did. It was his first attempt at a noble deed, coming from an untapped source within him. "Mr. Longfellow, I couldn't just stand there and watch. I'm glad I could help."

"Look, John, I have a ship leaving at the end of September. I always need a deckhand. Honestly, I don't believe you could handle it, as a new recruit you'll be treated harshly. Regardless, it's all I have for you. Think about it, and if you are still interested, come by in the morning, and we can discuss it."

"Sir, I'll be there. However, I have a much more urgent matter to discuss with you. It's a matter of a key—"

Once again, the troubled Romney interrupted John, not allowing him to breach the subject he dreaded would come up. "Look, we'll have to continue our talk in the morning. I need to attend to these men and talk to the dock captain. Excuse me, John, I must go."

Romney left John standing on the mostly deserted loading dock, feeling a sense of dejection that was becoming all too frequent. John had been unable to secure the key from Romney. With no key, he could not access the bank lockbox, so his morning was lost.

Chapter Seven

A Matter of Honor

John was now dreadfully past due for the meeting he had arranged with the employees of his parents' former estate. By the time he showed up, it was almost two-thirty in the afternoon, well past his promised lunch hour appointment. A surprising number of estate workers had remained, hoping to finalize their service and leave with sufficient pay to last until they could find new work.

Just as John walked through the door, a housemaid about John's age walked briskly up to him and slapped his face. She struck him with such force that her handprint left a bright red impression. John was so taken aback that he retreated outside to regain his composure. Taken by surprise, many of the older workers gasped. They were shocked at Mary's brash hostility toward their former employer, prompting several of the men to go and check on John. Mary's slap was yet another reminder of his newly acquired meager existence. He was being initiated into the work-a-day world, encounters he was just beginning to understand.

Ironically, it was Mary's father, Edward, who assured John that there would be no more trouble. "John, I don't approve of Mary's behavior. I'll speak with her later. It won't happen again." After a brief pause, Edward made an extra effort to assure John. "Right now, we all need each other. Please come back in and I will personally keep the peace."

John had, in a way, grown up with Mary Van Zandt, but it was mostly from a distance. John was not around much as he came and went to boarding schools, summer camps, family trips abroad and later off to university.

It was obviously a different world for Mary who had lived on the estate with her mother. As young girls often do, she dreamed of being with someone like John. She was too young at the time to understand that she would always be on the outside looking in.

As Mary grew older, she slowly began to realize that she would never be involved or partake in the opulent lifestyle that was set before her. As any of the older workers knew, a prideful attitude or a feeling of self-importance needed to be cruelly dealt with, using utmost self-control. Doing otherwise was dangerous. Until the issue of strict subordination was settled deep within, a worker's life on any estate could be a wretched existence. If a servant or employee ever crossed the line, thinking equality on any level, a dismissal would follow a scathing rebuke. Further, if a charge of insubordination was severe enough, a worker could be blacklisted, never to work in the trade again.

Edward and a few of the male estate workers escorted John back into the kitchen to face an uneasy crowd of anxious people. John's level of maturity was being forced to grow by leaps on a daily basis, but today's events would be a crowning achievement as he addressed the group. "Alright, everyone, before I get down to business, I believe Mary has something she needs to say to me. I'm here, Mary, have your say."

Mary felt embarrassed for lashing out at John in such an uncontrollable fashion, yet she was still provoked by John's apparent lack of concern for the workers. "John, I'm sorry for the disrespect I've shown you. Please forgive me... I have been taught better." John didn't have anything to say at this point, and since forgiveness was a completely foreign concept to him, he just nodded his head, signaling for her to finish. Mary bit her lip as she gathered her words to continue what turned out to be a heartfelt sentiment. "John, I have always looked up to you. And now, my disappointment is more than I can bear. You have turned out to be nothing more than a selfish and spoiled man who only thinks of himself. You'll have some answering to do for how you have treated these people."

Still bearing a bright red handprint on his face, John asked if there was anyone else who needed to speak. An always-vocal groundskeeper lamented about his dire future, and then pleaded with John to assure him and the others that he had the money owed them.

Unfortunately, John was empty handed, so this moment of truth was proving to be the toughest spot of his entire life. The pressure was enormous. "It pains me to tell you that my trip to the bank was not successful. I do not have any money for you today—" Before he could complete what he wanted to say, he was drowned out by the workers who began loudly asking questions, each trying to be heard over the others.

Edward Van Zandt stepped forward, raising his hands and signaling for the crowd to be silent. "Let's give John an opportunity to finish what he has to say. I think if you give him a chance, you'll find that he is with us in this."

John was a little surprised by Edward's declaration of confidence. With a look of reprieve, yet feeling a little confused, he continued, "Please hear me, I *am* with you in this. I have no money of my own. In fact, until I retrieve the money that my mum has set aside, I'm as penniless as anyone here today. Further, I have no position with China Tea, as I have been completely left out. And lastly, I have no promise of employment except as a cabin steward on some future voyage. To that end, my mum informed me from her deathbed that she had only saved a meager amount for our shared plight. As her loyal employees, she wanted me to give you half of the money she had put back, and the other half was to give me a new start—the sum total of my inheritance."

John paused to make a noble yet naive proclamation that was beyond the generous intentions of his mother. "I stand here today and pledge to you that any and all of the money that my mum has left at the bank will be split among you, keeping none for myself."

In the few moments, he took to catch his breath, a quiet hush fell, as no one spoke a word. It was apparent that John's passionate pleas were believable even if the facts were hard to bear. In a more subdued tone, John continued, "These are my plans; I have no other intentions. Tomorrow morning, I have yet another appointment with Romney Longfellow. He is in possession of the key to the safety deposit box where the money is being kept. Upon obtaining the key, no matter how long it takes, I will bring the money directly here. Please know that I have your welfare as my highest priority."

Edward was satisfied with John's contrite confessions as he stepped out and spoke to the quieted gathering. "I can vouch for what John has told you today. I have firsthand knowledge of the arrangements that Madeline Taylor made, and John speaks the truth. Additionally, what happened today was outside of his control. He had every intention of fulfilling his promise to be here at the noon hour—he was prevented from doing so."

Mary had been too quick to judge. She had no idea that John had been doing the best he could, to be honorable in their shared plight. Now that she knew John had made an honest attempt, she felt embarrassed. In an effort to amend her earlier overstepped display of contempt, Mary went too far in the opposite direction. In another impetuous display of pent-up emotion, Mary quickly made her way to John and threw her arms around him in what would be considered improper under any circumstance.

> *Mary quickly made her way to John and threw her arms around him in what would be considered improper under any circumstance.*

Even so, the "hug" was truly innocent and given with genuine regret. Nonetheless, it was still a passionate embrace.

Mary could not help how she felt about John. Even though she truly did not know him personally, the little time they had spent together over the years had captured her heart from an early age. In the real world, her feelings were only dreams, but this did not keep her from holding him tight. Being in the arms of a woman was nothing new for John. However, he knew there was a difference in Mary's "eager" attempt to make amends. Despite the inappropriateness of her embrace, there was a distinct yet unexplainable sense of virtue and innocence in her persona.

Even with their doubts assuaged, the estate workers were feeling demoralized as they displayed lost hope. One by one, the workers quietly thanked John for his efforts and tried to encourage him the best they could. Before anyone could leave, John spoke to them. "Please hear me carefully. I will leave the bank straight away and come here by noon tomorrow. I have no way of knowing what is owed to each of you, or how much severance would be fair. Please come to an amount by writing it down, and then give your accounting to Mr. Van Zandt. As I mentioned earlier, the money I retrieve from the bank is yours as a group."

John reached China Tea's offices in an early morning fog, a little rare for June. The ships were mystically shrouded, giving them a romantic appeal that betrayed the reality of their dirty and often brutal employment. Today's three-story climb up to Romney's office seemed a little easier as John was growing stronger by the day. This time, his visit began differently as John was ushered directly into Romney's office. The wall of windows that formed three sides of his office were fog cloaked, giving them a foreboding grey appearance, which darkened the room.

Romney was fidgety as he gruffly ordered John to have a seat. "Look, John, I made promises to your mum that I can't keep—everything is different now. Circumstances change on a daily basis, as you witnessed yesterday. I feel truly indebted to you for what you did, but my hands are tied. I can't offer the job I promised your mum to have for you. The deckhand position that I mentioned yesterday is all that is available, and as I said, I wouldn't wish it on anyone. John, these ship crews are a rough bunch, and trust me, you will be treated harshly."

John wasn't taking Romney's warning to heart because he somehow thought the lockbox held the turning point for his problems, and the dire working conditions would not be necessary. Respectfully, John skipped over the job opportunity for the moment to ask for the key to the lockbox. "Mr. Longfellow, I agree that there was a time when the offer of a deckhand position would have insulted me. However, today, I will not rule out anything. That being said, I would like to speak to you concerning a key that was left in your care by my mum. She spoke of it before she died. She specifically asked me to request the key from you at my earliest opportunity. Sir, there is an urgency connected with obtaining the key."

Romney was having a hard time controlling his emotions. He was feeling angry with himself, and angry at the situation that he had hoped would go away. He was also feeling guilty. He was deeply frustrated as he pondered how to break the truth to John. He knew there was a lot on the line, and John was going to take the brunt of the bad news. "Look here, lad, there is no money! The money's gone."

With an angry outburst, John chided his elder, "Sir! The safety deposit box would, by intention, be a private affair. The key should have only been held for safekeeping. How could you possibly know the contents of the lockbox without forfeiting your honor?"

Romney was struck by the naivety of this spoiled scamp who was displaying too much self-righteousness. Irritated, he began a string of lies. Trying to hide his real feelings, he spoke with a measured tone, "John, your mum entrusted the key to me as a friend and advisor. She kept important papers and a few valuables, which you'll find intact. The truth is, John, there was never any money. I didn't want to tell you this earlier because it meant your mum was lying to you. In her defense, she had intended to put some money away. In fact, we talked about it on several occasions. She was just never able to do it."

Provoked by Romney's blatant lies, John continued his highbrow rebuke, "Mr. Longfellow, what made you think there was any money in the lockbox? I never told you that I was expecting to find any money. And yet, at every mention of the lockbox, you seem obsessed with the topic of money. Sir, I believe you have tipped your hand!"

Romney was livid. If he could have strangled John, and not been caught, he would have. Romney was accustomed to lying and getting away with it, so John's remarks enraged him. "You're mad! The whole lot of you Taylors... you're all mad!

Get out of my office, and don't ever show your face around here again!"

John was still seated as he endured the punitive rant from Romney. In that harsh moment, John suddenly remembered the very odd occurrence when his mother was on her deathbed. Speaking from her sleep, she told him: *"John, you must get the key from Romney; your future depends on it."* Recalling his mother's imperative charge bolstered his courage, allowing him to remain remarkably calm, especially considering Romney's theatrics. "Mr. Longfellow, if I could just retrieve the key from you, I believe our business will be concluded... at least for the moment."

Romney was still seething as he took the key from his desk drawer and threw it at John. "I'm serious, John. We have no further business to discuss. Now take your key and be on your way... and don't come back!"

Chapter Eight
Confidentiality and the Key

John somehow knew that there was more, much more business to be conducted with Romney or at least with China Tea. He couldn't imagine what matter of enterprise could possibly cause their paths to cross, he just had an odd feeling about it. One thing was for sure: John would eventually hire someone to look into the financial scandal that Romney apparently perpetrated on his ailing mother. For the moment,

John would have to put the spiteful episode behind him as he tended to the matter at hand.

While making his cross-town trip from the shipping piers to the bank, John had settled in his mind that there would be no money in the safety deposit box, and, consequently, his day was going to be a very long and disappointing affair.

As he entered the in-town London business district, the cobblestone streets brought back pleasant memories of how he, as a young lad, tagged along with his father. As John contemplated those memories, he sadly shook his head at the last thought that occurred to him. *What a sad turn of events, considering my father's entire financial legacy may or may not be stashed in a bank lockbox.*

The massive granite-ensconced Bank of England had just opened its doors at John's 9:30 a.m. arrival. Once inside, he made his way over to the enormous rounded vault and presented his identification along with the numbered key to the bank clerk. As the clerk finished his cursory routine of documenting the transaction, a quick thought popped into John's mind, "Excuse me sir, is Romney Longfellow listed in your journal as an approved key holder for this lockbox?"

"No, Mr. Taylor, I don't see his name listed next to this box number. However, I do see Mr. Longfellow's name listed for the next three consecutive numbers following yours. You can see for yourself... 699, 700 and 701."

John was mystified, as well as intrigued. "Is my name or Madeline Taylor's name listed as an approved key holder on those numbered lockboxes?"

"No sir, John Wilson Taylor was listed but has since been lined through and marked as deceased. Was he your father?"

John didn't immediately answer as he thought through the implications of having four boxes in a row. It didn't seem so mysterious once he realized that someone from the China Tea Company rented the four boxes, and his father simply reserved a box for personal use. "Yes, John Wilson Taylor was my father. Why do you ask?"

"Well Mr. Taylor, I see here, at the bottom of the page that a John Wilson Taylor was also listed for boxes 718 and 719, with you as an approved key holder. Do you have either of those keys with you?"

"No, I don't. I wasn't aware of any other boxes. When were the boxes leased?"

"I don't have those records here. However, I can check for you while you peruse your lockbox."

Both men approached the massive walk-in safe and presented the guard with a matched set of keys that displayed the stamped number 698. Both keys were required to open the small vault-type drawer. In a ritualistic manner, each man inserted his key and turned them simultaneously. John pulled the steel drawer out and carried it to a private room meant for personal use.

John carefully emptied the contents of the lockbox onto the table. He didn't intend to be so cautious and wary, but in some ways, he was afraid of what he would find. Most of the papers were in envelopes, so he opened each one and took his time as he examined them. The majority of the paper documents were paid notes of some type, some business and some personal. He also found a few unimpressive pieces of jewelry that didn't appear worthy of taking up space in a safety deposit box. John wondered if Romney had just taken what he wanted or possibly replaced the more valuable pieces with worthless costume jewelry. Either way, it didn't matter much at this point. There was no use worrying over it now.

John was just about done when the bank clerk knocked on the privacy room door. "Sir, I have the details for you concerning boxes 718 and 719."

"Alright, what information do you have?"

"Boxes 718 and 719 were rented about three years ago. However, this is very interesting, Mr. Taylor. The boxes were rented by *"Anonymous,"* the lease is paid by Anonymous and Anonymous has signed in every month up until one year ago."

John's thoughts were immediately captivated with numerous possibilities of what this all meant. Even so, he wasn't going to allow his imagination to run away like it did with Romney's promised job. "How does one go about remaining anonymous and still prove who they are to sign in?"

The bank clerk seemed more than willing to discuss the ins and outs of the bank's business practices. "I can assure you that this is all perfectly legitimate. But, to answer your question, these transactions are managed by a special vice president who handles "discreet accounts." Only certain customers have access to him, and only they know who he is. It's a very secretive but necessary service the bank offers to its most discriminating customers."

John was being drawn into a mystery that was beginning to feel like a staged setup. "I see…. can you look again to see who else is on the approved list for box 698?"

"Yes, sir, but it will be a few minutes while I go and transcribe the names from the journal. By the way, did you find what you were looking for?" Without waiting for an answer, the bank clerk offered, "You might try the false bottom—most people forget about it."

> *"You might try the false bottom—most people forget about it."*

John's thoughts were being jerked around along with his emotions. He had all but given up hope on the original box 698, and looking hopefully to unlocking the mystery of box numbers 718 and 719. Now he was being brought back to a new possibility—a new hope. John reached for the box and felt around for a way to remove the bottom. Sure enough, in the corner was a slight groove that allowed for gripping. He pulled up the thin metal floor to reveal the slightest space large enough for a few sheets of paper or maybe a thin wedding band.

To his surprise, there was an envelope hidden in the secret compartment. John was nervous as he opened his mysterious find. The envelope contained a handwritten note that was unmistakably penned by his mother, which read: *My dear son, I hope you have remembered my instructions concerning my heart's desire to clear the family name. I much anticipate that you will be paying the house staff and estate workers their back wages, as well as their much-deserved severance. In this envelope is a key to lockbox 718. There you will find what you need to pay Dr. Andrew Murray the entire amount owed to him, as well as a small amount of additional funds to help you in your new journey.*

Love always, your mum, Madeline Taylor

John was having trouble controlling his emotions. The letter itself was a poignant reminder of his mother, bringing him to the verge of tears. Then, there was this great effort being laid out before him to make sure that those who had trusted in the family name were not cheated. Admiration rose up in John for the honorable intentions of his mother.

The bank clerk once again knocked on the door. "Sir, I have the complete list of names you requested. The only other name, not mentioned earlier, on the approved list was *Anonymous.*

"Thank you for looking. You've been quite helpful." John had already deduced as much. Since his mother's name was not on the approved list for boxes 718 and 719, he was able to make the assumption by the time he finished her letter.

In the process of the intervening conversation, the bank clerk had ventured into the private viewing room. He was standing next to the table where John had arranged the contents of the lockbox. In a matter-of-fact tone, John queried the bank clerk, "I must ask you. Are our conversations and these discoveries that you're privy to, held as confidential?" John felt as if this young man had a severe case of loose lips and wanted some assurance that an inquiring mind would not be given any information about the contents of his lockboxes.

"Well… I've never been asked that question."

In the stress of the moment, John made an overstepped response to the bank employee, "For god's sake man… what's the bank policy? Is all of this confidential or not?"

John's rebuke sent the bank clerk taking steps backward toward the door. The young assistant was a little wide-eyed as he responded to John's demand. "I'll get my manager."

John was feeling a sense of urgency and wanted a straight answer. This whole thing with the lockboxes was turning out to be a very secretive and muddled affair. He felt there was more going on than was known, appearing as if someone was behind the curtain pulling strings. Furthermore, one would have to assume that Romney was unaware of the hidden note and key when he pillaged the lockbox. John began to feel a looming and rather odd sense that he would be in danger if Romney were to find out about the hidden note and key.

Moments later the vault manager appeared outside the private viewing room. Apparently heeding bank policy, the manager beckoned John to speak with him outside the room. "Mr. Taylor, I understand you have some concerns with bank policy."

"Yes, I specifically have concerns about confidentiality. Your employee has become aware of certain information that must remain confidential. In his efforts to be helpful, he witnessed—" John stopped midsentence when he noticed the smug look on the vault manager's face. John now suspected that the manager had been informed about the hidden key and note and that there must be a conspiracy in play, possibly with

Romney at the center of it all. Trying not to let on, John continued, "Sir, I must have your word, as a bank manager, that the information discovered here today will remain confidential."

The vault manager curtly replied, "Sir, this *is* the Bank of England—need I say more?"

Not to be intimidated by the haughty snob, John demanded an affirmation of intent. "Yes, I request that you swear the information discovered here today will remain confidential."

In a pretentious reply, the vault manager retorted, "Of course, anything seen or heard is always held in the strictest of confidence."

John was not intending to make a threat as he concluded with the vault manager. "I will hold you personally responsible if I ever discover you have given this information to anyone. Do you understand? Now, please escort me to box 718."

The vault manager studied John for a few moments while he decided whether to have John escorted out of the bank for making "threats" against an officer of the bank, a very serious charge. He and John were engaged in a stare-down when the vault manager backed off and nodded to the young bank clerk to comply with John's request.

Once back in the private viewing room with the second lockbox, John decided he needed to finish up quickly. There was a sense that he should leave the bank immediately. He retrieved a complimentary cloth bag and hurriedly put the contents of both boxes in it. He checked the false bottom of the second box, found another hidden note, and stuffed it in the bag. John left the bank as promptly as possible, trying not to be too noticeable. For unknown reasons, he felt like he was in a race for his life.

Chapter Nine

Arresting Suspicion

Still commanding his rental carriage, John made his way to the outskirts of the city and rode onto the sprawling estate grounds of his former family home. He realized he was possibly taking in the gently rolling pastoral view for one of the last times. The familiar sights and sounds were spawning emotions that were difficult to bear. Even so, he knew things were changing around him—times were different. He was different. In many ways, he was experiencing a disconnect that enabled him to cope and rise to the difficult challenges that lay before him.

John tied up the carriage at the backside of the east wing where the oversized kitchen, storeroom, cold-room and general maintenance quarters were adjoined to the mansion via a massive dining hall. His earlier than anticipated arrival at the estate kitchen allowed him the time to go through the contents of the lockboxes before the appointed meeting.

John went to a worktable inside the dining room where he could sort through the bank bag. He had been in such a hurry when leaving the bank vault that he wasn't sure what he actually possessed. As before, most of the contents were in some type of envelope. Several thick envelopes looked and felt like they contained the pound sterling notes he desperately needed. His hands were shaking as he opened the first thick envelope to find various denominations of money. With a great sigh of relief, accompanied by a quick flush of tears, John instinctively bowed his head in a thankful posture. In a very real way, he experienced a heavy emotional load lift from his shoulders.

It was obvious the money was a compilation of odd bills that were collected and stashed over time, and not an orderly stack of bills that one would receive from a bank transaction. John sorted the bills so he could count the total, carefully stacking them by denomination. The total came to just under nine hundred pounds sterling, an amount he felt would be sufficient to compensate the estate staff. He placed the neatly arranged money back in the envelopes for later.

John felt he was ready to engage the workers who had shown varying degrees of nervous anticipation in his previous meetings with them. One potential concern was the lack of any recently kept records. He had no way of knowing the amounts owed to the individual workers. He had earlier decided he must invoke the honor system, hoping that the truth would prevail.

Edward Van Zandt was the perfect intermediary to collect the personal totals, which was due to each worker, so John asked him to help. John simply wanted to treat everyone fairly just as his mother had hoped.

It was now nearing the noon hour, and various employees began gathering in the kitchen for the meeting, as well as their midday meal. John was preparing to leave the large dining area where he had made his accounting of the money from the lockboxes. As he stood with the bank bag in hand, Edward walked through the doorway with several of the estate workers.

John was happy to see the men and anxious to share his good findings with them. "Edward, I was just coming to look for you. I have good news for everyone. Were you able to gather the IOUs from all the staff?"

With a measure of irritation in his voice, Edward questioned, "John, that doesn't matter right now. I have some bad news for you. There are two police officers outside who say you robbed the bank this morning. Can it be true, John?"

"No! Of course not! Hear me! This bag contains everything to prove otherwise. Nothing has been stolen. All of the money and documents came from a lockbox. There are handwritten notes from my mum explaining the money and how it's supposed to be used."

"I want to believe you, but it looks like you'll need to go and plead your case before the magistrate."

John was dumbfounded at the possibility of this heinous diversion, leaving him to make a desperate plea. "If I have to go, can you please take the bag and pay the workers? The notes from my mum will prove my innocence. Can you help me?"

"I can't take the bag, John. The authorities must determine your innocence. And, if as you say, the proof is in the bag, you'll need to turn it over to them."

"But Edward, I'm being framed. This must be a setup."

"I'm sorry, John. If I take the bag, I will be implicating myself as an accomplice. I cannot be of any help to you if I'm in jail with you. My best advice is to turn over the money and what evidence you have and go peacefully with the police."

John was devastated. He was really in this for the estate workers, and he was so close to making it right with them. "Alright, will you, at least go with me?"

"Of course, I will. I have no problem with that."

As the men turned to go and meet with the officers, John stopped in his tracks. "This is a hoax, a setup by Romney Longfellow. He is just trying to steal what he can from the second lockbox. My bet is that those two men out there are not even police officers. You have to believe me in this."

"Alright, John, I'll go and check out the men, but if they are from the precinct, then you will have to go with them."

"It's agreed—thanks for doing this."

Edward Van Zandt had a few connections within the parish police department. He was acquainted with Captain Yardley through a mutual friend. Edward stepped outside the kitchen to have a word with the waiting police officers. "Officers, I have spoken with John Taylor and he has agreed to go with you. He will be out momentarily."

In an oddly unprofessional manner, the men acted a little giddy, giving Edward good reason to continue his vetting process. He decided to lower the men's guard with small talk. "I heard your precinct was being commended by the mayor and your captain is going to receive an award. You are from the Fifth Precinct, aren't you?"

The two men appeared dumbfounded as they looked at each other and nodded in agreement to Edward's offhand questioning. "Oh yes, our captain's a great leader... remarkable man... deserves the highest honor."

"If I remember correctly, your precinct captain is Mr. Billingsley, is that right?"

"Oh yes, Captain Billingsley... best captain ever."

"Gentleman, would you excuse me, please? Give me a few moments, and I'll be right back."

Edward was satisfied that the men were imposters, but he wasn't yet sure the best way to handle them. He hurried back to meet with John and the other men. "John, you were right. This is a trap, but it has nothing to do with the bank or the proper authorities. It appears these men were sent to kidnap you. If I was guessing, you were to be robbed and possibly beaten for the contents of your lockboxes."

John had lived a sheltered life and had never been in a predicament like this before. "Edward, what do you think we should do?"

"I think we should call their bluff. Perhaps we can find out who sent them."

John liked the idea of playing along to try to expose for whom they were working. He was also learning to appreciate Edward's wisdom in a tenuous situation. "That's a great idea, but how can we do that?"

"Alright, here's the best way to handle this. Leave the bank bag here since we know they are here to steal it. Put it in the cupboard for now. We will simply go and confront them with the truth. Just follow my lead. Let's go."

John, Edward and the other men approached the imposters with a plan to find out as much as they could about their true intentions. Edward was not interested in reprisal until he got the information he wanted from the phony police officers. "Officers, this is John Taylor. Before I turn him over to you, I'll need to see some identification, as well as your orders from your precinct captain."

Surprisingly, the officers put up a convincing response. "We have our badges and the captain just told us to come out here and get John Taylor, as well as the stolen property. We will need it as evidence."

"Well, gentlemen, I believe you may have wasted your time and efforts. I am sorry to inform you that John did not have any stolen property on him when he arrived. Officers, we are willing to attest to his innocence by escorting you to the police station and swear an affidavit. We will substantiate that John Taylor did not possess stolen property when he arrived here at the Taylor estate."

The phony officers were provoked into an unprofessional rant, "He must have ditched the money. It will be a lot easier on everybody if he just shows us where he hid the cash, and we'll be on our way." At that moment, the henchmen realized their misspoken words revealed the ruse—they were found out.

Edward knew he needed more information, so he pressed the men. "Alright, men, the game is over. Before we turn you over to the real police, we want to know who you are working for."

"Not so quick!" The imposters backed off a few steps to secure a defensive stance as they pulled out their pistols and pointed them toward John and the men. "John, you'd better come with us. We'll need you to show us where you stashed the bank bag." Edward held out his arm to prevent John from moving, causing the thieves to be angered by the standoff. Exaggerating their threat, by waving their pistols, they yelled at John, "We're serious, John! Somebody's going to get hurt if you don't come with us!"

For reasons unknown to everyone present, Edward was not taking their threat seriously. He remained calm. Providentially, Edward was an expert marksman and used his flintlock regularly. He was also known as a local authority on black powder weaponry. He immediately knew the men were unable to carry out their threats because he could see that their pistols lacked the flintlock needed to fire their weapons.

In a brash move that appeared foolhardy, Edward brazenly approached the bandits, disregarding the obvious danger. Also knowing that their pistols were worthless as weapons, the robbers froze when Edward lunged toward them. He took hold of the pistol barrels before the imposters could react to his charge. Quickly following Edward's lead, the estate workers tackled the would-be robbers to the ground.

Edward's fearless control of the heart-pounding confrontation left the others breathless. "John, run to the tack room and get some rope. Let's get these scoundrels tied up."

The overpowered men were handily bound while a small crowd

...knowing that their pistols were worthless as weapons, the robbers froze when Edward lunged toward them.

of newly gathered estate workers and staff gawked at the rousing altercation. The latecomers to the skirmish erupted with questions about the "unlawful treatment" the police officers were receiving. To ease the ongoing confusion, the robbers were stripped of their police officers' uniforms and left outside in their long underwear, firmly tied to the hitching post.

Chapter Ten

Pilfered

John was anxious to get the meeting started, so he ushered the estate workers back inside the large kitchen area. There was important and needful business to conduct, and John was determined there would be no further delay. Even so, to carry on without interruption, he felt it necessary to explain the events of the day. "I know you all have questions, so let me explain what happened earlier this morning which led up to the altercation you just witnessed." John was forced to raise his hands to quiet the murmuring crowd. As soon as he had everyone's attention, he began the troubling account of his morning, "As you remember from yesterday, I went to Romney Longfellow to take possession of a key he was holding in trust for me. This important key was to open a bank lockbox that held money for your back pay, as well as a small amount for severance. At some peril, I obtained the promised key from Mr. Longfellow this morning. Much to my disappointment, he all but admitted that he took the money that my mum intended for you to have."

The workers angrily erupted with rumbling howls and hisses. Once again, John was forced to bring the crowd under control so he could continue. "After his admitted betrayal, Mr. Longfellow was very angry and would only turn over the lockbox key after I strongly insisted he do so. Once the key was in my possession, I made my way to the Bank of England. Upon arriving at the bank, I discovered my worst fears were true. The lockbox had been pilfered. However, upon the kindly advice of the vault attendant, I removed the false bottom of the box to find another key. This hidden key was for a second lockbox that contained an envelope of pound notes."

With the good news, the moody crowd couldn't be contained as they broke into cheers and whistles of elation. Smiling with satisfaction, John continued, "Please, allow me to conclude so I can get to the matter at hand."

All of the previous day's frustrations completely left John as a realization occurred to him. He could now see what a day-to-day existence entailed. Until now, John had never been close to the brink, so he had not been able to feel the tangible relief these common, hardworking people felt at that moment. The celebration seemed to continue until John was able to take to heart the significance of obtaining the money. It was then that someone spoke up and asked John to continue. "Go ahead, John, tell us what happened next."

With a much more humbled and quieted spirit, John continued. "I believe the confrontation many of you witnessed just outside these doors a few minutes ago was a result of the newly discovered key. I have to conclude that the secret key has been highly sought after by Mr. Longfellow." A sense of intrigue enveloped the gathered workers as they waited to hear what happened next. "Upon my departure from the bank, I can only speculate that he was immediately informed of the hidden key's existence. Hence, the thugs disguised as police officers. My guess is that their intention was to pretend an arrest in an effort to steal the contents of the second lockbox, as well as the money my mum left."

John wanted to get the whole ordeal behind him, so he concluded his explanation by saying, "This is all of the information I have, and, as you heard, there is much speculation involved with this mystery. There may be more to tell later after we turn the robbers over to the precinct police. Rather than spend any more valuable time discussing this further, let's get on with the business at hand. Edward, do you have the IOU slips from everyone?"

Edward immediately queried the anxious workers, "Alright everyone, if you want to get paid, I need your notations." Edward collected the remaining notations that he needed to final the tally and then assured the staff, "John and I will go into the next room and fill these requests as quickly as possible. A few of you men need to go and stand guard over our prisoners until we can get finished."

Fortunately, Madeline had collected the money in small denominations, so dividing the money was relatively easy with a few exceptions. The grand total of payments for the thirty-seven workers came to just under seven hundred pounds sterling, leaving a little over two hundred pounds sterling to be split among them according to John's earlier promise.

Completely inexperienced in handling money in this way, John asked for Edward's advice, "How do you think we should split the remaining money among the workers? Should we use seniority or merit? What do you think?"

Edward felt as if John was so focused on his efforts to treat the estate workers fairly that he hadn't realized how generous he had been. Additionally, John was accustomed to dealing with much larger monetary figures—a result of his previous exalted lifestyle, which left him unable to relate to the workers' relatively modest incomes. Edward attempted to guide John by consoling him in his efforts to be just. "John, you have already rounded up the figures quite generously—I believe you have been more than fair."

"It is important to me that I fulfill my mum's last wishes. Additionally, as you know, I vowed to give the workers all the money I found."

"Alright John, I won't argue your point, but let's poll the workers on how to split the money. Perhaps there is someone who is extra needy or as with any group of people... *extra greedy.*"

Back in the kitchen, Edward handed out the pay in a roll-call fashion. Almost everyone was pleasantly surprised by the extra pay that John had added to their calculations. As expected, a sense of curiosity followed when Edward asked, "Does anyone feel that more money is due them?"

Edward waited for the crowd to speak up and commit to their satisfaction with the pay given to them.

Satisfied, Edward continued, "John promised his mum that he would be generous with you for your loyalty. As you remember from yesterday's meeting, he made a heartfelt promise to distribute among you all the money he collected." Edward took a long pause, looking into their eyes, before continuing, "Before you answer the following question, please remember that the money Madeline Taylor had originally set aside for you was stolen, meaning that John had nothing to give you. Keeping that fact in mind, consider that the money he has distributed to you today was intended for another purpose." Edward didn't want to belabor his point, so he asked the crowd with a measure of finality, "Does anyone here feel they need more money, or do you know of someone here that needs more, but may be afraid to ask?"

The always-vocal yard worker, who had previously expressed his dire circumstances, jumped at the chance for more money. The others looked around at each other and ultimately expressed contentment with their pay. Someone yelled out their gratitude for John's extra efforts and expressed a desire to see John keep any extra money for himself. Except for the lone yard worker, the vote was unanimous for John to keep the extra money. Edward felt he had accomplished exactly what he desired. There was fairness all around.

Chapter Eleven
The Promise

Before the workers dispersed, John arranged for several volunteers to take the prisoners to the police station to press charges of impersonating a peace officer. The criminal offense could be easily proven, having possession of police uniforms, as well as multiple witnesses.

The adrenaline-charged events were making for a long day even though it was only midafternoon. John retreated to the kitchen to sit for a few minutes and take a well-deserved break from all the spent emotion.

John did not know that Edward had been personally involved with his parents as a close friend and advisor. Now that both of John's parents were gone, Edward needed to begin conveying important information to John; guidance that Madeline and Edward had carefully laid out to help John survive.

For weeks, Edward had wanted to have a serious talk with John, but the timing had not been right. Now, with the estate worker's pay distributed, he saw the opportunity. "John, may I sit with you? For some time now, I've wanted to share some matters with you?"

"By all means, pull up a chair and tell me what's on your mind."

"John, I don't know where to begin. There is so much you need to know going forward. I'll begin by saying that Mary and I have been praying for you."

John was a little put off by Edward's remark, causing him to reply with a somewhat puzzled tone, "I'm not certain what you mean. You're not a priest... how could you be praying for me?"

"I'm a follower of Christ, and I believe what the Bible says about those who choose to follow Him and obey His Word. You don't have to be a priest to pray to God."

"Well, thanks for your prayers, but I don't think following Christ is for me."

"John, in the midst of praying for you, I have become persuaded that you have a remarkable future ahead of you. Even so, I'm also convinced from reading the Bible, that you will not achieve your full potential without dedicating your life to Jesus Christ."

John was a little wide-eyed at Edward's passionate claim. "Look, I'm a good person and that should be enough. Besides, my parents gave lots of money to charities. They even have an orphanage named after them. I'm certain I've heard something about God wanting us to take care of the orphans. What else could God want?"

"John, you're absolutely right about taking care of the poor and orphans. By the way, I'm glad you mentioned your parents. There is a lot I need to tell you about them that may surprise you."

At Edward's second mention of having intimate knowledge concerning his parents, John became a little agitated. "Wait… stop. I'm a little confused. Earlier, you mentioned having firsthand information about the financial arrangements of the severance, and now you're telling me you have a lot you need to tell me about my parents. How is that possible?"

"Let me start by saying that I actually didn't work for your parents. They were just very close friends. Years ago, your father began confiding in me and asking for counsel when China Tea was having difficulties. And yes, we prayed about almost every important decision he faced."

John was allowing himself to become offended as his flickering aristocratic flame rose up within him. "You dare say! Who are you to have given my father counsel about anything?"

John's arrogance was to be expected, so Edward spoke to him on a level he could not refute. "John, I am aware that you really don't know me. My father was an Earl and consequently, I was educated at Cambridge University. But John, I've given up that life because it is not the one that God has planned for me."

John furrowed his brow and continued his disconcerted dialogue. "I'm beginning to think you've gone completely mad. You're not talking sense, man. I don't want to hear any more of this religious nonsense."

Edward understood John's response. His display of pride and arrogance was just the way he had acted, when as a young man, he was told of God's desire to intervene in his own life. "Please allow me to say one last thing about God's aspirations for you. I would then like to talk to you about a job offer."

John was still flustered by all the "religious" talk. Even so, out of respect, he relented to Edward's request. "Go ahead, but don't be so insistent with me."

"John, both of your parents turned their lives over to God. If they were here, they would tell you it was the best decision they ever made."

John was incensed by the implications Edward was making, considering how his parents died. John angrily slapped his hand down on the table and voiced his reply just under the audible tone of yelling. "Now I know you're mad! If God was so important to them, how could He just let them die the way He did?"

Edward's own life experiences with unexplained deaths allowed him to empathize with how John felt, responding in a sympathetic tone, "John, I know how you feel, but accidents will happen and people do get sick. That's just part of living. Knowing God is how you get through these difficulties unscathed. What happens to the body isn't overly important when you know your eternity is secure."

John's heart was aching with emotional pain; he spoke with moistened eyes, "But they didn't get through unscathed. Their world fell apart around them."

"John, listen to me. You can have peace in the midst of the storm. Your mum was in perfect peace when she died, and so was your father." Edward paused to give John a few moments to consider what he had just said before making a most important claim. "John, you can never know the moment when you will die, but you can be prepared when that time comes."

> *John, you can never know the moment when you will die, but you can be prepared when that time comes.*

John was emotionally charged as he wrestled in his mind, looking away, trying not to allow his feelings reveal his thoughts. He vividly remembered how his mother was serenely peaceful the day she died. Even so, her tranquil demeanor was beyond John's understanding.

Edward could see that John was struggling with his emotions and thoughts, so he waited until John re-engaged him. "John, when you know God the way your parents knew Him, then death becomes just a part of living… there is nothing to fear. You can live your life to the fullest when you have no fear."

John was resigned. He knew, deep down, much of what Edward said was the truth. He just wasn't ready to accept it for himself. Without saying a word, John looked down in a contemplative stare and gently nodded his head, affirming what

Edward had told him. After a long few minutes, with moistened eyes, John looked up and quietly asked about the job offer. "You mentioned employment. What kind of work do you have?"

"I own a printing company. I can teach you the trade if you are interested. When you get back from your trip to the Orient with China Tea, I would like to take you on as an apprentice. In the meantime, you are welcome to come by the office. I'll give you a tour of the shop and show you all that we do."

John was once again provoked, once again raising his voice, "What makes you think that I will be going on a voyage with China Tea, especially with Romney Longfellow trying to kill me?"

"John, you don't know that Mr. Longfellow means you harm. Right now, that's just speculation. The vault manager could have hired the robbers, or they could have just seen you leave the bank with the cloth bag and followed you. Besides, like I told you earlier, we've been praying for you, and I believe that your journey to the Orient is going to prepare you in some way for how God wants to use you. I have a feeling this trip is very important."

John's emotions were on edge; he was having trouble controlling his irritability. "So, is this your counsel to me? Are you telling me I have no choice in the matter? If I don't sail with China Tea, then somehow I'm of no use to God?"

"That is something *you* will have to pray about. What you do or don't do is between you and God, but don't take the gift of free will as a way out, running from His will for you. You will have to answer for how you respond to His call on your life."

"It doesn't seem to me that God is interested in how I feel about my future. It appears to me that everything I could hope for will be lost… that I can't determine my own future. How can anyone be happy doing what someone else wants them to do?"

"That's the beauty of knowing the Creator of the universe. He made you. He knows your strengths and weaknesses, your gifts and talents. His plans are tailor-made to give you the utmost fulfillment so you can enjoy your life. John, there are scarce few who find the fullness that God offers, *but it is only because the many who don't find it have chosen to refuse Him.* His abundant life is freely given to all those who will diligently seek Him. That's a sure promise He gives us in His Word."

Slowly, John's prideful anger and confusion began to lift, allowing points of Light to pierce the darkness of his shrouded mind. "Edward, this is all so new for me… talking about God as if He is involved in our everyday lives. That's just not the way I was taught. I thought God was supposed to be impersonal… *maybe* getting involved only when someone was *really good* or *really evil.* You know… sainthood for some and punishment for others, acts of God… that sort of thing. I don't know, Edward. I'm really muddled about religion."

"John, I have a great idea. Why don't you come to my home for the evening meal; Mary is a wonderful cook. I can explain more about God and the Bible."

John didn't intend to ignore Edward's invitation; he was just struggling with many unanswered questions, "That's another thing I'm confused about. I assumed you and Mary lived here on the estate."

"As I mentioned earlier, your parents were dear friends. Actually, we were closer than mere friends. We were, as the Bible describes, brothers and sisters in Christ. I realize you may not understand what this means, but our relationship was bound with the deepest kind of love... a type of love that only God can enable a person to possess. But, to answer your question, I have my own home and Mary has rejoined me there even as she has continued here with her employment."

Edward paused to determine if he should share the story of his broken marriage. After a few moments, he decided to give John a few needed details. "You mentioned earlier how you were doubtful that God is involved in our everyday lives. The Bible plainly tells us that He is. I can also tell you from personal experience that God cares greatly about the smallest details that concern us. If you are interested, I can share part of my story with you."

John was unsure if he wanted to continue talking about God, but Edward had his attention. "Edward, I have only known you for a few hours, yet I sense that I can trust you completely. Somehow, I feel that I need to hear your story. Please continue."

"Elizabeth, Mary's mum, and I were estranged early on in our marriage. And, it was mostly my fault. As a young husband, I lived an unseemly life that brought about a terrible strain to our relationship. Mary was just a young child when I left them. Fortunately, when all seemed to be lost, in my darkest hour, a rather miraculous change began in me. Looking back, I know now that God was drawing me so I could know Him. Later, when Mary was a young teenager, God began to move in all our lives, including your parents."

Edward realized that he had given John a lot of solemn details and didn't want to overwhelm him. "I don't mind explaining further if it will help you understand. In fact, my complete story illustrates how God *is* personal and cares about our everyday life."

John was finding himself intrigued. A window into his heart was opening up as he sensed an often-felt void being revealed once again. "I am interested... especially the part about how my parents became involved with knowing God."

Edward continued. "As I mentioned earlier, God was working to restore all of our lives. You'll see just how important your parents were to Mary and me. I had ruined any chance at having a good marriage because I was wild, arrogant and prideful—caught up in high society living. I became convinced that I had married beneath my social class, so I abandoned Elizabeth." Edward had to stop as tears flushed his eyes; he couldn't speak through the sorrows and regret. After a few crushing moments, he regained his composure and continued. "When I scorned Elizabeth, she was seen by our haughty circle of friends and acquaintances as being rejected, which ruined any social standing she had. She had no choice but to find her own way. She came here to work for your parents as a young pregnant woman."

Edward had to pause again. Revisiting the thoughts of abandoning his wife and unborn daughter tore at his heart, finding it hard to continue. "John, your parents were very gracious and generous to take Elizabeth in as she was obviously showing her pregnancy. They could have turned her away, but they didn't. Can you see how providential their generosity turned out to be?" And now, God is using me to bring you to know Him.

John was listening intently, trying to piece the events together in his mind. He gently nodded even though he did not know the answer to Edward's rhetorical question.

"You see, John, it was Mary and Elizabeth who eventually led your parents to genuinely know the Lord. In the midst of my betrayal and the pain I caused, God was turning around for good what was meant for destruction. Looking back, I can see it was part of His plan to bring your parents to know Him. Isn't that marvelous?"

Revisiting the truth of those divinely intertwined events was an inspiring reminder for Edward. He stopped his storytelling once again to meditate on God's goodness. He then continued with his story, "As a young father, I was blind to my selfish and arrogant ways. I did not begin to change until Mary was an adolescent. Sadly, by that time, the damage had been done; Mary didn't want to have anything to do with me.

Then, as I mentioned earlier, in a rather miraculous fashion, things started happening. In an extremely desperate time of my life, trying to escape my tortured soul, I went to a small country church to find help. The pastor led me to Jesus, the Savior of every man's soul who will turn to Him. At about the same time, Mary had a similar renewal experience brought about by a schoolmate whose family reached out to her. Afterward, about a year later, Elizabeth became a believer.

It wasn't long after that when it became apparent to all of us that God wanted to restore our family. The healing was a slow process because of the great amount of wounded emotions and deep hurt I inflicted upon my wife and Mary. Both needed to feel they could trust me; the healing came in stages. If it were not for God working on all of our hearts, there would have been bitterness and anger in their lives. For me, if God had not intervened, I would still have the torment of reckless abandon in my own life. His goodness and mercy were undeniable to anyone who knew of our predicament."

Edward paused to reflect on the testimony he had shared with John. It had been awhile since he had given such detail of his marriage. Even so, he felt it was something John needed to hear. "There is much more to the story, but I think it should wait for now. Will you please come and have dinner with us tonight?"

In many ways, John was on a new path, a path toward knowing God. "Edward, I can honestly say you have cleared up a lot of questions I've had concerning my parents and, of course, without wanting to admit it, about God as well. I sincerely appreciate the dinner invitation, but I need to go and visit with Dr. Murray. Thanks to you, I have some money to go towards what I owe him. Fulfilling my mum's wishes has become all-important to me. I'm beginning to see how she felt. The people who worked for her were very loyal and truly needful. If she hadn't been so diligent with putting the money aside, many of the estate workers would now be destitute. Perhaps tomorrow evening I'll be back this way, and I can stop by."

"Since you mentioned Dr. Murray, may I keep you for a few more minutes? He is a big part of my story that I'm certain will inspire you. You'll appreciate Andrew Murray even more as you see him in a different light. It's getting late, and we both need to go, so I'll keep it brief."

"Please, go ahead."

"Remember when I mentioned that I went to see a country preacher when I had reached a very low point in my life?"

"Yes."

"Andrew Murray and I go way back. We were in medical school together, at Oxford... before I changed my course of study and moved to Cambridge. It was Andrew who taught me and showed me the truth of God's Word and His desire to save me. If Andrew had not spent the time or shared with me from the Bible, I would have sought relief from a tavern and not a church. I believe that I literally owe my life to Andrew Murray. I was making my life, the road I was traveling on, rough and rocky. There is no telling how my life would have turned out if he had not shared the Truth with me in our dormitory. In much the same way, John, God loves you and wants to capture your heart and take you on a path He has prepared for you. When you're ready, I urge you to say 'yes' to Him."

Edward's enriching testimonies and heartfelt sentiments caused John to be much more receptive to his invitation to know God. "That's fair enough. Edward, thanks for sharing, especially your life story. I truly would like to hear more, but first thing in the morning, I need to go and see Dr. Murray. Just so you'll know, I've been thinking about visiting my sister and her husband, Paul. I want to stay with her for a few days just in case Romney Longfellow really is trying to ruin me. May I keep your invitation for dinner open without you thinking of me as rude?"

Edward could sense that the Lord was already working on the seeds planted in John's heart. "Of course, anytime you can come and see us would be seen as a privilege on our part. In the meantime, may I give you my Bible to read as you have a chance?"

"Oh, Edward, I couldn't—"

"No really, I insist. There is a promise in here that I don't want you to miss."

Chapter Twelve
Unanticipated Transformation

John was truly inspired by Edward Van Zandt's moving testimony of redemption. Since spending the afternoon with Edward, John sensed an odd awareness, feeling that the people in his life, at the moment, were trying either to kill him or get him saved. Either way, John wanted to flee the pressures closing in on him. Even so, a safe path was opening up for John. The path led straight to Dr. Murray, who John now knew to be a believer, and then to his religious sister. John felt that he was being drawn to God—unable to resist.

In the middle of the night, unable to sleep, John audibly conversed with himself in an effort to find his way. "But why? Why must I give up my dreams and aspirations to a God I can't see... to someone else's version of the truth? I've already lost so much; why do I have to give up everything?"

John remembered Edward's Bible and felt compelled to look through it. He thumbed through the pages but was unable to find what he was looking for—something that would let him off the hook. Anything that would allow him to see that Edward had made a mistake and none of his claims were real.

There it was... leaping off the page... Acts 4:12 *Neither is there salvation in any other: for there is none other name under heaven given among men, whereby we must be saved.* John quickly searched the context to see who the verse was referencing. Who is there salvation in and none other? Back up a few verses... there it is ... *the name of Jesus Christ of*

Nazareth, whom ye crucified, whom God raised from the dead, even by him doth this man stand here before you whole. Under his breath, John answered his own questioning. "The verse is talking about Jesus, just as Edward said."

John was seeing for himself the power of God's Word to reach his heart… to answer his deepest longings for the truth. He felt satisfied yet hungry for more. John continued reading the rest of the chapter and then turned to a few more pages, resigned to the fact that God would eventually win his heart. He had a sudden eagerness to get the day started and to make his way over to see Dr. Murray.

It was early, too early, to be knocking on anyone's door. John tied his carriage to the hitching post outside Dr. Murray's back door. With lantern in hand, he then began to pace around the yard, knowing it was inappropriate to be so untimely. John suddenly had a great idea. He would stall his still-rented carriage and start his day working off what he owed the doctor. Even if cleaning the stalls wouldn't earn him much against the debt, it might help him settle his racing thoughts.

Much to John's surprise, Andrew Murray came walking up the path that was adjacent to the barn, leading up from the chicken coops. With lantern in one hand and egg basket in the other, Dr. Murray hailed John from a distance. "John, what a wonder—you must've been up since four o'clock to get here at this time of day. Come give me a hand while I get some ham from the smokehouse. You do want some breakfast, don't you?"

John's sensibilities were shifting by the moment. He could see a genuine goodness resident in Dr. Murray that he had been unable to recognize until today. What he saw was not with his natural eyes. John was experiencing a clarity being made known to him. His spiritual eyes were being opened. In a divinely orchestrated moment in time, an opportunity was presenting itself to him—a call he felt he could now answer.

With a faint glow of morning light warming the ambiance, John spoke with heightened enthusiasm. "Dr. Murray, I have some great news. But first, let me tell you that I'm sorry for not coming back to see you when you requested. With my mum's funeral and all… by the way, thanks for coming. You'll be glad to hear my body has healed pretty well, but I'm still sore in a few places, though."

"So what's the good news that got you here at five-thirty in the morning?"

"Well, first, I've come across some money to apply toward the family account. I have no idea how much I owe, but I have decided to take you up on your offer and work off as much as you will let me, knowing you can't take the entire bill in trade. I plan to take employment with Edward Van Zandt, so eventually I will be able to pay the whole amount."

"Edward's a good man. So he offered you a job?"

"Well, he did say it would be a future offer. Even so, I'm confident he would give me something right now if I asked."

"Let's go inside. We can talk over breakfast."

As John and Andrew made their way toward the kitchen, Andrew sensed something was very wrong. "John, are you feeling all right? Do you have a fever?"

"No fever that I know of, and I feel good except for a few lingering bruises. Why do you ask?"

Andrew set aside the eggs and ham on the kitchen counter and turned to face John, addressing him in a concerned tone. "I'm afraid we're going to be skipping breakfast today. If what I suspect is true, then neither one of us is going to have an appetite. John, I need you to strip down to your underwear."

"What's happening, Dr. Murray?"

"John, you have a smell about you that can only be one thing. Any doctor or rancher knows the stench of rotting flesh. Do you have any open wounds?"

It was only a few moments when Dr. Murray implored, "My god, man! How'd you get these knots and welts on your head?"

"Oh, those... it's a long story. The truth is I took a few blows from a crowd with nightsticks down at the shipyard, day before last."

"These wounds are dreadful. You have several bad infections with a nice crop of young maggots. John, my boy, if you hadn't come today, and these open wounds had gone untreated, you could have become gravely ill.

John couldn't grasp the severity of the moment. "Why didn't I have more pain with the lumps on my head?"

Dr. Murray laughingly quipped, "God gave us men hard heads for a reason; we often put them in places they don't belong. Seriously, John, the scalp has fewer nerve endings, but you may also have some local nerve damage. Either way, I'm glad you came." Unexpectedly, a divine realization occurred to John. In the briefest of moments, he saw a glimpse of God's hand working in his life. "You know, Dr. Murray, it was by chance that I came here today. I felt compelled to bring you the money as soon as possible." John's heart was pricked as he confessed with moistened eyes, "You've saved my life twice in a month's time. I think Someone is trying to get my attention."

John's admission did not go unnoticed by Dr. Murray as he shifted to a serious-minded persona. He wanted to get started with the tedious procedure of mending John's injuries. "John, I need to put you under and shave your head. Next, I'll need to cut these wounds open and thoroughly clean them out. This is serious work that will take quite a while, considering the number of sutures I will have to make. I need to get started— what about it John?"

John was trying to be compliant even though things were happening quickly, "I know I can trust you, so go ahead and put me under." In a humble tone, John expressed his deepest appreciation as God continued to work on his heart. "Dr. Murray, I can't thank you enough for how you've taken care of me."

Andrew explained with a reassuring tone, "Alright, John, I'm going to use chloroform. It won't hold you long enough, so you'll get some morphine before you come to. Here goes...."

It took over three hours to complete the reconstructive work to John's scalp. Before the morphine wore off,

Dr. Murray reopened a few places on John's face where the earlier stitches had been compromised. If the facial wounds had not been corrected, a few marks might have remained more noticeable than desired. He then removed what was left of John's body cast.

Once his work was complete, Dr. Murray had made forty-five new sutures to properly close the open welts on John's scalp. This brought the total to ninety-eight stitches to John's head. Granted, these were fine sutures, necessary for a wound to the face or scalp.

John's unanticipated transformation over the last month should not be wished on anyone. Considering John's weight loss, baldhead, scars, bruises and stitches, he would barely be recognizable to anyone who knew him before the accident. If it were possible to compare the handsome John of four weeks earlier, by standing him next to the John of today, the visible differences would be shocking.

Chapter Thirteen
"...the two shall become one."

John began to revive around four o'clock that afternoon. Dr. Murray thought he would try to lighten John's grogginess with a well-placed tease, "John, are you hungry for the ham and eggs you missed this morning?"

John was lightheaded, making him a little disoriented. "I don't think I can eat anything right now, doctor. Tell me, was it as bad as you thought? What day is it anyway?"

"Take it easy, John, I was just kidding about the breakfast. You couldn't hold down any food right now anyway. But... if I know my morphine, you'll be very hungry a little later."

Dr. Murray helped John over to a chair so he could sit up awhile, helping to alleviate his grogginess. After giving John a sip of water, Andrew pulled up a stool and spoke to him as a patient, "I had to cut away quite a bit of dead flesh, so your scalp is going to feel a little tight for a while. By the way, I had to redo some of the sutures on your face, so altogether you look rather banged up. I suggest you stay here for a week or so and get well before going to visit your sister. It'd give us time to talk and you could do some light work around here and help me out... be good for both of us."

John took several moments to process Andrew's suggestions before responding, "Thanks, for your concern. Right now that sounds good; however, I would like to go see Edward in the next day or two. I promised him a return visit after a short stay with my sister—he'll be expecting me, and I don't want to concern him."

"How is Edward? I haven't seen him in months."

"Well, he's part of the reason I came so early this morning. Edward and I had a long talk yesterday about God and the Bible. He also told me how you started him on his journey to find God."

Andrew was instantly taken back to his college years. "Yes, we were both at Oxford University when we had several heated debates about the scriptures. It was during the last two months before he decided to change his course of study and move to Cambridge. I was glad to hear that he later found the Truth and received the Lord as his Savior. Since then he has never wavered, a real fireball—always the evangelist."

The story about Edward piqued John's interest. "Dr. Murray, do you mind if I ask you a rather personal question?"

"No, go ahead."

"How is it that a graduate of Oxford is practicing medicine on the outskirts of town?"

"Oh, John, you certainly know how to ask a tough question. It's a hurtful topic that I have never really come to terms with. I'm sorry to have to admit it. Even so, a man's reputation and honor are very near and dear to him. I have been deprived of both, as well as a fruitful marriage."

"I'm sorry, Dr. Murray, I shouldn't have broached such a personal subject."

Dr. Murray spoke with a somewhat reflective mood, "It's quite alright. It would probably do me good to talk about it more. The anger and resentment, which I've held onto, are nothing more than poisons that eat away at my sanity. As a man of faith, I should have let go of my disappointments years earlier."

John wasn't sure how to proceed with the conversation except to extend his gratitude and offer help. "You've done so much for me. If talking will help you, then please do so."

Andrew felt he should continue for John's sake, as well as his own. "John, my father was a Baron, and, as you know, that is the lowest rank of the aristocracy. At Oxford, I was trivialized and often shunned because of my peerage. I had to work incredibly hard to gain any credibility among my peers. Eventually, the extra effort did pay off with a few of my professors. I believe the worst part was that I had to work alone in the laboratory where collaboration is crucial."

Dr. Murray hesitated while deciding whether to continue with the most difficult part of his story. "My final exam and all my thesis work were duplicated and turned in by another student—my laboratory journals were meticulously copied as well. When the impersonated work was compared to mine, I was called before the board of regents to address the charge of cheating—my work was identical to that of a fellow graduating student. My lower social standing was all that stood in the way of being acquitted and having the real cheat exposed. I was never told who had deprived me of receiving the recognition I was due and the honor of a full diploma. John, I would have graduated at the top of my class instead of some imposter."

John was shocked at Dr. Murray's moving account of betrayal. Even though John had never done anything so damning, he knew others who had taken full advantage of their peerage. Now, he was seeing the human side of the injustices the upper classes often mete out. John could sincerely feel Andrew's cause for pain and resentment that had plagued him. "Dr. Murray, I can certainly see how you could carry your anger and how it would affect your life's work. A lesser man would not have been able to bear it. But how did the unjust treatment at medical school affect your marriage?"

Andrew lowered his head in shame at John's question. "The state of my marriage is the most heartrending part of my life, and, to tell you the truth, it's mostly my fault. I was a young man in love, attending my final year of medical school. Ruth stole my heart, and we married three months later. I was a man of the Bible and knew that I shouldn't marry a nonbeliever, but that is exactly what I did. At the time, I couldn't see how it would matter. John, it's not that she has rejected my faith. She just doesn't see how believing in God could be relevant for her own life. Trust me, John, if this situation ever presents itself to you, don't do what I did. Your desire to please God will be compromised if not extinguished."

Andrew paused for a moment to reflect on his thoughts before continuing. "Ruth was a city girl who relished the high society lifestyle she had grown up in. Unfortunately, the fiasco with my final exam left me with no choice but to take my medical practice to the commoner, which meant a life outside the social elite. Even though the charges against me were false, it didn't matter for many in our circle of friends and especially her family. My "supposed" diminished character is what they chose to believe rather than stand by me and seek the truth."

Dr. Murray felt a lighter heart as he shared his story with John. He felt that John needed to hear what he had to say, knowing that John too had fallen from the graces of nobility. "Ruth still loved me and she believed in me, but she wasn't willing to give up her opulent lifestyle that she loved so much. Rather than come with me to live a more meager existence, she chose, in her words, "a town and country marriage." I spend a few days in town when I get caught up with my work here, and Ruth visits me here in our country home when she has a lull in her social affairs."

John couldn't help asking the tough questions. He was wrestling with his own ebb and flow of sensibilities, trying to find the meaning of it all. "I don't see how it could matter. Can't you still be the Christian God wants you to be even if Ruth doesn't believe?"

"John, when two people join in marriage, the Bible says that the two shall become one. If this union is pulled in two directions, it will eventually be torn apart. Therefore, to remain married, one of the two must relinquish their aspirations, usually at great heartbreak. The scripture describes this division of hearts as being "unequally yoked." However, if two people marry, having an equal desire to pull in the same direction, much can be accomplished for God's Kingdom.

Unity between husband and wife is a must if you want your marriage to reach its full potential. You see, John, every person was designed and made by God to glorify Him. Anything less will leave your marriage empty and unfulfilled. John, please understand that Ruth and I are still faithful to each other; we just don't have the abundant life that God wants us to have in our marriage."

Chapter Fourteen
One Sows and Another Reaps

John wasn't sure why he was getting this weighty instruction on marriage; he hadn't ever considered taking a wife. "When I asked you about Oxford, I didn't realize there was so much behind the question."

"There's a reason we're having this conversation; more than we know right now. You won't understand all of this until another time. However, I felt that God wanted me to share with you about my marriage and how important it is to find a godly wife."

"I do appreciate your advice. I'm not certain when I'll use it, but it sounds right."

"You know, John, there is one thing lacking in all of this."

John was a little puzzled by Andrew's statement, but he also had a feeling he knew where the doctor was headed with his comment. "Let me guess. I need to become a Christian before I meet the godly woman who is to become my wife."

Dr. Murray felt like a proud father as he smiled at John's budding discernment. There was a certain joy in seeing John gain understanding while grasping his tutelage. "John, let me answer you by saying this. There is a woman, right now, as we speak, who is preparing her heart to be holy before God, so that you, her future husband, will not be disappointed. Her heart's desire is to be pleasing to God so she can be a blessing to you. God is setting aside the perfect wife for you, John. Yes, there is one thing lacking. Would God take a diligent and faithful woman and join her with a man who is not as diligent and faithful? Knowing that God is being faithful in His desire to give you the perfect wife, wouldn't it make sense to step into His plan for your life and follow Him with all your heart?"

> *Would God take a diligent and faithful woman and join her with a man who is not as diligent and faithful?*

It's not that John was trying to be difficult. However, inconsistencies were always a bother to him. "I don't mean to be disrespectful or question what you are telling me, but if you haven't lived what you are saying to me, then how do you know it's true?"

John's rather innocent yet penetrating question instantly brought a sharp prick of conviction and shame. Andrew, who had spoken from his heart, albeit through the pain of experience, was brought to tears. Tempered with years of regret for his impulsive decision, Andrew spoke through his tears, "You are absolutely right, and it makes the very point that I want you to see. My Christian testimony... my credibility is severely diminished because my marriage is not honoring God, as it should. You have every right to treat my words as worthless because I cannot stand before you and testify they are true for me. So naturally, what follows is to question whether any of what God tells us is true. The diminished and compromised course of my life is the crux of your very first question to me: *'how could it matter, as a Christian, whether Ruth is a believer or not?'*"

Andrew paused to collect his thoughts, giving John a chance to speak up. "There is more to marriage than I could have ever imagined. I thought the goal of marriage would be to try to find happiness through someone else. You know... find a woman who could please me and meet my needs."

"John, the greatest blessing a man can have is a wife who will walk by his side through every obstacle to achieve God's plan and purpose for his life. The only way that can happen is if you lay down your life for her and for God and not seek your own way, following Him only."

"You know, Dr. Murray, when I came this morning, I was very interested in your views of Christianity. Edward Van Zandt gave me a lot to think about last night. So much so, I was unable to sleep. In the early morning hours, I thumbed through the Bible that he gave me, and I read something that seemed very reassuring, especially in light of all that he told me. I thought God had given me direction and answered my doubts.

Now, having talked to you and remembering the trials that Edward has faced, I feel a little doubtful again."

"John, remember that Edward and I have shared our failures in hopes you will not make the same mistakes. Trust me, John, when I tell you that knowing Christ as my Savior is the greatest accomplishment that I will ever make. You will have struggles and disappointments, even heartbreak, but life will always be worth living when you know your heavenly Father and experience the enormous love that He has for you."

Doctor Murray's rebuttal to John's momentary lost hope washed away any resurgent doubts that had surfaced. "Dr. Murray, Edward told me quite plainly that there would be a day that I would be ready to receive Jesus as my Lord. He urged me to say 'yes' when that time came. I'm ready to say 'yes.' Would you please help me?"

"Yes, of course, John. However, before we pray, allow me to say one thing. What God has done for us is so profound it is beyond the capabilities of our intellect to grasp. Even so, the way you enter into His provision of Salvation is of the simplest means." Andrew paused to carefully select his words. "John, asking God to come into your life is only the beginning of your journey with Him. That is why Jesus used the term 'born again.' In much the same way a baby is unlearned and vulnerable, you will be in your faith. You must commit yourself to seeking Him in relationship and through His written Word. It is the only way you can live and grow in your faith. As I tell you this, I'm reminded of a verse that I read this morning that speaks directly to what I just said." Andrew took his Bible and found the verse, "Deuteronomy 30:20 says: *You can make this choice by loving the Lord your God, obeying him, and committing yourself firmly to him. This is the key to your life.* Take that Bible and thoroughly read it; treat it as food that will sustain you."

Dr. Murray paused as he searched John's facial expression for his willingness and desire to proceed. "John, if you're ready to receive Jesus, tell God what is on your heart. Talk to Him about your desire to walk in His ways. When you finish, I will pray as well."

John was eager in one regard but hesitant in another. Not sure what or how to speak to God, he began with halting and broken speech. "Lord God... I believe... this is my time to find You. I can see... how I have been on the... wrong path. I have hurt many people. I have done many things that were... wrong. Please forgive me for...all the mistakes I've made. I want to live for You... and be true to Your desires for my life. Help me to be the man that You created me to be. I need Your help. I want my life to be pleasing to You."

After a long pause, Andrew sealed John's earnest petition. "Heavenly Father, thank You for such a repentant heart seeking Your forgiveness. Please, give John the courage to say 'yes' to You over and over again. Draw him into deeper truths as You prepare him to be Your spokesman to the world, which is in need of Your great love and forgiveness. Lord, I ask You to protect him from those who would try to destroy him. Bring him through Your crucible that will prepare him for the work You desire to do in his life. I ask this in Jesus' name, Amen."

John was so moved by the reality of God's touch on his life that he could not hold back a flood of emotions. A sense of relief and elation moved him to tearfully thank Andrew for leading him to God.

John was reinvigorated and anxious to hear more wisdom and understanding from Andrew. The men continued talking until well past midnight.

Chapter Fifteen
Taking Care of Business

The next morning, John was once again ready to discuss how to pay the family debt owed to Dr. Murray. Over breakfast, John broached the subject of money. "Dr. Murray, my mum was very concerned about the debt we owe you. As I mentioned earlier, I now have some money to pay toward our account. If Edward does hire me, then I will pay you the balance as quickly as possible. I would also like to take you up on your offer to help around your place. However, I refuse to take any money in return for my labors. I can never repay you enough for all that you have done for me in the last several weeks. Not to mention the sacrificial care that you gave to my mum, especially not knowing if you would ever get paid for your work."

"John, I appreciate your sincerity and honorable intentions. Consider this proposal... only give me half of the money you have with you today. I don't want your good intentions to leave you destitute. We can work out a schedule for you to help me here two days a week. Then, if you do get employment with Edward, we'll discuss payments at that time."

John was happy with Andrew's offer, as well as the opportunity to resolve an important matter. "That sounds more than reasonable. Dr. Murray, I accept your proposal."

Dr. Murray needed to break some unpleasant news to John about Mr. Jenkins, the riding club owner. "Now… I have a tough question for you. What are you going to do about your charges at the riding stable? Mr. Jenkins has come here asking about you on two separate occasions. To be quite frank, I don't think he was overly concerned about your health. I believe he may be having a few financial problems of his own and could use the money you owe him. You need to make good on your obligation with Mr. Jenkins."

John had not forgotten his previous fateful conversation with Mr. Jenkins while in the throes of severe pain and reeling from being humiliated. "It looks like I may be working every day of the week for a long time; but yes, I will go and see him today. Do you mind if I go to the riding club after we finish breakfast and I clear the table?"

"I don't mind, but it's Friday, and he'll be gone nearly the whole day. He goes into town to buy supplies and I suppose does his banking for the week. Since he is usually back by four-thirty, why don't you do a few light duties around here until then? If you still feel well enough to ride down to the riding club, then you should go and take care of your business."

John was eager to get started with his chores—an unspoken symbol of his new beginnings. "If you will make a list of things you want me to do, I'll work through the list."

Dr. Murray chuckled at John's good intentions. "John, you don't even know which end of an axe to hold, and I'm certain you've never cleaned a horse stall. I think we'll need to spend some time together while I show you a few basics. I do admire your grit, and you have a good attitude. Those two traits alone will get you a long way in this life. Let's go see what you're made of." *Friday, June 16, 1865, was the first day in John's life to pick up a tool and put his hand to a task of manual labor.*

The lunchtime break was much anticipated and well deserved. Even though John was weak from his surgery, he proved up to the various tasks that Dr. Murray gave him to do. Once in the kitchen, Andrew needed to initiate a conversation with yet another awkward subject. Pointing to the table, Dr. Murray queried, "So John, you mentioned that you came across some money. Tell me about that. One just doesn't come across money in these days and times."

John wasn't sure about Dr. Murray's tone. His statement seemed more than curious, even tainted with an air of accusation. With the allegations of bank robbery still fresh on his mind, John momentarily hesitated as he pulled out his chair to be seated. "I'm not certain what you mean. The money came from one of two safety deposit boxes that my mum had secured. The money was left for me to make a new start, to pay you and the estate workers their back pay."

"Are you certain you have your facts straight? This is important, John."

"Well yes… What's this all about anyway?"

"A detective from the police department came by here on Wednesday, wanting to know if I'd seen you or knew where you were. He didn't give me any details but told me that it was important to let him know if you came by. I didn't want to say anything until I talked to you. Now, you show up with a sack of money. I felt I needed to ask you these pointed questions."

"I will tell you everything I know, and Edward Van Zandt can confirm what I tell you is the truth."

"What has Edward got to do with this?"

"Wednesday, while I was preparing to pay the estate employees their severance, two men dressed as police officers came to arrest me. Edward was instrumental in determining they were imposters. After we finished our business with the severance, we made a citizen's arrest and took them to the precinct to press charges. Unfortunately, we were unable to determine if they were being hired or were working on their own. Either way, they were there to steal what had been in the bank lockboxes. I don't know if they meant me harm, but I'm certain they would have done what was needed to get what they came after."

"So you think it is possible that the detective who came by here was after your mum's money?"

"I don't know why he was here. What I do know is that I haven't done anything wrong. But, yes, there seems to be a connection. Someone is desperate to put his hands on what I have. It's clear that if the detective is connected to the phony policemen, then there must be a conspiracy in play."

"Is there something other than money that could be valuable enough to go to all these efforts? Have you looked to see what else you have from the lockboxes that may be of value?"

John hadn't thought about anything the bags may have contained that would be of more value than the pound notes; it never occurred to him. "Since I left the bank on Wednesday morning, my thoughts and attention have been thoroughly consumed by one happening unfolding after another. Since paying the estate workers, I haven't thought much more about the bank bag." John paused to mentally run through the last few days, hoping to remember something. "While at the bank, I went through the first lockbox. I did not see anything of value. Moments later, I felt as if I needed to leave the bank as soon as possible, so I just dumped the contents of both boxes into the bag and quickly left."

"Perhaps you should go through the bag and see what you have. With a new perspective, it might help you understand why you are being pursued and if your life is in danger. You can use the front room for privacy. I don't need to know what you've got. Besides, I want to make our lunch."

John carefully went through the many documents and papers, some for the second time. Upon finding the second letter from his mother, he thoughtfully set it aside to read last. Continuing his search, he found a pleasant surprise. To his amazement, he found a small box that contained his mum's wedding ring and a beautiful jeweled pendant that appeared to complement the ring. The touching reminders of his mother brought a lump in his throat that almost moved him to tears. He also found another envelope that contained more money, just under the amount of fifty pounds sterling.

After spending ample time scrutinizing the contents of the bank bag, he was ready to see what his mother's letter held for him.

My dear son, by now you have paid Dr. Andrew Murray the full amount due him. The smaller amount you found in a separate envelope is for Mr. Jenkins of the riding club. I don't know how much we owe him, but the money I have left you should go a long way toward finalizing our debt to him. Please tell him how much I appreciate that he carried us. John, there are a few smaller debts we owe; please seek them out. The market carries a small balance, as well as the druggist. You should have enough money left to find a small cottage and settle into a new life. And finally, Mr. Edward Van Zandt has the key to box #719. I have instructed him to give it to you only when he feels you are ready. John, you can trust Edward completely.

Love Always, your mum, Madeline Taylor

John's mind was spinning as he began speaking aloud as if someone was in the room to hear him. "So Edward is the mysterious *Anonymous* from the bank vault." Mentally, John began putting together the bits of information that he knew from talking to Edward. Now, it was beginning to make perfect sense.

All of the recent revelations, as well as John's decision to yield his life to the Lord were creating a sense of optimism. John's immediate future seemed to be taking a turn for the better. The extra money set aside for Mr. Jenkins enhanced John's feeling of assurance. Adding to his sense of well-being, Dr. Murray was rapidly becoming more than John's doctor. He was now a friend, counselor and father figure.

John neatly placed the envelopes, as well as the jewelry back in his bag. Satisfied that he had accounted for everything in the bag, John was eager to give Dr. Murray a report. In an upbeat tone, he called out from the doctor's front room to the kitchen. "Dr. Murray, you must see this note from my mum."

As John made his way toward the kitchen, he had a sudden pervading thought. He needed to ask Dr. Murray something that had never occurred to him. Andrew was still busy making lunch, so he had not heard John call out to him. John queried Andrew with a new level of enthusiasm, "Dr. Murray, do you know how much I owe you... the total amount, including my mum's debt?"

"To be honest John, I have never added up the total. However, I have all of my journal entries so the amount can be tallied when needed. The fact is I'm not much of a bookkeeper." With a big grin, he quipped, "It's my only weakness. Why do you ask?"

John continued following a hunch, "I'm not very good with money. I guess my problem is that I don't know what things cost because I never had to be concerned about it. Do you have a guess on the amount?"

"Oh, let's see. It's probably not going to be more than… say… sixty or seventy pounds sterling."

John's gut feeling was true—he had enough to pay Andrew. With controlled elation, John ventured, "Well, Dr. Murray, can we keep our original arrangement except that I pay you most or all that I owe you?"

Andrew's curious facial expression hinted that he was baffled. "I'm confused. You have enough money with you to pay the whole amount?"

"Like I said, I didn't have any way to relate the money I had to the amount that I might owe you… but, yes, I have a little over two hundred pounds sterling to pay the family debts. My mum has mentioned several times that there would be money to live on. Even so, after considering the amount that Romney stole, I assumed there wouldn't be any money left after I paid everyone. That being said, even if I pay you the whole amount owed to you, I still want to come out here and help you just as we discussed earlier. Would that be all right?"

In a matter-of-fact way Andrew voiced, "Of course, I'd like that. Here, let's have some ham and bean soup."

John challenged Andrew's rather plainly spoken affirmation. "I'm sincere when I say I don't want this to change our plans. You have been good to me, and I want to return your kindness. I want to be a friend you can count on. Perhaps I can assist you in your research and in the process learn a few of the basics of medicine."

In a fatherly tone, Andrew moved the conversation along, "Does this mean you intend to pay Mr. Jenkins?"

"Yes, sir, it certainly does. That is one account I will be glad to pay off. He's been holding my pocket watch since I rented the carriage. I'll be happy to have my watch back—it was my father's, you know."

"Well, John, just a fair warning, Mr. Jenkins was anxious and on the verge of anger when he came to ask about you. My advice is to deal forthrightly with him. I think he's under a lot of pressure. He keeps meticulous records, so don't be afraid to ask to see them. It'll keep him honest, especially if he knows you have a lot of money on you, so don't let him know that. You'll be doing business with him in the future, so keep your dealings with him cordial."

"That's good advice. I'll remember that, thank you."

John was anxious to return to his earlier appeal concerning his mum's letter. "Dr. Murray, if you have time after lunch would you look at the letter my mum left for me in the safety deposit box?"

"Let me see the letter. I'll look it over while we eat." Andrew read Madeline's note with great interest. "John, this note is very interesting, to say the least. Looks like you have something to look forward to in the future... a little intrigue to keep you on your toes.

I noticed there is mention of a place to stay. My wife's in-town residence has a detached bungalow that she has been debating whether to rent out.

> *Looks like you have something to look forward to in the future... a little intrigue to keep you on your toes.*

Could be something you might consider. It's within a few blocks of Edward Van Zandt's printing company. It could work out for everyone, but it will be Ruth's decision. I won't have a say in the matter."

John's life was looking positive for him, as all things seemed to be coming together. "Thanks for your counsel concerning Mr. Jenkins, as well as the information on the bungalow. You have been a big help to me."

After a momentary pause, John proposed, "I have a thought… if you were to write a letter of introduction, I could stop by and see Mrs. Murray tomorrow, when I go to see Edward."

"John, I think you're getting ahead of yourself. Did you forget that you are being pursued? I suggest that you stay here as we discussed earlier… grow your beard as a disguise. The extra time will allow things to cool off as well. With the weight you've lost, commoner's clothing and a beard, you should be able to move about London without being recognized."

"Dr. Murray, you have a valid point, but I feel I must take a chance. I promised Edward that I would return to see him as soon as I finished my business with you. Since he is expecting me, I don't want to cause undue worry. Perhaps you can help me with an idea of how I can get to town undetected so that I can meet with Edward. My plans to visit my sister will just have to wait.

Andrew was a thinker. "Give me a little time, perhaps I can come up with an idea or two. In the meantime, finish cleaning the stalls and bring a week's worth of kindling up from the woodshed. By then it will be time to wash up and go see Mr. Jenkins. I promise, by the time you get back from seeing him, I'll be ready with a plan to get you safely to town."

John's short trip to the riding club was rather uneventful except for one excruciating disappointment—his pocket watch was not there. Since John was overdue returning the rental carriage, Mr. Jenkins lost faith in John's ability to keep his word about paying his family's debt. Mr. Jenkins needed the money, so he sold John's watch to De Beers Jewellery when he went to London earlier in the morning.

John returned the rented carriage and retrieved his horse while taking extra care to settle the riding club account in an amicable manner. He even remembered to thank Mr. Jenkins as his mother requested. Actually, John was so gracious and honoring that Mr. Jenkins was left wondering what had happened to him—a very good start for John's testimony as a new Christian.

Perhaps not all was lost concerning the pocket watch. De Beers Jewellery was in the "diamond district" not far from Ruth Murray's in-town home. John hoped he could retrieve it first thing Monday morning before he went to see her.

While John was taking care of his business at the riding club, Andrew was considering the possibility of taking John to town concealed in his carriage. That is when he suddenly got an irresistible urge to spend the weekend with his wife. Even though Ruth had recently been out to the country home, he now had a rekindled desire to see his wife. It made perfect sense for him to take John to see Edward. With growing anticipation, he eagerly began to prepare for his surprise visit. He then put together a change of clothes in a knapsack for John.

When John returned from the riding club, he found Dr. Murray waiting and ready with the carriage. Knowing that something was up, John confirmed what was evident. "Dr. Murray, you must have an idea for getting me to town."

"I have a grand plan which I think you'll like. We are both going to London. I'll tell you more on the way."

John now had his old horse back and began tying the reins to the back of the carriage when Andrew stopped him. "Anyone who is looking for you may recognize your horse; you'll need to leave it here. While you put him up, I have a few things I can do. Even so, you need to hurry—it's getting late."

Once they started for town, Andrew explained his intentions. "John, I'm going to spend the weekend with Ruth. After we talked last night, I have decided to try and bring our marriage around. I think it's time to make it right. First, we'll stop by Ruth's so I can introduce you to her. Then I'll drive you over to Edward's home. I'm certain he won't mind if you spend the weekend at his place. That's the best plan I could come up with. It seems to meet most of your concerns, and it gives me a chance to be with my wife."

"You are a genius, Dr. Murray."

"I've packed a change of clothes for you, as well as some food in the knapsack. Before we get much further down the road, I suggest you change your shirt and put on the bowler hat." In an apologetic tone mixed with male jesting,

Andrew quipped, "Oh... and John... you need to try and remember that you look dreadful. Your head is shaved, you have stitches showing on your face and head, and you're a little gaunt. The way you look is to your advantage, but try not to frighten Edward's sweet little daughter, Mary."

John replied, "I can assure you that Mary Van Zandt is quite able to defend herself from the likes of me. I don't believe she is the type that can be frightened easily." John sat silently as he reminisced about Mary's hotheaded rebuke that had previously sent him running. It certainly wasn't funny at the time, but looking back John found amusement and quietly laughed to himself.

Chapter Sixteen
With God's Help

Andrew Murray pulled the carriage around to the back of his wife's in-town residence and temporarily secured the horses. Even though it was not yet dusk, Ruth had her gas lit home glowing with lights. When she opened the door to Andrew, she was as radiant as her well-lit home. He was not sure what to think, as he had not seen her as joyful in years. "Oh, Ruth, you look beautiful!"

Ruth was pleasantly surprised by Andrew's unexpected but welcomed visit. Unknown to Andrew, Ruth had begun seeking God in a genuine manner; a change that began about six months earlier when she attended a Bible study. She had been reluctant to mention her newfound interest, fearing Andrew would push her too quickly. Over the ensuing months Ruth slowly, but surely, opened her heart to the truth of His Word. Sunday last, while at church, Ruth had a moment that she could only describe as *being touched by God*. She had yet to surrender her life to Him, but she was ready to do so.

With overflowing gladness, she welcomed her husband, "What a surprise! I wasn't expecting you—come in. I'm so happy you're here—this is wonderful."

Andrew couldn't believe what he was hearing. On most occasions when he would come to visit, he felt like he was merely stepping into her world; a bother to her. To hear her express such heartfelt enthusiasm was almost more than he could bear. With moistened eyes, Andrew was finding it hard to speak. "Ruth, I'm so glad I came."

An awkward moment passed. In recent years, their physical relationship had been guarded, so he didn't feel he could hold her the way he wanted. Ruth sensed his wariness and graciously stepped into his arms. Their embrace was all that any man could want. God was working a miracle in Ruth that immediately began to heal Andrew's wounded and broken heart. The change had been many years and countless prayers in the making.

A little embarrassed at his emotional reunion with his wife, Andrew introduced her to John. "Ruth, this is John Taylor, who has been under my care. He'll be working with me for the next few months while he heals."

Ruth didn't intend to step back into her former haughty persona, but she judged John to be a vagrant. She had often faulted Andrew for being too soft-hearted, trying to help those that she felt he shouldn't bother with. "Oh... I see..." On the verge of tears, Ruth broke down, "Oh, Andrew, must you do this to me? Did you have to bring this man to my house?"

Ruth began weeping into her hands with prideful despair. Andrew was somewhat bewildered by the unfolding drama. He knew that on one hand, she was misjudging the situation, and on the other hand, he knew that even if she was right about John, she was wrong in her treatment of him.

John made a bold move, attempting to bring clarity to the moment of Ruth's flawed reaction. "Mrs. Murray, I'm John Taylor of the China Tea Trading Company... the worldwide shipping line. I was in a terrible accident, and since your husband is known as the best facial surgeon in London, naturally I went to him for help."

Had Ruth's tears of distress been faked? With a lifetime of practice and perfected form, no one could say for sure, but her recovery was quick and sure. "Oh my... please forgive me for my tactless indiscretion." Her canned response made her realize that she had fallen back into a prideful routine that she wanted to stop. In a more repentant gesture, Ruth looked down and took a more humble composure. "I'm sorry for my rush to judgment. Actually, it is a nasty habit I've been trying to break. I have been judging others for so long it seems impossible to stop. Please forgive me."

Andrew and John couldn't help but look at each with a brief stare of wonderment. Andrew had never known his wife to be humbled, much less repentant. In much the same manner, John was in awe of the woman who graciously defied Andrew's unintentional portrayal of her. Ruth took it all in, knowing they had every right to be wary. After a few moments, Andrew found his verbal footing and spoke through his newly acquired encouragement. "Ruth, I've been praying for our marriage. I'm beginning to see that this is going to be a wonderful time for us."

Ruth did not mean to disregard Andrew's remark; she just was not ready to talk about a future so radically different—one that she knew he was expecting. Ruth's highly refined social skills provided a cover for guarding her emotions as she casually shifted into her amiable hostess mode. "You men must be hungry. I was just beginning the evening meal when you drove up. John, will you be staying for supper?"

"Mrs. Murray, that is an invitation that is difficult to turn down. However, I'm expected by a friend here in town. Otherwise, I would be delighted. Thank you for your hospitality. It is very gracious of you to include me."

"Well, perhaps you can join Andrew and me tomorrow for services at Metropolitan Tabernacle. Charles Spurgeon is expected back from Europe. He's been gone since late April you know."

Charles Spurgeon

Andrew was astounded and elated at the unexpected pronouncement from his wife. Not to upset the moment, Andrew quickly reined in his shock and eloquently reaffirmed his wife's invitation, "Yes, John, we would be delighted if you could join us."

John was carried along by the momentum of pleasantries and hospitality. "I've only known Mr. Spurgeon by name, as I have never been to his church or heard him preach." John had more to say, but suddenly had a lump in his throat. He felt prompted to speak to Ruth about his recent conversion. His urge to share was countered by a strange feeling of anxiety. His heart was pounding with expectancy, yet laced with an odd dread. How could his remarkable Salvation experience bring such an unfamiliar fear? He felt a deep sense of denial clouding his thoughts giving him a heart-wrenching decision to make.

> *John felt a deep sense of denial clouding his thoughts giving him a heart-wrenching decision to make.*

John broke through his fear with an untested faith that ultimately prevailed. "I think going to hear Mr. Spurgeon would be just the thing I need to do. I just received Jesus Christ as my Savior on Thursday. Andrew was kind enough to explain to me about God's love and His power to save. It was quite a remarkable experience for me. Thank you for asking. I'll speak to Mr. Van Zandt about the service. I'm confident that he and his daughter, Mary, will want to go as well. May we plan on seeing you there?"

Ruth eagerly replied with a hopeful concern, "John, I do hope our two parties can find each other tomorrow. It's a very large church. Afterward, I want to hear more about your conversion. I've been considering joining the church as well."

It would be natural for Ruth to equate conversion with joining the church. It was within her realm of understanding, considering her society-minded experiences. Unfortunately, status is only sustainable with heavy doses of pride to undergird its foundation. And pride is often a cruel disqualifier for authentic salvation. In any case, God is able to deliver the lowest, as well as the proudest among us. Besides, He had already begun a good work in Ruth; He was certainly able to finish it.

It was getting late, so Andrew had no choice but to find a break in the conversation, "Ruth, I'm going to drive John over to Edward Van Zandt's home. I shouldn't be gone long. Would that give you enough time to finish preparing supper?"

"Yes, Andrew, I'll be waiting for your return." As a gracious host, Ruth especially liked cooking for others. She possessed the gift of hospitality that she had perfected over her lifetime. "I'll see you soon."

Andrew was no longer harboring even the slightest amount of reservation about his improvised trip to town. He could see how God was working in his life through John and now Ruth. Andrew also realized that he had been stuck in his faith, having reached what he felt was a dead end or a plateau. At the moment, he was actually experiencing a sense of peace and joy, something that had been eluding him for a long time.

The two men had much to talk about as they struck out for Edward's home. Andrew shared about his elation and thankfulness for Ruth while John spoke of his struggle to share his salvation experience. In the midst of his resistance to testify, John found the courage when an inner voice allowed him to know that Ruth needed to hear his testimony. He felt assurance that she needed to be nudged along in the process of turning her life over to God.

In the final few minutes before reaching Edward's home, Andrew gave John some advice. "John, you should listen to what Edward has to say when he counsels you. He is extraordinarily wise and very knowledgeable. His guidance is rich with God's Word. Few people know these things about him because he doesn't try to make himself known. He has seen more, accomplished more and traveled to more places than most people might achieve in two lifetimes. He's been to mainland China on numerous occasions, as well as much of the Orient. Edward is also a major supporter of Spurgeon's China Mission—he's as good as they come."

Edward was out in the yard, having finished tending the horses when he saw John and Andrew coming up the lane. He quickly finished his last chore of lighting the gas lamp so he could greet them when they arrived. Edward walked toward them, striking a casual cadence intended to match their arrival. "Well, well, well, what have we here? Gentlemen, it's always a pleasure to have good friends drop by."

The three men engaged in an enthusiastic round of handshakes and small talk before the conversation turned more serious. Andrew needed to broach an important matter. "It's good to see you, Edward. John filled me in on some excitement you two encountered at the Taylor Estate last Wednesday."

Nodding in agreement to Andrew's assessment of the ordeal with the bogus police officers, Edward quipped, "Those scoundrels had us going for a bit, but they gave themselves up straightaway."

Andrew didn't intend to leave John out of the conversation as he continued his discussion with Edward. With an overriding parental compulsion, he needed to make sure that Edward knew right up front about the potential for a conspiracy against John. "Edward, we may have another rogue to contend with. John and I have talked at length, and we've decided that he must stay hidden until things cool off and he can grow his beard. Would it be all right if he stayed here for a few days? He could then move on to spend some time with his sister."

"Of course, I think I can arrange that." Turning toward John with an enthusiastic invitation, Edward offered, "John, this will give you a chance to come by the office and see the work we do at the printing company. Why don't we all go inside and I'll get us some tea."

Andrew was anxious to get home. The likelihood of being robbed increased by the hour once the sun went down, so he did not like being out after dark in the city. "Edward, I can't stay. My wife is waiting for me to return, but I know I'm leaving John in good hands, so I'll be on my way."

Edward and John waved him off while standing on the gravel driveway. "Godspeed, my friend."

The two men watched as Andrew briskly drove off down the lane, longing to be with his wife. If what he felt was true, his life was about to begin a new chapter—a chapter he had longed to write. Now he could with God's help.

Chapter Seventeen
Unto the Least of These

Turning toward the house, the men slowly walked to the front porch of the comfortable yet humble home where Edward and Mary lived.

John was glad that Andrew had told him so much about Edward. It helped him understand why a Cambridge-educated aristocrat would give up his social position and live modestly. Even so, John didn't know the half of it. His youth and immaturity could not see past his relatively naive and one-sided concept of life. There was much for John to learn about Edward, and he would.

Edward was truly glad for the moment; he had wanted John to visit. "Mary and I have been looking forward to your visit. I hope you haven't eaten."

"I had a filling lunch with Andrew, but I think I must have worked it off. I cleaned the stables this morning and hauled firewood this afternoon, so I am looking forward to having dinner." Edward chuckled when John showed him his blistered hands.

Giving a glance toward the kitchen, Edward expressed his delight in Mary. "I think Mary must have been expecting you to come tonight as she has been putting together a special meal."

"You have told me on several occasions that she is a very good cook, so I am looking forward to seeing for myself." Mary had made a distinct impression on John last Wednesday, leaving him thinking of her often. He was anxious to catch a glimpse of Mary, and having looked toward the kitchen several times, her absence was noticeable. "Where is Mary; I haven't seen her?"

"Mary is with the neighbors right now, but she'll be back in about an hour. May I get you some tea in the meantime?"

"Oh yes, tea sounds good." John had a lot to talk to Edward about but wasn't sure where to begin his conversation. "I have some good news. I took your advice and answered the call that God was making on my life. Thursday afternoon, Dr. Murray led me to pray for Salvation in Jesus."

Edward was visibly moved by John's conversion. "John, that is wonderful news. I am happy for you. I can tell you, John, in all sincerity, that God has great plans for you if you will surrender your life to Him."

"Edward, several days ago, while we were at the estate, you mentioned that God had plans for me. I didn't know what you meant, nor could I conceive of such a thing. However, since I asked the Lord to save me, I have had several moments of profound optimism in a way that I have never experienced before. I believe God has been allowing me to see the world more clearly and to experience His goodness."

"You are experiencing God's abundance, and, as you said, the goodness that he has set for anyone who will trust Him completely. One thing you will discover as you grow and mature in your faith is that you must walk in total surrender to the Lord. When you do, those moments of peace and optimism will become a constant in your life."

"Edward, that sounds encouraging and you make it sound easy. But, it seems impossible to give up the way I have learned to live. I have always known how to get what I want… or at least, I thought I did."

"John, before we come to Christ, we are naturally inclined to satisfy every whim, making every effort to get what we want. But, when you yield to God's call on your life, then your life becomes about Him. This is where most new converts lose the meaning of what God has done for them."

"I am not quite sure what you mean."

"Many people feel that if they give all to Christ, they are going to "miss out" on the good things in life. Nothing could be further from the truth. Complete trust, faith and dependence on God will open up His treasury of abundant provision."

"Is that how God has worked in your life?

"John, before I answer your question, allow me to give you an illustration. I have numerous people who work for me. As a businessman and company owner, I am constantly looking for employees who I can trust with more responsibility, even someone who could take over and manage the company. Now, would I choose someone who is half-hearted, shows up late, has a bad attitude and misses work regularly?"

"Well, of course not."

"In that case, I would reward my most trusted employee with all the good things that come with higher responsibility."

"So, complete devotion enables God to bless me with His good things."

"Yes, faithfulness is a requirement that allows God to release His bounty of blessings. The scripture tells us that every good and perfect gift comes from God.

Now for your question about me. You must understand that faith is personal. The Holy Spirit will lead and guide me in directions that will fit me and suit how God made me, and He will do the same for you. What I mean by that is you cannot allow others to dictate how you live your life before the Lord. Moreover, for those who do not know the Lord, the Bible plainly teaches that the unsaved person cannot and will not understand the dictates of scriptural principles. The things that I do may not make sense to others because I am following the leading of the Holy Spirit."

John was trying to make the connection. "I think that I am following you."

"Do you remember your reaction when I told you that my father was an Earl?"

John's recollection made Edward's point perfectly clear. "Yes… I do remember. I couldn't believe that anyone would willingly give up fame, fortune and status for a seemingly meager lifestyle."

"John, for me, the good things in life are the *true riches* that God speaks of in Scripture. I have found that earthly things are empty, and will never satisfy the longings of my heart. That is why I have invested all that I have in God's Kingdom."

"Andrew was right. He said you were very wise and that I should listen to what you say. Tell me how a person can make such a wholehearted decision to invest all, as you have?"

"Let's go back to your night with Andrew when you decided to receive Jesus as your Savior. Scripture tells us that you were born again to a new life. Your old way of living is completely gone. Even so, you must decide on a daily basis to surrender and let go of the old life. The difficulty of letting go of the old is determined by how much you embrace the new. For example, it would be difficult to throw your arms around someone with a convincing embrace while at the same time holding onto a corpse. That sounds grotesque, but that is an accurate description of what we try to do when we fail to let go of our old life and embrace the new."

"That is quite a graphic depiction, but I can see your point. You do have a way of helping me understand God's directions. Do you think we can get together on a regular basis so you can teach me how to grow in my faith?"

"John, I would be delighted to help you, but you must seek God personally. God says that He is a rewarder of those who diligently seek Him. I have found that in doing otherwise, you will begin to live out your faith through my experiences with God, and not your own."

John took a moment to consider Edward's forthright guidance. John responded in a more sober but grateful tone, reflecting the significance of Edward's charge. "Thank you for the instruction on the need for total surrender. I believe I understand what you have said. And as you mentioned, it is a matter of deciding to let go of my old life."

"John, I have one last thought to share with you before Mary returns. I believe what I have to say will sum up what we have been discussing. The scriptures tell us that *we are bought with a price… we are no longer our own, but slaves to Him, for His bidding.* That means we belong to Him and He is a good Master. Most importantly, we were made to be in relationship with Him. It is only in Him and through Him that you can reach your full potential that He has for you. Your ultimate destiny will be determined by your willingness to be consumed for His purposes. You can trust Him, John."

> *Your ultimate destiny will be determined by your willingness to be consumed for His purposes.*

John could not help but be assured by Edward's heartfelt passion. There was an unmistakable anointing on Edward's words of encouragement. "You inspire me to have such confidence in God. How could I say no to Him?"

"John, most men travail with God over the smallest of issues… an indication their hearts aren't fully given over to Him. It's the saddest of occupations to have a divided heart. All gladness will escape the man who sits on the fence, wavering back and forth—a miserable life to live as a Christian."

John immediately related to what Edward was saying. "I think I experienced that feeling earlier. One part of me wanted to tell Ruth Murray about how I received Christ. I struggled inwardly until I realized that I must tell her; it was something she needed to hear. It was travail, just like you said. By the way, Ruth invited me, you and Mary to hear Charles Spurgeon speak tomorrow at Metropolitan Tabernacle."

"I would delight in going with you to church tomorrow, but as for Mr. Spurgeon, he is still in Europe for a few more weeks. It was my understanding that he would be gone all of May and June. Nonetheless, Mary and I will join you and the Murrays. The three of us can take our carriage and ride there together."

"Ruth didn't mention the time the church service started. However, she did want to meet afterward… that is if we see them. She mentioned it was a very large church and was hopeful that we would find them among the crowds of people."

John felt a sudden urgency about Mary and expressed his concern, "Not to change the subject, but it's dark now and Mary is not back. Will she be all right?"

"She should be back soon; she's just down the lane. Mary takes the evening meal to a family who has fallen on rough times and then stops by to check on an elderly widow. There is no need to worry, she's fine. Once she returns, it will only take a few minutes to finish preparing our meal."

John listened intently as Edward gave further details of Mary's nightly routine. At first, he hesitated to ask an obvious question, but then his curiosity won over his reluctance. "Why would Mary go to your neighbor's first and feed them before you have eaten? It seems more appropriate to give them what you have left since they are the ones in the beggarly state."

"Oh, John, what a great question you've asked. You see, as a family, we are committed to doing things God's way. There is great blessing reserved for those who follow His principles. Proverbs 4:13 tells us very plainly: *"Take hold of my instructions; don't let them go. Guard them, for they are the key to life."*

"I'm interested to know more about how to apply God's instructions to everyday life. So teach me the principles that you are practicing in Mary's example."

"Well, there are at least two scriptures that come to mind that will help explain. The most well-known is in the book of Matthew where Jesus instructs us to attend to the poor and destitute as if we were serving Him. And then in the book of Mark we are told that to be counted as first in God's Kingdom, then we have to become last and a servant to all."

This was all new to John, so he completely missed the connection that Edward was trying to make. "I'm not certain I understand."

"I have a good example. In your mum's house, did your servants eat first and then serve you?"

John raised his brow at such absurdity, "Well... no... of course not."

"Well then follow this. Jesus is our King and we are His servants. And as I said earlier when we do good works toward the least, the poorest, we are doing our good deeds as if to Him who is our Lord and Master of the House; therefore, we don't eat until they do."

Edward's real-life illustration was perfectly clear to John, but the concept of *being last and a servant to all* was going to take a while to grasp. "I perceive that God's way is contrary to how a person would naturally go about conducting one's life."

"John, you're absolutely correct. In fact, that is one way to tell if you are doing the right thing according to His Word. Knowing that God's way often opposes your natural inclinations can often help you know what to do."

John's knowledge of God's ways was being stretched, and at the same time, his former perspectives were being challenged. "I can see I've got much to learn."

After a brief pause, Edward struck a curious tone, "John, I'm surprised you haven't asked about the key mentioned in the letter your mum left for you in the safety deposit box."

"Well, a lot has held my attention since I left the bank on Wednesday. As you know, I received some injuries from a scuffle at the loading docks, so Dr. Murray had to do emergency surgery on my scalp. I was out nearly all day on Thursday." John lifted his hat slightly to reveal the stubbles and bandages before continuing, "Yesterday afternoon was the first time I was able to thoroughly look through my bank bag to discover the contents of the second lockbox. When I read the note from my mum that is when I discovered you were the anonymous key holder as listed by the bank. Because she indicated you would surrender the key when you thought I was ready, that was good enough for me. Honestly, there hasn't been time to think of anything other than God calling me to surrender my life to Him."

"John, trust me, when the time is right, we'll have a proper discussion about the key."

As if on cue, Mary's rather noisy entrance through the back door could be heard in the front room where John and Edward were finishing their conversation. Her clumsy arrival was caused by a small wooden crate of potatoes she was trying to carry with one hand and a gunnysack full of dirty laundry in the other. With her hands full, Mary had to push and kick her way through the doorway.

When Mary entered the front room to let her father know she was back, the resulting comedic effect was delightful. At the sight of John, she gasped, realizing that her noisy entrance had been much less than ladylike. Still not completely in charge of her emotions, Mary gushed as John gawked at her stupefied pose. "Oh, John! I didn't

Mary Van Zandt

know you were here." Mary's mounting embarrassment prompted a flight to her room.

Edward smiled at the incident, knowing how Mary felt about John. Surveying John's facial expression of wonderment brought a heartwarming observation from Edward, "Isn't she the most charming young lady you have ever seen?"

John's life had changed by epic proportions since his last personal encounter with Mary. His entire outlook on life was different. He was finding that what he once thought was lowly and unappealing was, in fact, more genuine and satisfying than anything he could have ever wanted from his past.

The women he had previously known were selfishly opportunistic just as he had been. The games people played in an effort to seize power, money or influence were enough to make the 'new" John nauseated. These unfolding personal revelations were rapidly escalating John's esteem and reverence for the genuine people he now had in his life. The inner beauty that was so evident in Mary was creating a sense of rapture that John had never before experienced.

After an extended pause, John gathered his wits enough to respond to Edward's expressions of pleasure in his daughter. With an awkward and stumbling response, John uttered, "Oh... yes... sheer beaut—I mean pleasantly charming and lovely. What more could a man ask for a woman?" John immediately realized his last sentence was a bit forward, so he tried to apologize. "Edward, I'm sorry, that was inappropriate. I didn't inten—"

Edward stopped him midsentence. "John, I knew what you meant. It's quite alright." With a bit more humor, knowing that Mary was going to be in her room for a while, Edward mused, "By the way, just in case you haven't gathered by now, it may be a while before we eat."

As Mary invaded his thoughts, John became naively tentative as his sensibilities were reeling. The room became strangely silent as he contemplated his new feelings about Mary. *In the ensuing moments, the stain from his former lack of morality was being washed from him. In a divine encounter, John was translated to possess the innocence of a younger man.* John knew that he had been touched by God. He also realized that somehow he was being given a second chance at virtue. As wonderful and rewarding as his renewal experience was for him, he needed to re-engage Edward. "I'm sorry for my inattentiveness, but I just experienced a rather profound sense of God's forgiveness. Please forgive my stupor."

"John, God's favor is upon you and I'm glad for you."

Not wanting to leave the reverent moment, John asked about church. "Do you regularly attend Metropolitan Tabernacle?"

"Yes, Mary and I do attend regularly. However, I teach and sometimes preach at a small church near here, so I obviously miss going on those days. I am on the board of directors at Metropolitan Tabernacle and I have a direct connection to Mr. Spurgeon's China Mission, as well as other ministries within his larger church. But, I must be honest, John, part of my heart is with my neighbors and their welfare, both physical and spiritual. Even so, I willingly lend my experience and talents to help Mr. Spurgeon in his far-reaching ministries."

John continued to be astounded at the depth of Edward's commitment to God's call on his life. "I am looking forward to learning what God has for me to do."

"You are unique, and God will use your talents and gifts at His good pleasure, if you will allow Him. If you will do that,

He will be glorified, and you will be raised up to your highest level of fulfillment and satisfaction for living. Your life will have extraordinary breadth of meaning, allowing you to leave a praiseworthy legacy—the burning desire of every good man. And that, my friend, is a blessing that God grants to those who will diligently seek Him." John listened intently to Edward's wisdom.

As if to punctuate her father's anointed charge, a redefined Mary reappeared. She had changed from her plain, work-worn, grey flannel smock-frock to a fastidious floral design that she reserved for special occasions. Her dress was by no means of Victorian pomposity, but rather an artistic dress a middle-class commoner might wear to a special occasion. The kind of dress she wore no longer mattered to John. By now, he was enamored with Mary and longing to talk with her.

Edward decided to break up the gawking session and move everyone to the kitchen table. "Mary, what needs to be done to serve the evening meal?"

Mary's youthful coyness wore off quickly when the matters at hand tempered her reactive emotional romp. "Oh, father, everything is ready. I just need to stir the pot so I can serve everyone. By the way, Mrs. Haley gave us some red potatoes from her garden."

John felt enriched and pleasured as their lengthy conversations carried late into the day. The evening's exchange with Edward and Mary was different from any previous personal encounter from his past. The topics were positive and uplifting, as well as varied in depth and subject. Within his former circle of friends, John was accustomed to shallow and selfish talk that one would never really count as meaningful discourse.

It was getting late, and the evening would inevitably have to end. Nothing can go on forever, not even the good things. The moment came when John needed to be escorted to his sleeping quarters.

Edward lit two lanterns and gave one to John as they walked across the rather expansive backyard toward the stables. Attached to the barn was a two-room guesthouse, the former living quarters of the grounds keeper and stable manager. It was comfortable, neat and clean, yet very different from what John had been accustomed. The truth was that John's outlook had changed so much over the last few weeks that Edward's meager provision no longer mattered. "John, I hope this is suitable; this is all I have to offer."

"This is quite agreeable. I'll be fine. Thanks for your hospitality and friendship."

"Just so you'll know, the church is four miles from here. Even though the sanctuary will seat five thousand souls, if we want to have a place to sit, we will need to be there an hour before the service starts. The carriage traffic will be terrible so we will want to leave here by eight o'clock. I'll be tending the livestock by six o'clock. Would you like for me to wake you then?"

"Sir, I'll be awake and dressed by six. Would it be all right if I help you with your chores? Dr. Murray taught me how to clean stalls; I could, at least, do that. I want to make my way here and not be a draw upon your household."

"Let's put the stalls off until Monday. I don't think you want to spend your Sunday smelling like a barnyard. Otherwise, I would appreciate your help; the work will get done that much faster."

Edward turned to leave but thought he should inform John about an important part of his and Mary's Sundays. "Oh, one other thing about tomorrow; Mary and I fast our Sunday meals. Instead of breakfast, we will be undertaking a short devotional with a time of prayer. That usually takes us up to the time we leave for church. Of course, I won't make this a requirement for you, but you're free to join us."

John was once again seeing the ever-emerging contrast between the world he once knew and the realities of biblical Christianity. "I'm confident I'll survive a day without eating; it won't be the first time I've missed a meal. I am also certain you have good reasons for your Sunday routine. Perhaps you can explain it to me sometime."

"How about in the morning we make the purpose of our Sunday fast the topic of our devotional."

"I look forward to it."

"Oh... I almost forgot... you saw the privy on the way out to the barn?" After receiving a nod from John, Edward continued, "Good, I'll see you in the morning. I'll be the one making all the noise just outside your window about 6:00 a.m."

After Edward left John's quarters, and as the light of Edward's lantern faded into the night, John shook his head in silence—*he had never used an outdoor latrine.*

Chapter Eighteen
Overwhelming Sense of Well-Being

In nineteenth century London, it was not unusual for a commoner to miss various meals on a weekly basis, but not the breakfast meal, especially if he was gainfully employed. Life was a strenuous affair, and nourishment to begin the day was a requisite, that is if you wanted to have a productive day. Ah, but Sunday was a bit of a peculiarity with its reputation for being a day of rest. Nonetheless, there would be no meals prepared in the Van Zandt home.

John slept well considering his unfamiliar surroundings and intimate proximity to barnyard animals. The year's longest days occur in the middle of June, so John's early rise meant that it was dawning at 5:30 a.m. He was up at first light and dressed well before the chores would start the day.

Waiting for 6:00 a.m. to near, John paced for a few minutes deep in thought. Among all the other concerns and anticipations, one topic was steadily making its way to the forefront of his thoughts—a bath. Once the morning chores were done, John was determined to get thoroughly clean for one of the most significant days since his mother's funeral. Attending church as an adult was completely new to him, so he wanted to be clean. Hopefully, his desire for a bath and a change of clothes would set well with Edward.

In anticipation of Edward's imminent arrival for the morning chores, John left his sleeping quarters to take in a perfect June morning before his day began. He had not walked far when he saw Edward across the yard drawing water. John was a little surprised because the well-house was not in his line of sight from the guesthouse. Edward had already started his morning ritual, which began with pumping water into the watering trough. John hit his stride and hurried to greet Edward to see how he could help. "Good morning. I didn't see you come this way. What chore can I do first?"

Edward's routine was so habitual he was able to look at John and speak without slowing his labors. "John, my good man, I have a better idea. You look a bit scruffy with your stubble, and since this is your first time to attend church, I think you would feel more comfortable if you had a bath and clean clothes. Mary has heated the water, and I have laid out a suit that I think will fit you. Mary has agreed to come and help me with the chores so you will have complete privacy. Oh, and John, your suit is plain for a reason. Remember, we cannot allow you to be recognized. I also put out two hats for you to try on."

John was grateful for Edward's insight, as well as his fatherly support. "I truly wanted to help you with the chores, but you're right about needing to look presentable. I was hoping to get a chance to clean up this morning before church. I promise I'll make it up to you on Monday."

The Van Zandt home was upper middle class, which meant that it was built with a separate room for bathing. Even so, the facilities would still be considered primitive by the elite upper class. It didn't matter to John; he was just thankful to have hot water and a tub. After a quick but thorough scrubbing, John tried on the hand-me-down suit that Edward had set out. Since Edward was slightly larger and taller, the suit was a somewhat loose, making John's appearance a bit sloppy. All the same, it was more presentable than what he had been wearing. After a long glance in the ornate floor mirror, John rationalized that once he regained his weight and purchased a new pair of boots, the suit would look just fine.

The older, more worn, brown bowler hat fit best, but it didn't match his grey suit, so he decided to wear the black hat even though it was slightly loose. Being choosy about matching colors meant that John had retained enough of his former vanity to ensure he was decently attired. One advantage of the plain ill-fitting suit was it would help ensure his disguise. Those who knew him would never expect John to be dressed as a working class fellow—it would be unthinkable.

The timing was perfect. John had just finished cleaning his bathroom mess when Edward and Mary entered the kitchen through the back door. Mary had spent her time gathering her daily basket of eggs while Edward milked their two cows.  The trio converged in the kitchen with John displaying his borrowed Sunday best.

Edward was in an exceptionally good mood and couldn't help but offer a manly tease at the sight of John's scrubbed clean look. "I have to say you clean up pretty good for a nobleman." Edward's jovial tone carried the humorous tongue-in-cheek pun to its good intention.

John took the lighthearted remark with a bashful smile. "I think this will do just fine. When this whole affair with the police is behind me, I will be sure to return your suit to you. It will be a pleasurable day when I can wear my own clothes again."

"That suit is yours to keep as long as you need it. Just in case you haven't noticed, I outgrew it long ago. If you want to take a seat, Mary and I will only be a few minutes while we change clothes and freshen up. Do you still have the Bible I gave you last week?"

"Yes, sir."

"While we're changing would you please look up Proverbs 3:9 and Deuteronomy 26:10? You can look in the front of the Bible for the list of books and page numbers. We won't be long."

John wasn't entirely unfamiliar with the Bible. He had attended several classes at the university that required its study. Even so, he had little retention of its merits.

Edward was first to finish making himself ready for church. He was eager to see what John had discovered from the scripture verses. "Were you able to derive anything from the verses I gave you?"

"I'm not certain about verse ten of the Deuteronomy reference, but as I read down through verse nineteen, I did see more of what you were talking about last night... about putting God first by honoring His ways... just like you explained. I cannot say with confidence that I understood verse nine of the Proverbs reference you gave me."

Edward knew these verses on "firstfruits" were going to need more time to explain. Even so, he could give John something to consider. "John, both of these verses refer to giving God the first portion of everything that He's given us. Sunday is the first day of the week, so we give it to Him completely. It is known as the principle of firstfruits. Fasting our Sunday meals is our own personal way of yielding to Him. It is not something He requires of anyone. It's something that the Van Zandt's freely choose to do to honor His principle of firstfruits."

John wasn't following completely. He did recall that both Andrew and Edward mentioned putting God first, so that part he understood. "I'll need to trust you with the firstfruits part. Perhaps you can go over it again when we have more time."

The Bible contains many major themes and principles that God wants us to build into our lives.

"The Bible contains many major themes and principles that God wants us to build into our lives. He weaves these principles as threads through the stories and accounts of God's people in the Bible. Once these principles are pointed out, anyone who is diligent can see them reoccur many times in scripture. For instance, the principle of firstfruits is woven throughout the old and new testaments. Grasping these vital underlying truths and applying them will change everything for the true believer."

John was finding Edward's instruction very helpful. "I'm hoping you won't grow weary of teaching me—this is all so interesting. Can you give an example of a prominent theme that I need to apply to my life?"

"First, let me make a significant distinction that few people ever grasp with their heart. The truth is most people want to add God's Word to their current way of thinking *or doing*. You cannot add God's Word to your life—*it has to become your life. God's Word should eventually define everything about you—it becomes who you are.*"

The completeness of surrender that Edward continued to speak to John was making him a little uncomfortable. He felt he had to comment, but how could he without challenging Edward's point? John merely needed to express how he knew most people would react to Edward's assertions. "Pardon me for speaking frankly, but it seems that living for God is all consuming, leaving little time for anything else. With so much effort devoted to the intricacies of following this or that and doing things a certain way, how can a person have enough time or freedom to accomplish anything for God?"

"What a great question. There are many, many, scriptures that speak directly to that concern. For instance Matthew 6:33 comes to mind, saying: *But seek ye first the kingdom of God, and his righteousness; and all these things shall be added unto you.* We don't have enough time this morning to cover your question thoroughly. However, trust me in this: God honors His Word when you honor His Word—*that is the essence of a principle.* Any educated person knows that when a principle is properly applied, then the attributes of that principle are brought to bear."

John was beginning to see the overwhelming wisdom of knowing and applying God's Word. "I'm sorry to admit this, but all my life I have relegated religion to the simpleton and the uneducated. Yet, as we talk, I am seeing the profoundness of God's Kingdom. The awe-inspiring totality of God's provision for His people is intricate and full of wonder. I think what you are saying is that God is not asking us to have blind faith. There is indeed substance to what He asks us to believe."

"Yes! Exactly! I am delighted to see how God has given you a great mind and an open heart. It's getting late, but I want to make one last comment before we go. For now, listen carefully, and later we can talk more about this. *Having an understanding mind is a gift from God. Remember that God knows everything about everything. Therefore, it is only by knowing God that we can have the greatest potential for divine revelation, which is pure truth. When we seek to know the Maker of the universe, He will make known to us the secrets of the universe. However, His wisdom and understanding will only be given to those He can trust, which comes by faithfulness and obedience.* And that, my young friend, brings us full circle to your question."

Incredibly, John was taking in the deeper truths that Edward was sharing. "That was a mouthful, but I think I understand what you were saying. When we seek Him first, He honors His promise to give us everything we need, as well as to meet us in the midst of our deepest concerns. So it becomes obvious that the time spent pursuing Him is returned to us by His giving us the ability to operate at a higher capacity of productivity."

Edward was more than impressed with John's ability to comprehend these essential truths; truths that many spend a lifetime trying to fathom. "John, I am convinced that you will be a scholar of unmatched persuasion. However, we'll have to continue this discussion later because it's after eight, and we need to be going."

As Edward, Mary and John climbed into their black horse-drawn carriage, there was an evident splendor about the morning; the day was set to be extraordinary. Yes, the weather was perfect, but there was much more in play. The feel-good ambiance was far beyond a worldly sensory experience that brought a feeling of elation to John. It was much more.

As they got underway, John couldn't hold back his exhilaration. He had never known anything to equate to what he was feeling. "Edward, I am experiencing what I can only describe as an overwhelming sense of well-being."

"Ah, that, my friend, is the peace of God resting upon you. Personally, I relish those special occasions, which usually come after spending time with God and reading His word. You can look it up later in Philippians 4:6-7."

John was resting in the warmth of knowing that God was touching him with His goodness. He raised his voice to speak over the odd rhythmic symphony of noises created by the moving carriage and the clomping of hooves. He felt compelled to offer his esteem, "Your command of the scriptures is admirable, to say the least." Turning to Mary, John broke their unspoken pact of silence. "Is he always this way… I mean his knowledge of scripture?"

Mary's shyness had peaked, leaving her wordless in her own realm of profound contentment. Rather, she nodded with an approving smile that added to John's happiness. It was apparent she didn't want to spoil the blissful moment with words.

As the noisy carriage ride reached a deafening rumble at full stride, conversing became impractical, leaving the jubilant commuters to settle into their own private thoughts. The imposed silence created the perfect opportunity to savor the glorious morning vistas as they fleetingly passed as a blur. The four-mile jaunt toward the downtown London church passed quickly until the trio approached the last ten blocks. Just as Edward predicted, the frenzied downtown traffic evolved into a slow crawl.

Chapter Nineteen

Casting a Broader Net

Carriages jammed the streets, jockeying for a place to park near the church building. John suggested walking any distance necessary to avoid the noise and dust. "A nice long walk is certainly agreeable to me on such a calm and sunny morning. May I propose tying-up the reins in the West Square? We can then enjoy a brisk stroll to Elephant and Castle Streets."

The morning walk was indeed pleasant until nearing Charles Spurgeon's downtown London church. While walking amidst the emerging clamor, John recognized his sister, Veronica. Her family was held up in the seemingly unmanageable hubbub of animals, pedestrians, hansoms, coaches and carriages. John was elated as he expectantly ran over to her stalled carriage to exchange a brief greeting in hopes of arranging a later reunion. Much to his dismay, his sister did not recognize him and rudely brushed him off. Frustrated and hurt John protested, "Veronica, it's me!"

Veronica would not be bothered by the riffraff that clogged the streets of London. On any given day, it was not uncommon to be approached by panhandlers numerous times, begging for any kind of handout. The only way to avoid being engulfed by a mass of beggars was to not be seen as a soft touch. On a gut level, in a primeval sort of way, any untamed compassion was suppressed or endured as a matter of survival. Callously, the easiest way for a member of the aristocracy to prevail was to maintain a wide gulf, separating them from the "idlers." It was considered an acceptable attitude and part of living in the Victorian era. And so it was with the vast majority of well-to-do church goers—ignoring the considerable raft of dire poverty, as well as the overwhelming need that surrounded them.

John would have undoubtedly felt the same way just four weeks earlier. But today, he wasn't sure what was happening to him. He was having trouble comprehending his dilemma because he was suspended between the two worlds of lack and plenty. Unlike his sister, who maintained a gulf of separation, John had been given *the only Bridge* between the two extremes, the Seed growing within his heart.

As John kept pace with Veronica's slow-moving carriage, he received an epiphany and spoke again to his sister with a solemn plea. "Sister, you should consider casting a broader net."

In the midst of a revelatory moment, Veronica recognized John's voice, which tore at the veil of her hardened heart. Her countenance was still captured with sternness, as she looked straight into the eyes of John's accusing voice. His visage continued to betray her sight. She only knew John as a proud and vain brother who had relished the upper ascendancy of their shared peerage. Even while staring into her brother's face, there was a refusal to acknowledge him on the deepest level. How could it be?

John wasn't going to give up as he perilously walked alongside his sister's carriage. He said the only thing he knew might explain the one-sided rift. In a lighthearted yet formal protocol, meant to break the sullen moment, John broadcast a heartfelt proclamation to his aloof sister, "Veronica Ann Wheaton, I, John Francis Taylor, met and received the Lord Jesus as my Savior Thursday last."

John's rather unorthodox announcement shifted the sibling standoff. Veronica's sentiments of disdain were transformed into feelings of embarrassment. Even so, the chill was broken, and Veronica changed her tone to that of muted concern, "Come see us as soon as you can. I want to know what has happened to you." She was still not completely cognizant of what was taking place, bound by prideful arrogance, not thinking for a moment that John was there to attend church.

John left the street to rejoin Edward and Mary, who had followed along with his halted pace while engaging Veronica. Edward wanted to offer consolation to John's eye-opening encounter. "John, I don't think that meeting Veronica here under these circumstances was an accident—there is a purpose in it. I can personally see how your story is something she needs to hear."

Edward felt he should mention a very important fact that John probably wasn't aware of. "Just so you'll know, Veronica looked for you at your mum's funeral. I was watching her when she finally located you. While you were fully engaged in the affairs of the day, she chose not to approach you, walking away instead. I hope you two can work things out."

Without a doubt, John had been operating with tunnel vision the day of his mother's funeral. Even so, he wasn't aware of any overriding conflict other than their usual differences about her overbearing religious talk. Perhaps the poignancy of the moment and the need to avoid ill feelings caused her to back away.

Until Edward mentioned the day of his mother's funeral, John had not thought about missing his sister that day. But now, his curiosity was piqued, especially since his life was being radically changed, making his upcoming visit to his sister's house much anticipated. Hopefully, with John's new-found walk with the Lord, there would be enough in common to make his stay a welcomed if not a celebrated affair.

Chapter Twenty

"Come and see..."

John felt a sense of great joy as the Metropolitan Tabernacle congregation began singing with such exuberance yet comforting repose. He had been to church on occasion as a young lad, but his reasons for attending were quite different than today. *Having* to be at church and *wanting* to be there makes all the difference. *The causable attendance of a hungry and thirsty soul engenders a virgin canvas to be painted upon by the Painter of grand masterpieces, enabling life-changing encounters involving the heart.*

John Taylor was spellbound by the booming voice that carried its invitation to the gathered crowd, "Come and see..."

"...The shutters of every window are open. The key is put into every lock and every door is thrown wide open. Investigation is courted upon every point—the Gospel stands

145

at her door and says, "Come in here, come and see." You have this short sentence, "Come and see," as, first of all, an encouragement to enquirers. Many of you are like John's disciples.

They had heard John preach and they believed his word and when they saw Christ, to whom John pointed, they followed Him. But not knowing Him, they followed Him with a question upon the tip of their tongues—"Master, where do You dwell?" He said, "Come and see." You also are anxious to know Christ. You have heard His Word preached by some of His witnesses and you want to know Him personally for yourselves. You have a pressing question to put tonight and Jesus encourages you to ask. No—to come and get your own answer with your own eyes. "Come," He says, "Come and see ... "

(excerpt from C.H. Spurgeon's June 18ᵗʰ 1865 sermon (as read) at the Metropolitan Tabernacle)

For the duration of Spurgeon's sermon, John's four-day-old decision to follow Christ was opened up to him in a crystal-clear fashion. He now knew with certainty what had been accomplished last Thursday when he opened his heart to answer the greatest invitation ever extended. He had chosen to receive the most valuable gift ever presented to mankind.

After the service ended, John and the Van Zandt's began looking for the Murrays to continue their day with them. Was it by chance that Ruth and Andrew Murray stepped out from behind a massive iron pillar to stumble upon John's entourage as they exited the church? Edward would be quick to say that it wasn't—coincidence was not in his vocabulary.

It was clear that Ruth had been weeping, so much so her shawl was damp with tears. The fortuitous reunion was just what she needed. The familiarity of kindred spirits brought a measure of reassurance that promised a harbor for her convicted heart—a safe mooring of trusted friends. *For it is in the grabbing hold of the Lifeline, tossed to a drowning sinner, that necessitates the release of one's grip on the entangling false hopes this world offers. The intervening occasion, between the heartrending release and securing a firm grasp of God's amazing grace, can be a frightening lapse of time. A net of reassuring friends charged with such care offers the welcomed reassurance of tendered hope.*

Ruth anxiously entreated her newly discovered old friends, "Can you spend the afternoon with us?" Ruth was overripe with a need to answer God's call to "come and see." She had been ready, but now, today, she was experiencing birthing pangs, if you will—it was her time to be born again.

Edward was the consummate evangelist who had witnessed many people who were in the throes of surrender. He was always moved with the enormity of such an occasion. Being translated from the realm of darkness to the kingdom of Light is the greatest miracle this side of heaven. Jesus himself said, "*...he that believeth on me,...greater works than these shall he do...*" Edward knew to his core the utmost privilege of being a part of the *greater works* that Jesus spoke.

In the sanguine moment of opportunity, Edward spoke for John and Mary, "Ruth, Andrew, it would be our pleasure to share our afternoon with you. Thank you for the invitation."

Edward knew that their planned meal-less Sunday would most likely give way to the Ruth's need, so he called John aside to ask for his understanding. "John, for now, please go along with the fact we most likely will be breaking our customary Sunday fast. There is scriptural precedence, so I don't want you to be entertaining the idea of hypocrisy. I'll be happy to explain what I mean by all of this later. Are you all right with that?"

Of course, John was not in tune with the unfolding occasion of Ruth's imminent conversion; he had no way of knowing the way Edward did. Nor did he realize how fasting the midday meal might affect Ruth. She most likely wouldn't understand its intended meaning, thereby creating a stumbling block for her. So, with his complete trust in Edward's leadership, John acquiesced with

> *...with his complete trust in Edward's leadership, John acquiesced with a broad, reverently blissful smile.*

a broad, reverently blissful smile.

Ruth's spirited independence often prompted her to outpace her husband's more subdued, even-keeled personality. Even so, Andrew spoke with enthusiasm, restating Ruth's earlier invitation, "Ruth and I would enjoy having you join us for lunch at The Mitre on Fleet Street. Afterward, we can all meet at our in-town residence and continue the afternoon together, enjoying a cup of tea."

"We'd be delighted. Shall we meet in say… thirty minutes?"

"Better make it an hour considering this crush of traffic."

Edward knew he would not face the same difficulties, so he offered, "We'll see you at Mitre Restaurant. Just in case we arrive first, we'll reserve a table."

Just outside the church building, the two groups split up and headed in opposite directions. John, Edward and Mary walked north eight blocks toward West Square while Andrew and Ruth located their carriage just east of the church building on Elephant Street.

Chapter Twenty-One
London's Finest

John had often eaten at the posh Mitre Restaurant, a white-glove enclave for the upper class, so he thought nothing of walking into his familiar meeting place. It wasn't until his eyes met an inquiring face that he realized he had made a serious mistake. It had even escaped Edward's methodical train of thoughts. John felt exposed. His only choice was to maintain his composure and continue walking to the back of the restaurant where he cornered Edward. "I completely forgot about being seen and recognized."

"John, it's my fault. I was so focused on Ruth's conversion that everything else completely slipped my mind."

John spoke his first thoughts aloud, "Don't worry, I have an idea. If you can help me quietly exit out the back to the alleyway, I'll walk to Ruth's home and wait there until you arrive."

Trying not to overreact, Edward attempted to assuage John's fears. "Do you think anyone has recognized you since we arrived?"

"I'm not certain. I thought I saw someone I knew, but I'm not convinced he recognized me. At this point, I would have to say no."

"John, if you haven't been identified, then it would be safer to stay here. Perhaps we can all leave out the back when we finish. You're safer if we all stick together. From what we know right now, there appears to be a bounty for your capture. If you leave without us, you could be spotted."

"Yes, but if I stay, all of you will be in dang—" John stopped midsentence when he saw a figure coming toward them, maintaining a determined stride. Without thinking, John bolted through a pair of doors leading to the kitchen, which allowed him to escape out the back exit to the rubbish-strewn alley.

Edward was able to halt the man's chase by blocking his path and engaging him in forced conversation. His successful intervention allowed him to bring attention to the aggressor's disruptive behavior. As would be quite typical for the upper-crust patrons, there was only so much tolerance for such a disturbance. A humiliating hush fell over the restaurant, drawing all eyes to the men.

After a very long minute, the din of conversations slowly resumed. Highly irritated, the would-be assailant brusquely turned to leave, but Edward was prepared. With convincing merit, he administered a rather harsh clenching grip to the stranger's upper arm, spinning him around to face him again. Edward bore a stern smile as he pointed to an empty chair. In an uncompromising tone, he firmly queried, "How can I help you? You seem to need assistance of some sort?"

The stranger was indignant. "Look, you; I know your type, always sticking your nose where it doesn't belong. Anyway, it's too late for your friend. He has probably been taken away by now. It'll be a long time before you'll ever see him again, *and* if you know what's good for you, you'll stay right here while I walk out."

Unknown to the two men who were entangled in a perilous dance of words and threats, Mary had slipped away to summon the police. Surely, it would only be a matter of time before the ordeal was discreetly handled and brought to an end. Not evident to the temporal realm was a raging battle for the numerous souls who were trying to respond to Spurgeon's rousing call to salvation. The heavenly principalities are ruled by demonic forces assigned to defeat God's plans by disrupting the lives of those who seek His refuge.

Seemingly out of nowhere, two uniformed officers appeared. They acted quickly, intent on putting Edward under arrest for disturbing the peace. Coincidentally, Captain Yardley of Precinct 5 witnessed the whole affair while sitting at a nearby table. He had chosen to keep silent as Edward deftly handled the presumed troublemaker. However, the scene radically escalated when the police officers began trying to handcuff Edward.

Fortunately, Captain Yardley took control and waved off the two officers. "It's alright, men, I'll take it from here." Then without a word, the captain gave the determined stranger an exaggerated head motion, signaling him to leave. Unknown to Edward, the aggressive stranger was a plainclothes detective. "Mr. Van Zandt, would you please join me at my table? We need to talk."

Meanwhile, outside, John was ducking in and out of alleyways, unsure if he was being pursued. In a bit of irony he *was* being followed, but not by anyone intent on doing him harm.

Shortly before her death, Madeline Taylor employed Bradley to look out after John. Madeline suspected that her son was in danger and would be more so after her death. Her solution was to confide in Edward to help protect John, so a closely guarded agreement was made to provide John with bodily protection. Bradley was a natural choice as John's shadow and secret bodyguard because of his cadet training. Bradley came from a distinguished military family, having attended the Royal Military Academy where he received the most intensive hand-to-hand combat training of the time.

Interestingly, Edward's profound wisdom led him to instruct Bradley to limit his interference with the natural order of events that were to shape John's life, thereby reducing any unintended consequences. Trying to protect John and balance their friendship had proven to be difficult—one reason Bradley had been less visible, especially since John's riding accident.

As Andrew and Ruth approached the Mitre Restaurant for their lunchtime meeting, Andrew caught a glimpse of John briskly crossing the street a half block ahead. Sensing something was wrong, he quickly pulled over to help Ruth out of the carriage, removing her from harm's way. He then escorted her into an ice cream emporium, where he pleaded with her to wait for him. "John's in trouble. Please stay here while I go and help him. If I don't come back within fifteen minutes, go to The Mitre restaurant and find Edward; tell him what's going on."

Ruth bravely responded, "I'll do as you say, but Andrew please be careful."

Andrew ran out of the confectionary shop and jumped into his carriage, whipping it into the still crowded street. He then headed toward the location where he had seen John cross the street.

Seemingly from out of nowhere, Bradley stepped from behind a parked hansom. "Keep going and don't stop." He ran alongside Andrew's carriage long enough to adjust his stride, allowing him to jump in. Bradley yelled above the clamor of the street noise, "We need to catch up to John." Pointing to an ornate multistory building, Bradley continued, "I saw him run toward the Escobar Hotel. I think he may have gone in."

Back inside the restaurant, Captain Yardley began making assertions that were troubling to Edward. The captain spoke unnaturally slow which added stress to the tense conversation.

His unhurried speech was deceiving, but the truth was that Captain Yardley was very intelligent and cunning. It was often that a prideful or arrogant criminal suspect would assume the captain was stupid. That mistake would invariably lead the suspect to slip up while being interrogated.

Captain Yardley got right to the point. "Edward, I understand you have a reputation as an upstanding citizen, so I'm not going to arrest you today for disturbing the peace. But please realize that I could take you in on charges of impeding the duties of a peace officer."

Inwardly, Edward questioned the captain's motives. "I'm sorry, Captain Yardley, but your detective was in plain clothes and he threatened me, as well as John Taylor. My actions could only be seen as self-defense."

"Edward, are you certain about any threats you may have heard? Detective O'Hare can be somewhat overzealous at times, but he is one of the best men I have on the force. Furthermore, I'm afraid you don't know the overall circumstances, so your perspective is a bit clouded."

Just as Edward was about to respond to Captain Yardley's claim, Ruth Murray caught his attention as she anxiously waved from across the room. Edward was in a tough spot. His conversation with the captain was very serious, yet Ruth obviously needed him, possibly with information about John. Edward did the only thing he could. Without letting on, he excused himself from the captain. Turning to Mary, he quietly spoke to her, "Mary, please go to Ruth. Escort her to our table while the captain and I conclude our discussion."

Edward purposely delayed returning to his previous conversation with the captain while he watched Mary interact with Ruth. Satisfied with what he saw, Edward returned to his discussion. "Captain, please help me understand why your detective was pursuing Mr. Taylor so aggressively. If your observations of him are somewhat casual, why have you assigned your most persuasive detective to detain him?"

Before the captain could answer, Mary reappeared with a confidential message for Edward. She whispered to her father, "Mrs. Murray says it's important that you not say anything to the captain before you speak with her."

Surprisingly, Edward didn't hesitate to curtail his conversation. "Captain Yardley, I'm afraid I need to take leave of our conversation. An emergency has come to my attention. Is there anything you have to tell me that can't wait?"

Captain Yardley was incensed by his loss of control and gruffly snapped, "Only this. We are considering John Taylor to be a "person of interest." It is apparent that you are involved with him and know of his whereabouts. I'm afraid I'll have to ask you to come see me at the station tomorrow morning at 9:00 a.m."

"I believe I can see you in the morning. However, I will need to go by my office first so it could be a little later... that is if you are willing to allow it. If so, I'll make every effort to be in your office by no later than 10:00 a.m."

The captain forcefully pressed his point, "Be there in the morning. If you choose not to come, I can make this very serious for your family, as well as John Taylor."

Ruth didn't want to be seen by Captain Yardley, so she stepped into an alcove near the maître d' station and waited for Edward to come to the front of the restaurant. Captain Yardley had his back to her when she gestured to Edward, so she was almost certain the captain was not aware of her presence.

As Edward approached, she nervously pulled him aside. "Edward, you must be careful. Captain Yardley can be very disarming, but he has another side—he is known to be dreadfully ruthless. Be extraordinarily guarded with what you say and how you say it. Do not find yourself on his bad side."

> *"Edward, you must be careful. Captain Yardley can be very disarming, but he has another side—he is known to be dreadfully ruthless."*

Appearing a little baffled by Ruth's sobering remarks, Edward protested, "He was certainly ill-tempered with me, but I understood he is London's finest… up for some kind of an award."

"You have to trust me, Edward. Yes, he has been very effective in cleaning up the crime in his precinct, but only because the mayor has overlooked his tactics. Those on the inside have smoothed over a great deal of his brutal schemes. He has also had several rather high profile mistresses who have suffered from his violence—one of whom suddenly disappeared after she tried to get help."

"Thanks for telling me. You may have saved me from a lot of trouble. I was also getting a little impatient with his remarks, so I appreciate you retrieving me. By the way, where is Andrew?"

"Oh, my! I forgot... that's why I came here in the first place. Just as we arrived for our luncheon appointment, Andrew spotted John running across the street and feared the worst. Andrew wanted to spare me harm, so he ushered me into the ice cream shop down the street, instructing me to find you. I can't be certain about this, but when I left the ice cream parlor, I may have seen them entering the Escobar Hotel."

Chapter Twenty-Two
"Watering others..."

The two groups of close friends were finally able to reunite, but it was not as planned—over lunch at the luxurious Mitre restaurant. Their disrupted dinner meeting was unfortunate. However, the unplanned encounter with Captain Yardley would prove to be extremely important, giving them further clues about John's elevated status as a fugitive. Even so, Edward was determined to see that Ruth had her opportunity to turn her life over to God.

While gathered in the grand lobby of the elegant Escobar Hotel, Edward took the lead in formulating a strategy to meet at the Murray's in-town residence. There was no way to know if further attempts would be made to apprehend John.

Edward suggested splitting into two groups; each would take a long and exaggerated route to the Murray's home. John would go with Andrew and Bradley, hiding in their carriage as they left in one direction. Edward, Ruth and Mary would take an opposite route. The final instruction was to make every assurance that all danger was clear before making the final turn toward Ruth's home.

No one could say if the extra precautions had been necessary. All that mattered was that the group of six reconvened as planned, without incident. Once safely together at the Murray's home, Bradley insisted on standing watch at least for a brief period.

Ruth was quite the hostess, a gift she thoroughly enjoyed expressing. Regrettably, there would be no midday meal as the hour had passed to prepare dinner for six people. Ruth only had the cold crumpets that she had prepared before church. Even so, a spot of tea served with crumpets and jam would have to suffice. Once everyone was seated in her meticulously decorated and furnished parlor, she began serving what little she had to offer.

Interestingly, in the typical upper-class Victorian home, much would have been made over Ruth's meager selection of food available for her guests. In some circles, her lack of preparation, no matter the cause, would have been considered dreadful, but not in this home and certainly not with these friends. Besides, Ruth had grown weary with much of the high-minded goings-on especially since she had been attending her Bible study group and attending church. She even began doing some of her own housework and preparing her weekend meals—something she enjoyed doing anyway. Nevertheless, if her friends discovered that Ruth was doing menial tasks, she could suffer a rebuke from her now tedious social connections. And sadly, if she continued, Ruth could be open to humiliation or a snub.

The uniquely stressful events of the day seemed to fade rather quickly as the enjoyment of close fellowship eased any lingering anxieties. The gathering began anew and unfolded as it originally should have.

It was not uncommon for friends or relatives to spend entire evenings together discussing various topics of the day. Parlor games were extremely popular among the middle and upper classes that looked forward to an evening of fun. After a quick but rousing game of *Minister's Cat,* which was followed by a laughter-filled time of playing a game of *Consequences,* Ruth expressed an earnest desire to hear more about John's conversion experience.

Turning to John, she asked to hear more of his story. "John, yesterday you mentioned that you received Jesus Christ as your Savior. I have heard many stories from my new friends that tell how God has changed them. Tell me more about what happened to you."

John happily gave a rather detailed testimony of how God had intervened in his life. As he pieced the story together for Ruth, the truth of God's goodness caused him to become a little emotional. Looking back, he too could see just how much God had done in his life.

"The ladies in my Bible study have mentioned how I must be saved, but no one has been quite so bold in proclaiming the reality of it as you. I do hope that I can experience God the same way that you have. I have such a yearning to know Him." At that moment, Ruth was reminded of a topic that had been on her mind, so she turned to Edward for his opinion. "Andrew and I have been discussing one of Charles Spurgeon's sermons that he gave in April. I want to know what you think about the following paragraph. I have the complete sermon here; may I read a portion of it?"

"Certainly, I hope I can help."

"All right then, this is what he said: 'Watering others will make you humble. You will find better people in the world than yourself. You will be astonished to find how much grace there is where you thought there was none, and how much knowledge some have gained while you, as yet, have made little progress with far greater opportunities.'"

Edward did not want to diminish Andrew's proper leadership in his own home. Rather than answer the question directly, Edward wisely sought to encourage and build up Andrew's rightful place as Ruth's spiritual leader. "Andrew, I would like to hear your thoughts on this. For me, I will have to think on it for a few minutes. Go ahead. What are your ideas?"

As it turned out, Andrew was eager to share his opinion, as well as a personal testimony. "Well, since Ruth gave me this sermon to read, I've had a chance to consider the whole of Spurgeon's thoughts. I have to confess, I have been refreshed with a new sense of purpose that has come over me. It has been a long time since I felt so invigorated for the Lord's work. In fact, this paragraph that Ruth is asking about touched me deeply."

Edward could see the Lord working in both Ruth and Andrew. It was thrilling to see how God was restoring their marriage relationship in such a remarkable way. "What did Spurgeon say that touched you so deeply?"

Andrew continued, "In so many ways I had shelved my faith. I had allowed my circumstances to dictate my efficacy for His calling on my life. And, just as Spurgeon stated, I did so while others of lesser opportunity progressed on. I am thankful for being guided back to Him. I have been prayerful about my condition and can happily say that I'm plotting a new course for my life, as well as my marriage."

Edward knew that Ruth just needed reassurance going forward, and who better to give it than her own repentant husband? He was not going to spoil the moment. "I have to say that about sums it up for me as well. I think we all could relate to allowing an unfortunate circumstance detour us in our walk with Christ. Ruth, does that answer your questions about the sermon?"

"I think so for now, but I do have a concern. I have no walk with Christ; at least not the way I understand it from the ladies in my Bible study group, or as John explained earlier."

A moment of truth was bearing down on Ruth's seeking heart, as she tearfully confessed, "To be honest, I can see now how I have hindered my husband in his desire to be the Christian he has always wanted to be." Turning to Andrew,

Ruth spoke with brokenness as she asked Andrew to forgive her. She then made a heartfelt confession of repentance. "Over the last few months, I have had a growing desire to honor you as my husband… in a real way, not just to be manipulative. I want our marriage to be all that it can be, and I have come to the conclusion that God has the answer for where we've strayed. My deepest desire is to know God the way you do and the way Edward knows Him. I want His wisdom and strength so I can be who He wants me to be and not what someone at the women's club thinks I should be. I know, from spending time with the ladies in the Bible study group, that I will never be perfect. Even so, there are many qualities they possess that can only be obtained from knowing God and the Bible. I want those qualities for myself."

Andrew was tearful to hear his wife speak with such clarity and willingness to yield her life to God. He had spent many hours in prayer over the years, and now to hear his wife express these godly desires brought the deepest joy and elation. "My dearest Ruth, you bring me the greatest joy tonight." Andrew looked deep into his wife's eyes and saw a hungry and thirsty soul coming to the Fountain to drink. He was reminded of John 4:15 when the woman at the well inquired of Jesus: *"…Sir, give me this water, that I thirst not, …"*

Closely engaged, husband and wife were moved to the point of joyful tears as they relished in the moment God had orchestrated through the prayers of a faithful husband. "May I read you a passage out of Romans?" Ruth nodded yes. "Ruth, the Bible clearly describes what we must do to enter into God's

Kingdom to begin a walk with Jesus. This is one scripture that tells us plainly: *"If you confess with your mouth that Jesus is Lord and believe in your heart that God raised him from the dead, you will be saved. For it is by believing in your heart that you are made right with God, and it is by confessing with your mouth that you are saved."*

Ruth perked up as she remembered. "I've heard Charles Spurgeon mention that same verse several times over the last two months—it seems *too* simple."

"It *is* simple, but just as I told John on Thursday, your confession here today is just the beginning of your pilgrimage with God. Much like a young child, it is a daily walk of *growing and becoming*; not a one-time profession."

"Andrew, I want to begin again... I want a fresh start. The things I used to count as important have left me unhappy and lonely. Those who I have considered as friends don't really care about me; it's mostly about how they can use me to get what they want. I can now see how I need God in my life. Can you pray with me so I can have God in my life?"

Andrew never thought he would hear Ruth express such life-changing sentiments. She was indeed ready to pray—ready to receive a new life in Christ. "Ruth, it's as simple as we discussed earlier. God looks on the heart. As we confess our sins, He is faithful and just to forgive us and to cleanse us from all unrighteousness. Why don't you pray to God and tell Him what's on your heart? When you finish, I will pray as well."

"Dear God, I'm sorry for thinking I didn't need You. Thank You for showing me the truth of how I am supposed to live, and thank You for giving me such a wonderful and faithful husband. Because Andrew has had You in his life, he was able to love me when I was unlovable. I want You to be in my life so I can love my husband as I should. Take my life and use it for Your purposes; I yield myself to You now as Your servant. Be my Lord. Amen."

This was truly a holy moment. A breathtaking reverence filled the room, causing a hush to envelop the six gathered friends. The quietness lasted for several minutes as each person considered the wonder of Ruth being translated into God's kingdom, forever to be with Him. With godly compassion, Andrew thanked God for His overflowing love and His provision for eternal

> *A breathtaking reverence filled the room, causing a hush to envelop the six gathered friends.*

life. John was so moved with gratitude that he couldn't hold it back. "Ruth, in the days before I got saved, both Edward and Andrew assured me that giving my life to God would be the best decision I would ever make. It's true. The joy and peace are unspeakable."

The worshipful atmosphere of thanksgiving slowly transformed into an air of congratulatory celebration. Even so, the afternoon would soon turn to evening and Edward and Mary would need to leave for home.

Chapter Twenty-Three
The Pocket Watch

John realized that he had a dilemma. He needed to visit his sister Veronica, yet he had no transportation. He also desperately wanted to reclaim his pocket watch from De Beers Jewellery. John was concerned that his watch would be gone if he didn't make it to the jewelers early Monday morning, a chance he did not want to take. He chose to settle the issue of travel first.

Asking Andrew for a ride was the most logical choice since his sister's estate was only a four-mile detour from the usual route to his country office. However, John also knew that Andrew should be spending precious time with his wife. Even so, John had little choice but to query him, "Dr. Murray, is there a chance you will be returning to your country home tomorrow?"

John's pragmatic query seemed to slightly dampen the Murrays' joyful mood. "John, I haven't thought about it with all that's happened today. Why do you ask?"

John was feeling a little selfish as he voiced his need. "As you may recall, my sister has extended an invitation for me to visit her. It would be the perfect opportunity to get out of London for a few days. And since the Wheaton estate is only slightly out of your way, I would like to ride along… that is if you are returning to your office."

"Let me have some time to discuss it with Ruth, and I'll speak with you later."

"I'll certainly respect whatever you and Ruth decide. I'm confident I can find another way if you two want to spend more time together while you are in town."

John turned his attention to the challenge of reclaiming his watch. With the police looking for him, it would be impossible to consider going to retrieve the watch himself. Also knowing that Edward was probably  going to be under surveillance for a while, his only option was to ask Bradley. "Bradley, I need a favor of you as well. Is it possible for you to go by De Beers Jewellery tomorrow morning and reclaim my watch?"

Bradley had already retrieved John's watch from the jewelers, knowing firsthand about the anxious sale by Mr. Jenkins. Bradley was staying in one of the hunter's cabins at the riding club, allowing him to maintain close proximity to John. Friday morning, before Mr. Jenkins left for his weekly trip to London, Bradley overheard Roger having a heated discussion with him. That is when Mr. Jenkins stormed out of his office over their disagreement about his decision to sell the watch, breaking his promise to keep it as security. Once Mr. Jenkins rode out of sight, Bradley followed him to De Beers Jewellery.

Knowing that John would be surprised, Bradley wanted to make the most of it. "Do you happen to mean *this* pocket watch?" Bradley lifted John's watch from his own watch-pocket and opened it for John to see.

John was dumbfounded. "How did you know?"

Bradley simply stated, "I was at the riding club when Mr. Jenkins left for London, and that's when Roger approached me and asked me to go and redeem the watch. He even gave me the money out of his own pocket to pay for it. I have to tell you that they don't come any more noble than Roger. Whether Mr. Jenkins reimbursed him when you paid off your account is doubtful—you might want to look into it."

Bradley's loyalty, as well as Roger's sacrificial acts left John overwhelmed, only to say, "You know as well as anyone that few if any of my former friends would have thought to do this. Thank you so much… and yes, I will make certain Roger is reimbursed."

Bradley had another concern that he felt John was not considering or had not thought about. He pulled John aside to talk privately with him. "John, I don't think you should be traveling to see your sister while carrying your bank bag or your watch for that matter. You will be exposed to highway robbers, and whoever is trying to kidnap you. You should consider taking a few shillings with you and leave your valuables with one of us."

Just as Bradley finished making his point, an insightful plan popped into John's mind. The puzzle pieces seemed to fall into place. "Bradley, thanks for your advice. I just thought of a way to resolve some of my immediate concerns, as well as yours. If my idea works, then I'll be able to do as you suggest."

John had remembered Andrew's offhand proposal to rent Ruth's detached bungalow. The location was ideal just as Andrew had mentioned earlier. John approached the seated group of friends and addressed Andrew and Ruth with his question about the cottage. "I know it's nearing the time for everyone to leave, but I have some thoughts that will involve just about everyone here. First, I want to thank each of you for your extraordinary efforts to help me through the last few weeks. Some of those efforts have saved my life. It is beyond words to express how much I appreciate all you have done for me. I also want to say that I will try my best to live up to your high regard for me."

John paused to collect his thoughts. While he was speaking, he remembered something Andrew said in a previous discussion. "I can now see firsthand what Andrew shared with me last week. I didn't understand it then, but I do now. Andrew, you said something like this: 'Christians are known by the love they have for one another.' I can certainly attest to that truth—it has become very clear to me. I have never known the depth of genuine love that each of you has shown me... so thank you all."

The group collectively received John's gratitude, but it was Edward who spoke. "John, I mentioned to you last week that we have been praying for you. In these times of prayer, God has impressed on me that His plans for you are extraordinary. You will do mighty exploits for Him. John, we all see it in you. We are honored to be a part of the great things that God has planned for you."

John was profoundly humbled. The depth of respect these kinds of words bestowed, and their powerful implications, would leave anyone at a loss for words. How could anyone respond except to be honored and grateful? After a solemn moment of reflection, John gathered his words, "Thank you for your faith in me, as well as your guidance. Earlier, I mentioned some ideas; I would like to get your input."

Andrew answered for the group, "By all means, what's on your mind?"

"Andrew, Ruth, is it true that your bungalow may be for rent? If so, I would like to consider renting it."

Ruth was elated. "I've been holding it... not knowing why... now I do. Yes, of course, it's yours if you want to take it."

"The location is ideal, so I don't even have to look at it." John was struck with a thought—he should ask the cost since renting was new to him. He awkwardly asked, "Do you know how much you will be asking as rent?"

The question caught Ruth off guard. She looked to Andrew for help with John's query. Andrew had already calculated the cottage would bring thirty pounds sterling on a yearly basis. Even so, he also knew that John would not be able to afford that much rent, so he offered him a compromise. "John, would you be willing to look after Ruth's home while she's away, as well as do some chores and odd jobs around the property?"

"Yes, of course. As I mentioned earlier, I can never repay you for all that you've done for me, so yes, anything you need, I'll do."

"Good, I think we can make a deal then. I would be willing to set the rent at an even one pound sterling per month if you can help us out around the house."

John had no inkling that Andrew was charging him less than half the going rate. All John knew was that having the cottage would resolve one of his primary needs of the moment. "I would like to pay you now for six months. This way, when I get back from visiting my sister, I will have a place to stay. The paid up rent will also give me time to start earning a living. Would that be satisfactory?"

Andrew was impressed with John's growing command of handling his personal affairs. "Ruth will show you the cottage. After you look at it, you can pay her the six pounds sterling, provided you still want to rent it. If so, we have an agreement."

John was still in need of transportation. "There is one last favor to ask. I have had a change in plans. When you decide to return to your office, I would like to travel with you with no detour. Going with you will allow me to retrieve my horse and take care of a personal matter at the riding club. I can then take the back roads to my sister's home."

"John, Ruth and I have decided that we will leave in the morning for our country home. You are certainly welcome to come along."

Chapter Twenty-Four

Victorian Courtship

As the evening of wonder and fellowship came to a close, John still had one last burning question to resolve. Its importance had been growing by the hour, but this request would be directed to Edward. Mary had captured John's heart.

His feelings for Mary began Saturday evening when Edward explained her evening routine of unselfish devotion, giving care to her neighbors. Then a few minutes later, when he saw Mary holding the crate of potatoes, he knew she would someday be his wife. Her apparent virtues and innocence were indelibly etched on his heart. From those life-changing moments until now, John was convinced he wanted to know everything about her; to experience the depth of who she was.

John was nervous. He wanted to be proper in the way he asked Edward for permission to begin a courtship with Mary. He did the best he could. "Edward, before I go to look at Ruth's cottage, may I have a private word with you?"

"Of course, we can talk in the kitchen."

John knew a little of what to expect. He had been raised to honor the strictest code of courtship. Nevertheless, even though he had been subjected to exacting Victorian standards, his previous lifestyle was spent in efforts to subvert them. Reaping the emptiness of his past behavior had invariably produced regrets. This time, he was going to do it right.

John squared his shoulders, stood taller and cleared his throat. "Edward, this is a very serious matter of which I'm not well versed. As you know, I have come a long way in the past few months. I am not the same person I was just a few weeks ago. The life you live with God is how I want to live my life. What I mean to say is that I have witnessed the virtues of honor, courage, brotherly love and devotion in your family, as

> *As you know, I have come a long way in the past few weeks. I am not the same person I was just a few days ago.*

well as in all those who are present here tonight. I want those same virtues for my family as well."

Edward was inwardly moved by John's sincere observations and heartfelt assurances. Even so, that didn't keep Edward from being amused by John's longwinded appeal. He couldn't let on that he knew where John was headed with his desire to seek his permission to court Mary. "John, you are most eloquent and earnest, but what are you trying to say?"

"Sir, I would like your permission to court Mary. Of course, my intentions are to follow the strictest formalities that you set forth."

"Well, John, I can't speak for Mary. I will talk with her about your wishes over the next few weeks and see how she feels. Would that be satisfactory?"

"Mr. Van Zandt. I couldn't ask for anything more. I appreciate that you took the time to hear me and gave me the opportunity to ask."

"John, don't get me wrong, I think you are a fine young man... you know that. Even so, Mary and I will want to pray about this and take some time to hear what the Lord has to say. I suggest you do the same. There is more to a marriage than physical attraction."

Edward was forced to pause. His last statement was a poignant reminder of his deceased wife, Elizabeth, and the mistakes he had made in their relationship. He immediately knew that John would need to hear the rest of his story concerning Mary's mother. It was certainly in order since she would not be around to be Mary's chaperone.

Edward continued with moistened eyes. "John, whether or not I accept your proposal to court Mary does not reflect on you... is that clear? It is paramount that we all do as the Lord wills."

John wasn't certain why Edward was so moved with emotion. "Yes, of course, I understand completely. I wouldn't expect anything less."

Edward knew he needed to explain why he had to pause. "I was just prompted to say this as well. John, I will want the opportunity to share the complete story about my marriage to Elizabeth—there are some things you need to know. I would be remiss if you heard the truth later and not from me. When you get back from your visit with your sister, we'll talk about all of this. Would that suit you?"

"Yes, I respect your authority completely. What you have to say is of utmost importance to me, and I look forward to spending more time with you when I get back. I also want to pay a visit to your printing company as well. What you have told me so far about your company sounds interesting."

John needed advice about his last major concern. "There is one last matter before I go with Ruth. I need to ask your counsel about the bank bag. I plan to rent Ruth's cottage today. Do you think it would be safe to leave the money and papers in the cottage? Ideally, the bag would be most secure back in the safety deposit box, but neither of us can access it until we find out what is going on with the police."

Edward didn't think John's question was so difficult. He just needed help thinking it through. Edward simply enumerated the logical points aloud. "If your presence here can remain a secret… and if no one finds out the bag is hidden here, then it should be safe. Remember that whoever is after the contents of your bag will be asking questions of everyone. That includes your sister, as well as every person here tonight. I wouldn't tell anyone where you've actually placed it. You may not have thought about this, but anyone who knows the whereabouts of your bank bag will be in danger as well. If you think about it from that perspective, you will be more likely to keep its location to yourself."

"Thank you. I appreciate your sound guidance. I should be getting back to Ruth so she can show me the cottage. Thanks again for your help."

Chapter Twenty-Five

The Cottage

John couldn't believe how agreeable and spacious his new cottage turned out to be. It even had indoor plumbing. The cottage was furnished, and as Ruth was quick to point out, the Third Street Livery was one block down and one block over. John could board his horse very conveniently. Otherwise, he could walk to most of the other needful places in the neighborhood. The market, the bank, the bookstore and a men's clothier were all close by. Moreover, if he were to secure a position with Edward's printing company, it was only a few blocks away as well.

John was anxious to say 'yes' to Ruth and give her the six month's rent. "I'll take it. Your cottage is much more than I expected. You can be assured that I'll take good care of it, as well as help with the main house just as we agreed."

While retrieving the six one-pound notes from his bank bag, it occurred to him that the amount of rent money seemed too low compared to what he was getting in return. He had to be honest. "Mrs. Murray, I think this cottage should rent for more than what you've asked."

"It's all right, John. Andrew knew what he was doing. You just do what you two men agreed to, and all will be well."

"Thanks for helping me out like this; you and Andrew have been more than generous. If I'm going to be traveling with you and Andrew in the morning, that means I'll be sleeping here tonight in my new cottage."

Ruth responded in an almost motherly tone. "Yes, it does; I'm happy you like it. I think our arrangement will benefit all of us. John, I need to return to the others. Take your time and look around as you wish."

"Thank you. I will only be a few minutes. I want to stow my bank bag while I'm here. Tell the others not to leave before I can bid them farewell."

Everyone was careful to stay clear of the street view as the group gathered in the rear yard where the carriages were parked. Edward had his carriage ready to leave with Mary already seated in the front. As John approached from the cottage, Mary's engaging smile stopped him in his tracks. His repressed infatuation surfaced, causing a momentary distraction.

Amused at John's rapture, Bradley called out from his mount, "John, I'll be at the riding club in the morning. Perhaps I'll see you there." Bradley could see that John was too preoccupied to hear him, so he rode over to break his daze. "John, I'll see you at the riding club in the morning."

John was a little embarrassed by his obvious display of fondness but quickly recovered his manly bearing. He falsely cleared his throat, buying him time to clear the romantic cobwebs that entangled his thoughts. Now he could respond to Bradley. "It will probably be late morning before I get to the riding club. However, I will look for you when I arrive. Godspeed, my friend."

By now, Edward was seated in the carriage and ready to go. He cautioned John as he bid everyone farewell. "John, be aware of what is going on around you at all times and don't talk to anyone about any of the troubles. I am meeting with Captain Yardley in the morning to discover the underlying cause of this harassment. Hopefully, I'll see you in a few weeks with a good report."

"You be careful as well. I am looking forward to our planned meeting when I return."

As the guests rolled onto the streets of downtown London, Andrew turned to John. "John, I know you are anxious to leave, but I do not want to be in a rush tomorrow morning. Ruth wants to make a leisurely breakfast for the three of us while you and I make preparations for Ruth's absence. When we are done, then we will leave."

John was up and dressed extra early, giving him time to look over his newly rented cottage. He further utilized the time to search for a safe hiding spot for his bank bag. He found several places that were convenient, but would be too obvious for an experienced thief. While searching, he discovered a loose floorboard that was partially covered by the bed. Satisfied that he had found a safe place, John decided to pry the board free and see if it would do. It appeared to be the perfect place to hide his bank bag.

John took some money before he hid the bag, taking enough to repay Roger plus enough to cover a short list of his own expenses. He carefully stuffed the bag under the floor and rearranged the furniture so the bed completely covered the loose floorboard. He hoped that Ruth would not object.

After breakfast, Andrew, Ruth and John cleaned the kitchen and readied Ruth's house for her extended stay with Andrew at their country home. The carriage rolled out onto the streets of London right on time. It was another splendid day to be on the road even if the Monday morning, in-town traffic was dreadful. That would be Andrew's assessment, being a country gentleman and not a city dweller. Even so, the day's glorious beginning was the perfect metaphor for each of the three travelers bound for the countryside. All three were beginning a fresh new chapter in their lives, which promised to be just as splendid and glorious. Andrew, Ruth and John had each made solemn, life-changing commitments before God and man.

Chapter Twenty-Six
The English Patient

Hopefully, this would be the last time John would have to ride on the floor of a carriage—a very rough way to travel. Since his accident, it seemed as if John had been riding prone for one reason or another. Today he needed to stay hidden from sight. Needless to say, his only decent suit was in pitiful shape by the time they reached the edge of town.

Once they reached Haggerston, John sat up in the back seat and attempted to brush the dirt off his suit. One thing he needed was some new clothing. He hoped that while staying with his sister, he could go to the nearest small town and have a new suit made, along with a new pair of boots.

The trip to Andrew's country home office proved to be uneventful even as they pulled into the large open area separating the house and stables. Andrew escorted Ruth inside the house while John put the carriage away. The livestock had been unattended for two days, which meant there was a lot of work to do. From the looks of things, it might take the rest of the morning. If so, he would just have to leave for the riding club after lunch. John's schedule was certainly flexible. He just wanted to have enough time to see Bradley before he left for his sister's estate. John started pumping water and cleaning stalls, hoping to get his work done so he could be on his way.

It was almost noon when John completed all the work he knew to do. After he had finished, the stables were cleaner and better organized than they had been in years. The truth is

Dr. Murray was simply unable to do everything, so he had to let some things go. He admitted needing help and anxiously coveted John's desire to come back and lend him a hand. John was more than willing.

After John had dusted himself off a bit, he headed up to the house. When he neared the back door, he heard an argument in progress. During the pauses, he could hear Ruth crying with an occasional loud sob. John wasn't sure what to do because he had never been in a situation quite like this. He didn't feel like he should interrupt, so he went back to the stables to consider what would be right.

After a few minutes of pacing in the breezeway that separated the stall areas, it occurred to him that he should pray. But how? He had heard Edward and Andrew pray for others, so he just began talking to the Lord as if He were right there with him. After a few minutes, he ran out of things to say. He sensed a lighter burden, so he just thanked the Lord for the work He would do in righting any wrongs. He felt like he shouldn't go near the house, so he decided to remain in the stables until something changed.

It wasn't long before Andrew and Ruth walked out arm-in-arm and greeted John. Both were smiling even though Ruth's face was tear stained and her eyes were red from crying. Ruth spoke first, "John, I want to apologize for keeping Andrew inside with me, knowing you needed help out here."

John wanted to interrupt her, but she raised her hand to stop him from speaking. Ruth continued, "I began to regret my decision to spend more time here with Andrew. I'm sorry. I have been quite absorbed with self-pity. Then a miraculous thing just happened... it suddenly became all right. In an instant, something in me just changed—I was fine with everything. I just wanted to tell you that you are a big part of why Andrew and I are on this new journey together. Thank you for that."

> *I'm sorry... I have been quite absorbed with self-pity. Then a miraculous thing just happened... it suddenly became all right.*

John was secretly spellbound. To see God answer a childlike prayer in such an astonishing fashion was a remarkable experience. His very first intercessory prayer. John must have appeared awestruck because Andrew asked if he was all right. "John, you look pale... you must be hungry. Come, let's go in and get something to eat—everything is ready."

With lunch done, it was now early afternoon so John was anxious to leave. The day was quickly slipping away, and he still had a lot of ground to cover once he took care of repaying Roger. John was regretful for how his morning had been delayed, knowing that Bradley may have left the riding club. Even so, he couldn't help how late it was.

By the time John reached the riding club, he realized that his horse appeared a little stiff, apparently from being stalled so long. It wasn't a normal limp though. He would need to have Roger examine his horse while he met with Bradley.

Roger saw John coming and walked out to greet him as he dismounted. "Roger, you're just the person I need to see. I want to personally thank you for your help in retrieving my watch."

"Think nothing of it. You would have done the same for me."

"Bradley told me you might be out some money. Did Mr. Jenkins think to reimburse you with the money I gave him?"

"Mr. Jenkins and I don't always see things the same way... I never said anything to him about it."

"I have the money to repay you. How much did you give Bradley?"

"I gave him two quid, but I don't think he spent it all. I'll get the change next time I see him."

"Here's your two quid and keep whatever Bradley gives you. I'll settle up with him later and pay him for the trouble he went through to get the watch."

"No, I can't take all this money... I'll look like a bandit."

"Roger, the watch is really important to me. You did me a great favor... so take the money."

"Oh, alright, John... just this time."

John had to smile at Roger's humorous candor. With an unspent chuckle, John asked, "I assume Bradley's gone. When did he leave?"

"Oh, I haven't seen him today. He didn't show up this weekend like normal."

John gasped. Bradley was like a rock. If he said he was going to be somewhere or do something, neither heaven or hell could prevent him from doing it.

"Have you been here the whole time?"

"For heaven's sake man, I can't be everywhere at once. Besides, a chap has to take his leave when nature calls. In any case, between Mr. Jenkins and me, we would know if Bradley had been here. You can go ask him if you want. He is in his office."

"By the way, while I go and talk to Mr. Jenkins, can you take a look at my horse? He has been stalled for two days and I think he may be stiff. His gait is off... but not a natural limp."

"Indeed, Sir."

John was worried and feeling anxious as he hurried to the club headquarters to find Mr. Jenkins. He was outside talking to a potential customer, so John held back until they were finished talking. Mr. Jenkins would be furious if interrupted while trying to sign up a new member. Much of Mr. Jenkins' financial woes stemmed from the fact that he had doubled the size of his club and needed to add patrons, as well as boarders.

"Mr. Jenkins, I'm sorry to bother you, but I'm looking for Bradley. He was supposed to meet me here, and according to Roger he hasn't been here today."

"Bradley's been staying in one of the hunting cabins for over a month. Roger wouldn't necessarily know whether he was here or not. Bradley often uses the back road when he comes and goes. John, he's not out there every night; he stays other places too. Your welcome to ride out to see if Bradley is there."

"Which cabin is he in?"

"He's in one of the remote cabins in the north pasture this side of Sloan's Creek."

"Can I use one of your horses? Mine may be lame. Roger is looking him over right now."

"Well, let's go see what the problem is. In either case, I have a mount saddled up front where Roger is working—you can ride out from there."

Roger was finishing his examination of John's horse when the two men approached. Roger was still on one knee prodding the steed's hindquarters when Mr. Jenkins inquired, "What seems to be the problem?"

Roger stood and faced John as he relayed his opinion. "John, it looks like something attacked your horse while he was stalled. Both hindquarters have cuts. If it was a wildcat, your horse was in a fight for his life. If I was guessing, the fight left his stall torn to bits. You're lucky he's alive at all."

"Is he going to be all right?"

"If he doesn't get the fever, he'll be all right; otherwise, he'll just need a few weeks to heal up. He'll need to be walked every day but not ridden. If he does get the fever… I'm sorry, John… we'll have to put him down."

"How long will it take before we know?"

"In a couple of days, he'll start acting real sick if he's not going to make it."

Mr. Jenkins offered to board him for free until it could be determined if John's horse was sick and then put him down if he was. "John, I'll take care of this for you. You don't have to worry he'll get the best of care. We'll do right by you and your horse. Here, take 'Wilkie' and go check on Bradley. I want to know what you find. When you come back, we can discuss renting Wilkie until your horse mends."

"Thank you for your help. If I remember right, it's a half hour ride down and back."

"John, Wilkie can run, and she loves it. It won't take that long. In fact, if you're not back here in twenty minutes, I'm going down there. Don't make me go after you." Smiling, John took Mr. Jenkins' remarks as a challenge, so he bolted off in the direction of the north pasture.

Even from a distance, John could see Bradley's horse tied to the gate of the makeshift three-sided stall. Panic was setting in by the time John flung open the door to the one-room cabin. Bradley was on the floor and lifeless. John carefully rolled him over to check his breathing and discovered a good breath, as well as a strong heartbeat. He was badly beaten and covered with blood. There were only a few signs of a struggle, which meant that he was either asleep when he was attacked or he didn't fight back. That's when John saw the rope burns on his wrists—he'd been tied up while being brutalized.

John had no choice but to race back to the stables and secure a wagon. He hadn't been gone very long, so Mr. Jenkins was surprised at first when he saw John riding in. Mr. Jenkins then got worried when John showed no signs of slowing down as he should have. Mr. Jenkins didn't like hard riding close-in nor did he appreciate dangerous stops that could kill someone on the ground who wasn't paying attention. "My god, man! What are you doing? I didn't say you could run her into the building!"

John was yelling loudly to be heard over the commotion of his hard stop. "Bradley's been brutally beaten! Someone has got to him and left him for dead. We need to get down there with a wagon."

"Roger, tack up the wagon and meet us down at the north meadow cabin. Let's go, John."

By the time Roger could get to the cabin with the wagon, the two men had revived Bradley with some cool water from the nearby creek. They stripped the bed and wrapped him in sheets so they could carry him without doing further damage to his body. By the time Roger turned the wagon in a large circle to make the return trip, John and Mr. Jenkins were ready to hoist Bradley in the back of the wagon.

By necessity, the trip back toward the riding club was a slow process—the meadow fields were uneven and soft in many places. However, once on the road toward Dr. Murray's, the much smoother lane allowed for a faster pace. Mr. Jenkins could not continue because he was unable to leave the riding club unattended, so he hailed the two men on. "Godspeed!"

When the wagon made its chaotic arrival, Dr. Murray was with a patient, so it was Ruth who went to check on the men as they loudly pulled up to the rear entrance of the office. Bradley was going to need the doctor's multiuse emergency room, so Dr. Murray quickly moved his patient to the next room to spare him the gore. Even a hardened country fellow, could pale at the sight of blood.

Gripping the folds in the sheeting, the two men carried Bradley into the emergency room. It was an awkward affair, a noisy disturbance made with ample amounts of stumbling, bumping and groaning. The unorthodox method used to get Bradley onto the exam table would have been very unnerving in the office of a city doctor. On the other hand, in a country doctor's office, especially one located so close to a rough-and-tumble riding club, this type of occurrence happened often.

Without hesitating, Ruth began to clean the blood and dirt from Bradley's face and neck, something that would have been unimaginable for her to do just a few weeks earlier. As Ruth progressed with her first aid, it became apparent that Bradley was going to recover despite all the welts, cuts and bruises with nothing that looked overly serious.

About the time Ruth was done with her work, Andrew had excused himself from his patient to take a quick look at Bradley. "Ruth, look in the hutch and get the bottle of Phenol that just came in from Germany; it's the large brown bottle on the left. Use some gauze and wash his wounds with it. I'll be through with Mr. Ramsey in a few minutes." Before he left the room, Andrew called out over his shoulder, "He looks dehydrated. Give him something to drink."

The doctor was right about the water. Bradley promptly perked up and had begun talking by the time Dr. Murray returned to check on him. After a thorough examination, Dr. Murray determined that Bradley would eventually recover with no lasting injuries.

John's curiosity was immediate and pertinent, "Dr. Murray, what did you have Ruth apply to Bradley's wounds—what was in the brown bottle?"

"That, my dear fellow, is Phenol; a new wound dressing I have been researching. I am honored to be one of many doctors who are conducting therapeutic trials here in England, as well as Germany and France. The results will be collected and reviewed to help determine its effectiveness to prevent the fever."

John instantly made the connection and was not afraid to ask. "Will it work on animals?"

"They've already tried Phenol on animals; it's how they first determine a use for new medicines. When a drug works on animals, then they try it on humans. Why do you ask?"

John had the answer he wanted to hear. He turned to Roger and motioned him to come closer to hear what Dr. Murray was saying. "My horse has some lacerations from a fight with a wildcat. Roger said my horse could get the fever from the cuts. Can we try the Phenol on my horse's cuts?"

"Alright, John, but you have to understand there are no promises; it may not help. Roger, I will fill a small bottle for you to take with you. Make certain the wounds are cleaned first, and then dab on the Phenol twice a day."

Roger was eager to get back to the riding club and get started using the Phenol. "Don't worry, John, I have a good feeling about this. By the way, what are you going to do about Wilkie? You are coming back to the stables, aren't you?"

Bradley had been watching and listening to the conversation about the Phenol. He encouraged John to ride back with Roger to see about renting Wilkie. Before the men left, Bradley motioned for John to come near. "We've got to talk when you get back."

Chapter Twenty-Seven
What Must I do?

John was bothered by the thought that Bradley's injuries appeared to be a result of the madness surrounding the lockboxes. Because he was worried about Bradley's condition, John made his trip to the riding club as short as possible. He quickly arranged to rent Wilkie for a couple of weeks. By then his own horse should be healed. The two weeks would also allow him a perfect timeframe to visit his sister, Veronica.

When John got back to Dr. Murray's, Bradley was eating some of the same soup that Andrew had prepared earlier in the day. Bradley had not eaten since Sunday when he shared the cold leftover crumpets that Ruth served to the group.

Having eaten, Bradley was feeling much better, so he readily initiated a conversation with John. Andrew and Ruth stood to leave the room, but Bradley asked them to remain to be included in the discussion. "John, I'll get right to the point. A couple of Captain Yardley's men came to pay me a visit; they were waiting for me when I got to the cabin. I didn't have a chance because they jumped me when I came through the door. I told them that I didn't have any information to give them, and that I was not aware of your dealings with the bank. I will say this: Yardley wants what was in your lockboxes."

Bradley had to stop talking for a few moments as he felt some pain creep in. The numbness was receding, allowing a dull throbbing ache to surface. "Andrew, as soon as we finish here, I'm going to need something for this pain."

"I can take care of it; just tell me when you're ready."

"John, I'll make this quick. After they had beaten me, they stood just outside the cabin and talked for a while. They spoke of a reward being offered for the contents of your lockboxes, and Captain Yardley is in the middle of all of it. Here is the worst part: the word is out on the streets among the criminal element. He doesn't care who gets your bank bag as long as he collects the reward. This is a real mess, John. My question to you is: What is in your bank bag that is worth all that has happened? You need to think about it before someone gets killed."

Bradley's tough talk was sobering for John, who was pale-faced for two reasons. First, he saw himself as directly responsible for Bradley's injuries, and second, he *hadn't* thoroughly thought through what could be so valuable to cause the deadly realities that were disrupting lives and causing harm. Somehow, he thought his problems would go away once he disappeared for a few weeks.

John spoke slowly and methodically as he mentally went through a sequence of events. "Andrew, you know I went through every piece of paper in my possession. It was here, in your front room, remember? There was nothing in the bank bag that appeared to be of great value. Of course, I have the pound notes, but that isn't enough money to warrant the mayhem we've endured. Then there was my mum's wedding ring and a pendant, but again their worth is mostly sentimental. There wasn't a key for the third lockbo—" John jumped to his feet in a fit of sheer panic severely startling everyone.

Alarmed, Andrew countered John's panic, "My god, man! What is it?"

John was gripped with his train of thought, "It's obvious they don't know what was in the boxes, but they do know *what should have been in the box*. We don't know what they know, so we're mystified."

"Come on, John. That's been evident from the start… is that it?"

John was so focused on his revelation that he didn't process Andrew's retort. John's extreme anxiety was palpable.

John continued his discourse of thinking aloud, "If they get their hands on the bank bag... what they are looking for will not be there because it is obviously in the third box. There was no key for the third box, only a note from my mum stating that Edward was not only in possession of the key, but that he knew the details concerning the contents of the last unopened lockbox. That puts him and Mary in mortal danger. *We have got to destroy that note by some means... at any cost!*"

John began trembling with the terrorizing thought of Mary or Edward being brutally beaten by a gang of thugs. With mounting resolve, John spoke with determined grit. "I've got to get that note even if it kills me. I will not have anyone else brutalized for money or whatever else Romney Longfellow thinks is so valuable. I'll leave tonight and go to the cottage. I'll burn the note, and it'll be over and done with. I'll be the only one they can harm."

Andrew needed to calm John and reason with him. "John, you need to sit back down and listen to what I have to say. Let's take a minute and think this through point by point. First, do you think Edward would allow himself or Mary to come to harm over material possessions? He would give them what they are after and not think twice about it, even if it meant having to restore what may have been yours. John, Edward is a man of integrity and honor."

John was angry and loudly rebuked Andrew, "I don't care about money or material possessions—you've missed my point entirely. Can't you see how some criminal could thoughtlessly take advantage of Mary, or beat Edward for malicious pleasure—it happens all the time. *I'm not going to let that happen!"*

John's passionate outrage was sobering. Bradley could relate to John's charges because of his own beating. Even so, he wanted to stop John from going to the cottage; he would have to use reason to help John think more clearly. "Alright, John, let's say you go to the cottage. Have you considered that they may be waiting for you to come? My guess is they have it staked out. All they need to do is wait for you to reveal the location of the bank bag and then ambush you—it will all be over. *They will have what they want, and you will have handed it to them.* John, think about this. The visit they paid me could have been nothing more than to set a trap for you—to provoke you into doing exactly what you're planning to do."

John was still standing, but once he took in Bradley's sensible rationale, he sat hard as he became demoralized. It all seemed so pointless and futile—he felt powerless to do anything. John crumpled and bent over, trying to hide his almost silent weeping. He was crushed over his helplessness to do anything—to ward off the impending danger to two people he dearly loved.

Andrew understood that times like these are often precisely orchestrated by God to bring his people to the end of themselves. Otherwise, they would never allow Him to be their provider and deliverer—their anchor in the storms of life. "John, you're in a safe place. You belong to God now, and He is fiercely protective of those who belong to Him. However, there is a requirement for Him to move on your behalf."

Even though John was still harboring some anger, Andrew's comments sparked an odd sense of curiosity. The Truth was calling out to John, but the whisper wasn't completely discernible to his yet unrenewed mind. The Spirit within him could hear; nonetheless, John's natural thinking was masking the pure-sweet beckoning—*come*. John looked up to lock eyes with Andrew. For the moment, there was a limitless expression of compassion in Andrew's countenance— John couldn't resist the call. "What must I do?"

"You must be willing to allow Him to move on your behalf. He tells in His Word; repeated over and over again. *Be still and know that I am Your God—the battle is Mine says the Lord of Host.* John, it's the safest place to be. Let's talk to Him about it—let's pray.*"

Chapter Twenty-Eight
See For Yourself

London Police Station earlier the same day 9:30 a.m.

Edward walked into the precinct headquarters for his Monday morning appointment with Captain Yardley. His deputy assistant, Eben Boles, met Edward in the waiting area to escort him back to the captain's office.

Edward Van Zandt was not a notable person in his own sight. Nevertheless, anyone who knew of him, especially members of Spurgeon's church, held a reverent awe of his personage. As the two men made their way through various assemblages of office workers, detectives and police officers, Edward was greeted with respectful gestures of acknowledgment. He couldn't say for certain, but many of their eyes seemed to cry out: *save us* from… something. Edward could only speculate. Remembering Ruth's fearful mention of Captain Yardley, it appeared these faithful public servants needed to be protected from their own police captain.

Edward had not forgotten Ruth's warning about dealing with the treacherous two-faced captain. There was only one way to proceed with the interview, and frankly, it was the only way Edward knew. It was a powerful lesson that he had learned early in his life on how to conduct his business—tell the whole truth no matter the perceived cost.

Edward made an unusual move to speak first. He did so with such strength of position that Captain Yardley was completely diverted from his plan to deceitfully wrestle information from Edward. "I know why I'm here… I know what you want… and I'm perfectly willing to satisfy your demands without going through the needless pretense, so let's cut to the quick."

Captain Yardley was doubtful; it was ingrained in him. In fact, success in his profession demanded that he be suspicious. Even so, in a highly unprofessional manner, the captain haughtily probed in a cynical tone, "Tell me what you think I want."

Edward began with a brief but necessary background. "John Taylor was left without an inheritance from his parent's estate. There are some who will not believe that is the case. Madeline Taylor left a paltry amount of money with instructions to pay the family debts. John has done that. He has less than two-hundred pounds sterling to start a new life."

Captain Yardley was agitated, "I thought you said: 'cut to the quick.' I'm not interested in this drivel."

Edward continued to tell it exactly how it was. "You and I both know that there is a plainclothes detective on a stakeout at the Bank of England. He's been there for over four weeks. Your detective has been posted there, during banking hours, since Madeline Taylor's death. We also know that you only allowed John to retrieve the contents of his safety deposit boxes so you could take what was in them. It is also evident that there has been a desperate attempt to subdue him ever since that day."

Still holding his smug attitude, the captain countered, "Like I told you yesterday, John Taylor is a person of interest. He will remain under suspicion until we talk to him. We believe you have the sway to bring him in."

Edward was ready to give the captain what he wanted. "Captain, John does not have the key to the third lockbox. I have it. *He was never intended to have it.* There was no key in the second lockbox, only a note to John, explaining that I had the key."

Suddenly, Edward had the captain's keen interest. Captain Yardley had been leaning back in his chair displaying his contempt via his body language. When Edward mentioned having the third key everything changed; the captain sat upright, tipping his hand.

The dirty captain tried to recover from exposing himself, but it was too late, and he knew it. Although Edward had outplayed the captain, he didn't let on because he wasn't through. "Captain Yardley, you're going to be disappointed. There is nothing in the third lockbox except a note from John's mum explaining her intentions. You can see for yourself."

"That's preposterous! Why would anyone engage in such tomfoolery?"

"That's preposterous! Why would anyone engage in such tomfoolery?"

"I'm certainly willing to explain, but I'm convinced you're not interested in the noble intentions of a mum trying to guide her son."

"For god's sake, man, you're mad."

Edward had defanged the beast, depriving the captain the thrill of the hunt. Trying to regain some kind of edge while displaying complete disgust, the captain unexpectedly grunted, "You've got two minutes to convince me. Then we're going down to the bank and have a look. What you have to say had better be good. I've got the power to see you rot in a jail cell. You best get started."

"If you will allow me to finish, everything will make perfect sense."

"I'm serious Edward; you've got less than two minutes."

"Before his mum's death, John was on a wrong path, set for destruction. She knew he would not survive in the future without the family money. Mrs. Taylor asked me to help her prepare John for a more meager future, and this was her idea of how to do it.

"Madeline had been to the Orient on several occasions. She remembered an old Chinese parable that told a story with similar circumstances to the one she faced with John. The young man in the story was spoiled and arrogant like John. The Chinese parents set up a series of trials that would challenge their son, forcing him to make the hard decisions to grow and mature. The notes to John, as well as the money, were supposed to guide him to make the right choices. He passed the tests splendidly. There was much more to John than anyone guessed."

"That's it. I'm supposed to believe that ridiculous fairy tale. Who do you think you're dealing with?"

"There is an interesting twist—I still have one minute. Something happened that Mrs. Taylor had not counted on. John, through his riding accident, found God, and he turned around even without the tests his mum scripted for him."

The captain was getting flustered and confused. "Wait a minute. Let's back up... I just thought of something. Why is the box empty?"

"When you read the note... I'm assuming we're still going to the bank... you'll see that the fortunate future Madeline envisioned for her son was not of fame or fortune, but in acquiring the values she intended for him to learn through the tests. And like I said earlier, there was little money to give him anyway."

Incredibly, the callous captain was becoming intrigued, although holding on to his suspicions. He didn't ask Edward to continue but didn't stop him when he did. "As I was saying, John found God and turned around. He was set on a new course of contentment and peace without the trappings of material possessions that were causing his early downfall—the very intentions his mum set out to accomplish."

Captain Yardley found himself going down a path that was painful for him. "That's it... no more of this God stuff. My mum was a fanatic just like you. She dragged me to church every time the doors were open. I hate her for the things she did to me in the name of God. She twisted my ear and slapped me around until I couldn't see straight. I have the utmost contempt for you religious zealots. So I don't buy any of this nonsense you're telling me."

Captain Yardley started to stand up, signaling his dismissal of the meeting, but today he was not in control. Edward stayed seated and in an oddly surreal way, the captain sat back down in such a resigned and submissive manner that his deputy assistant became wide-eyed. He knew his captain well, and this was completely out of character for him.

Edward continued, "If I prove to you that I'm telling the truth, will you stop harassing John and his associates? Will you stop pursuing a lawful citizen, denying him of his legal rights to peace and security?"

Yardley sarcastically retorted, "First of all, you can't prove anything. Second, I am the one who is responsible for upholding the law and determining who has broken the law.

You can't persuade me of anything; it's a matter of investigating the facts."

Edward continued unabated, "Captain Yardley, we both know that the sentry you posted at the bank was there to monitor the safety deposit box that is in question. You should know that I haven't signed in with the vault manager in over a year; that I can prove. Therefore, what's in the lockbox hasn't been disturbed, altered, added to or taken away from. It's exactly as I described it, and I'm willing to show you. All you'll find is a letter from a mum to her son."

"Seeing is believing. You had better not be bluffing, or you'll be in jail for contempt and any other charges I can drum up."

The men agreed to meet at the bank at 2:00 p.m. That would give Edward time to go by his office and if possible, go home to check on Mary and have a midday meal as well.

Likewise, the captain made good use of the intervening time. Unknown to Edward, Captain Yardley made a crosstown visit to see Romney Longfellow. The unresolved and disturbing matters concerning John Taylor and Edward Van Zandt were discussed at length. Romney ordered the captain to verify Edward's claims and then lay off if they appeared to be true. Romney's intention was to let the whole situation cool down for a few months. He would bide his time until the right moment.

Edward returned early to the bank so he could arrange for his anonymous status to be verified with the vice president in charge of discreet accounts. "Good Morning Mr. Dobbs. I hope all is well with you today."

"Yes, quite agreeable except for the riff-raff of the London streets that I have to endure every morning."

Edward continued with the business at hand. "Mr. Dobbs, I have a favor to ask that I believe may be outside the ordinary bank policy. I have an appointment with police Captain Yardley to open and view the contents of my lockbox. He will be here in ten minutes. Would you be willing to facilitate the meeting as a senior officer of the bank?"

Mr. Dobbs curtly responded, "Unfortunately, I cannot allow my identity to be disclosed under any circumstance. It would be a violation of bank policy that could potentially bring unwanted scrutiny to our wealthiest bank customers."

"It is important that I have a member of bank management present."

Mr. Dobbs continued his snobbish rebuke in a more aggravated tone, "If you insist, you will need a court order and the transaction will have to take place after normal banking hours. Mr. Van Zandt, understand that I have never had a client place me in the position of having to resort to enforcing a bank policy."

Edward was dumbfounded. "Excuse me. I don't want to sound disrespectful to you or the bank management, but wouldn't a court order bring *more* scrutiny?

"Mr. Van Zandt, please understand there is nothing I can do."

"I fully understand your concerns. So to not bring further undue stress upon you, I would be happy to have another bank officer assist me. You could witness my signature as usual and then simply have another senior officer escort me downstairs to assist me at the vault."

The vice president stared at Edward with a smug look of disdain for several long moments and then quipped, "Just a minute." He left Edward standing as he huffed out of his office.

The bank executive returned very quickly, bearing a rather dramatic change in demeanor. In a reconciliatory manner, he quickly had Edward signed in and ready to meet with Captain Yardley, precisely at the appointed time.

To say that something was up would be an understatement. With a full entourage, Captain Yardley had chosen to assume his public relations role to foster his appearance as a "knight in shining armor." He was going to use this paltry charade, involving John's lockbox, to enhance his public image. The pretentious captain gave a commendable performance. He was all smiles and cordial to everyone who greeted him. Oddly, all normal bank procedures pertaining the bank vault were forfeited. He was escorted into the vault as if he were the King of England.

Continuing to act as if he were the grand master of ceremonies, Captain Yardley gestured toward Edward to approach the heralded lockbox. With the broadest smile, the captain entreated Edward, "My good man… let's peruse your lockbox… shall we?"

The captain was playing it both ways. If Edward was lying, then justice would be swift and sure for all to see. If he wasn't, the elaborate fanfare would be a cover for the ill-intended conduct of a very dirty public servant.

The envelope that Madeline Taylor left for her son was sealed with a wax impression, signifying its very private nature. There was also a narrow red ribbon that encircled the envelope in both directions, and tied with a bow, further attesting to the intimacy that was reserved for only one intended reader and no one else. What was meant to be a sacred exchange between loved ones was now being desecrated in a public spectacle—a violation of all human decency.

Captain Yardley was aware of what he had done. If he continued, he would be seen as the two-faced monster he was. Realizing that the small envelope could only contain the letter that Edward had described, he cheerfully announced, "Everything looks in order here; I believe this case is duly dismissed. Edward, you are free to go. You need not fear any of my men further investigating this case. Give my regards to Mr. Taylor."

It was a few minutes before 3:00 p.m. and Edward felt compelled to find a way to inform John of Captain Yardley's very public dismissal of his person-of-interest status. Interestingly, Edward did not want to disclose the details of how the dismissal came about. Not that he wanted to hide anything from John, he just wanted to remain true to his mother's original desires. John was not yet ready to receive what was in the lockbox.

It was impossible for Edward to miss any more time from his company business, so he hired a messenger to ride out to the Murray's with a note for John. The significance of the message was paramount to his well-being. A mounted rider could make the trip in under an hour, which meant that John should have the news by no later than four o'clock.

The messenger knocked on the front door to Dr. Murray's country office just at the conclusion of an anointed time of prayer. Andrew excused himself to answer the door. As he stood in the doorway reading the note from Edward, Andrew's knees began to wobble; he was accustomed to waiting days or even months for answered prayer. He slowly returned to the front room where he and the others had finished praying only minutes earlier. Without speaking, Andrew handed John the note from Edward.

John was flooded with relief as he read the urgent note from Edward. It was truly a moment of God's timely provision—*God knew John's need before he even thought to ask.* Andrew was right when he told John to allow God to fight his battles. It was in John's moment of utter helplessness that he chose to surrender, trusting God no matter the outcome. It was a lesson well-learned.

Chapter Twenty-Nine
Sister Veronica

John's wearisome circumstances were finally giving way to a truly bright future. His responsibilities at his family estate were completed and he was now able to travel about without the fear of being arrested or kidnapped. He could finally be underway to see his sister, Veronica.

John had been longing to visit his sister since their chance encounter on the previous Sunday morning. Even though he was unsure where he stood with her, he was anxious to explain what had happened to him. John knew that Veronica would have a sense of obligation to help him; she had been trying to *rescue* him for years. Even so, there had been a strain of sorts between them, so he wasn't sure how long he should stay without causing further wariness.

Veronica had always been too insistent with her religious talk, creating an edginess to her persuasive arguments about God that were not appealing. On the other hand, when Edward spoke about the Lord, John felt a thirst to know God and felt drawn to Him. Perhaps Veronica would have a different frame of mind toward John since he had begun his own journey to know God. He hoped that their new common ground would allow them to build on their relationship.

Wilkie was up for the trip and eager to get going. However, despite Wilkie's need to run, John was not in the mood. He felt like he had been running for weeks. His body was tired, and his mind was just starting to recover from the emotional trauma that had reached a tumultuous culmination just an hour earlier. John wanted to enjoy a relaxed pace that would still allow him to travel the eight miles to Veronica's home in less than two hours. That would leave him plenty of time to help his brother-in-law, Paul Wheaton, finish his evening work routine.

Even though the Wheaton lineage was firmly entrenched in the English aristocracy, Paul Wheaton was a quiet, hardworking and reverent man. He owned a large working estate near Stratford, twelve miles east of metropolitan London. Of course, Paul had numerous employees who helped operate his massive sheep ranching operation. Nonetheless, he enjoyed working side-by-side with his men.

Paul and Veronica were in their early thirties and childless, having lost two children to miscarriages. They had given up hope for a large family they both had desired, and with it, a certain capacity to experience joy had been lost as well. Their dream of a bustling family with children underfoot was not to be.

Anyone could see that religion was a big part of the Wheaton family. Even so, was their faithful church attendance hypocritical? Was their involvement in a prayer group, as well as their support of Spurgeon's China Mission only for display? No family is perfect and never will be. For it's our imperfections that qualify each of us to need God's forgiveness. *Facing our frailties and our fallibility eventually produces the desperation required to grope for God and find Him. Our blindness to recognize that He has always been there is revealed—He has been reaching out to us all along with His unquenchable love.*

Veronica was no stranger to high society peerage that entitled her to privilege. As the daughter of John Wilson Taylor, a wealthy shipping magnate, she had been raised with every advantage—something she held dear.

As is often the case with a professing Christian, Veronica's position of status regularly forced her to compromise the biblical values that were important to her. She was frequently angry with herself, often feeling guilty, for the choices she had made that were contrary to her faith.

The conflict in Veronica's soul had played out over and over again until a week earlier when a series of events began to bring clarity to her dilemma. Early one morning she read Matthew 6:24: *No man can serve two masters: for either he will hate the one, and love the other; or else he will hold to the one, and despise the other. Ye cannot serve God and mammon.* She had read that verse before, but somehow never related its meaning to her own life. Then yesterday, when she was on her way to church, her own brother could not break through her arrogant pride and self-righteousness. At the last moment, before she rode off and left him standing in the congested streets of in-town London, he spoke the words that penetrated her heart.

In her moment of divine revelation, the deepest meanings of "not being able to serve two masters" was opened to her— her heart was pricked. In a most profound way, she was able to see her impasse as God saw it. She could clearly see how her prideful religiosity had held her hostage, preventing her from serving God without compromise.

Her confrontation with John on the streets of London almost broke her heart when she realized that John must have been in trouble. Her pride had blinded her until John ripped back the veil to reveal her hardened heart. Her revelatory moment combined with John's apparent distress had left her mournful, desperately wanting to right a wrong.

In a feeble attempt to appease her moment of failure, Veronica had called out to John: *"Come see us as soon as you can.... I want to know what happened to you."* As her carriage lurched away, she had no way of knowing if he had heard her desperate cry, drowned in the clamor of the crowded cobblestone streets near the church.

Even a life-changing epiphany is just a beginning. The essence of any truth taken to heart must be worked out until its results are observable, often taking months or even years. Veronica continued to struggle, but with a God-given vision to hold on to, she would overcome her divided heart.

Eventually, Veronica's need for approval from her peers, slowly gave way to an enduring respect for her husband. Ironically, it was Paul's unwavering ability to not compromise his beliefs that had been a point of contention for her. His faithfulness was a constant reminder to her of her lukewarm state. In the end, it was his securely grounded faith that inspired her to persevere.

Veronica was standing on the second-story veranda, taking in the rolling countryside, when she saw John approach from the north on Darby Road. She would not have been expecting his arrival from that direction, so she remained long enough to make sure. Since Veronica had last seen her brother, she had vowed not to exclude anyone from the Gospel even if it meant getting her hands dirty in the slums of London. With her freshly renewed desire to love to the uttermost, Veronica rushed downstairs to greet her battle-weary brother.

John was truly in need of a well-deserved rest, a chance to fully mend and to chart a new course. His last few weeks had been spent responding to, as well as recuperating from, circumstances that seemed bent on destroying him.

The time he anticipated spending with his sister would be the perfect opportunity to grow strong in more ways than just his physical renewal. With Veronica's knowledge of the Bible, he saw an opportunity to grow spiritually as well. He had resisted her many efforts to share God's Word with him, but now he was able to appreciate what she could tell him.

> *With Veronica's knowledge of the Bible, he saw an opportunity to grow spiritually as well.*

As he rode up to the oversized stone-stepped entrance, Veronica rushed out to meet him. Her unexpected gladness surprised him. There was a connection that had not existed before—no longer just siblings, they were brother and sister in Christ.

The conditions were ripe for John to spend a generous amount of time with Paul and Veronica. By God's grace, any mending in their three hearts was done before John arrived.

What had not been possible before, God orchestrated a way for their relationships to quickly flourish, allowing them to form a close bond.

Over the next two weeks, John, Veronica and Paul grew in understanding, wisdom and grace just as the proverb states: *as iron sharpens iron, so a friend sharpens a friend.* And so it was that John was ready to start his life anew, leaving the refuge and safety of his sister's country estate.

Chapter Thirty
Web of Treachery

The rest and renewal that John experienced while staying with his sister were much needed. He regained his weight and sported a neatly trimmed full-grown beard. He also took the opportunity to buy two new changes of clothes, as well as travel bags to transport them. Interestingly, John chose suits in the style that a middle-class manager might wear and not the elaborate aristocratic attire of the elite, who donned top hats and coattails.

John left his sister's estate relatively early on Monday for his trip back to London. By necessity, he would return to the riding club first. He needed to find out how his injured horse was faring. As much as he had grown fond of Wilkie, she was just on loan. From the riding stables, John would then go by to see Dr. Murray to get an update on Bradley.

John gave Wilkie every opportunity to run as they sprinted back to the riding club. It was exhilarating to be her mount as she ran all out the last half mile to the club. As usual, Roger was out tending to the boarded horses when he saw John ride up to the arena. Wilkie was lathered and wet, as she shivered with contentment—John would miss riding her.

"John, I was wondering if you would come back. Wilkie's such a great horse I thought perhaps you had run off with her. By the way, we decided to name your horse, *Slayer*. Turns out he killed that wildcat with a direct hit to the head—Doc Murray found its corpse just outside the back of his barn."

"Well, how's Slayer doing?"

"He healed up just fine. You know, I am fairly confident that Doc's medicine may have saved your horse. John, I'm sorry to be the one who has to tell you, but Slayer can't run as he should. The cuts were deep enough to cause some muscle damage—been hobbled, I'm afraid."

John winced at the thought of the vicious attack that earned Slayer his new name. "So he'll never be able to gallop or sprint?"

"Sorry, John, I'm afraid not. He'll fade in the stretch. But, don't worry, Mr. Jenkins has an offer I think you'll find agreeable."

"Thanks for all your help, Roger. Where is he?"

"If he is not in his office, he won't be far from it."

John left Wilkie tied up at the arena and walked over to the club headquarters to find Mr. Jenkins. He was just inside the doorway talking to his new bookkeeper, so John waited outside until they finished. Mr. Jenkins was in an exceptionally good mood as he greeted John. "I'm glad to see you. Your horse is healthy, but I'm afraid he's not going to get you out of any trouble; he's been hobbled."

"Roger just told me. Can't he be worked through the injury?"

"Anything's possible, John. I learned long ago these creatures will surprise you if you give them half a chance. In any event, I have an offer for you. You know I'm in the horse trading business, so I'm prepared to make you a trade. We can use Slayer around here on weekends for the ladies and children to ride—be a great asset. Give me £01/5 along with Slayer, and Wilkie will be all yours."

It took John a few moments to try to calculate if the deal was fair. He still didn't have a command for what things should cost, but he was learning. "We have a deal. However, you might want to think about renaming Slayer—not a very appropriate name, considering who'll be riding him."

"You have a point. By the way, I have something for Bradley. Can you give him this when you see him?" Mr. Jenkins handed John a Bible and a bag of belongings that were left in the cabin the day Bradley was rushed to see Dr. Murray.

John was a little annoyed, and it was evident in his tone. "You haven't checked on Bradley since I left here two weeks ago?"

"Calm down, John. Bradley's fine. Roger went down to see him. He just forgot to take Bradley his belongings. He only spent one night with Dr. Murray and apparently didn't want to come by here when he left for town, which surprised me. Roger says that Dr. Murray gave him a clean bill of health."

John noticed the Bible was splattered with blood, which caused him to get a lump in his throat, prompting him to finish his business and move on to see Dr. Murray. "Can you put the £01/5 on my account?"

"John, when you get a job, we'll talk about an account. I hope you understand."

"Of course, you're absolutely right. What was I thinking?"

Once John put Bradley's possessions in his new saddlebags and paid Mr. Jenkins, he wanted to leave quickly. He was eager to find Bradley.

It was a little before ten o'clock when John rode up to Dr. Murray's home office. He quickly discovered that Ruth wanted to take a break from the country for a few days. Even though she wasn't a country lady, she was living up to her new resolve to be with and honor her husband. All in all their new life together looked promising. Even so, she needed an escape to her home in town. Andrew would reunite with her over the weekend. John's offer to drive Ruth into town was wholeheartedly appreciated.

Before they left, John needed to know more about Bradley. "Dr. Murray, what can you tell me about Bradley? Is he all right? What I mean is… was he acting normally?"

"John, he was just fine physically. Nevertheless, he was hell-bent on getting to town. I could never get him to admit it, but I was afraid he was going to exact vengeance on the two men who beat him. I kept him here as long as I could, trying to reason with him. Whether he took my advice or not, I can't say."

John was crushed. If Bradley had become violent with the brutes who came after him, the fragile truce with Captain Yardley would be called off—no one would be safe. John wanted to get to London as quickly as possible, but he had already committed to helping Ruth. In a politely anxious tone, John questioned Ruth, "Mrs. Murray, when would you like to leave?"

Ruth sensed John's worry. "All I need to do is pack my bag; give me five minutes."

John was relieved as he imagined the delay to be minimal. "I'll go ready the carriage while you get your things together. I would like to make the trip as quickly as we can. I'm worried about Bradley."

Dr. Murray spoke up with concern. "John, don't drive that carriage too fast. Plenty of people have been killed in overturned buggies. I'm serious; I should know. I've had to deal with their broken and dying bodies." Andrew caught himself before he let slip how Edward's wife was killed in a runaway carriage accident. That was Edward's story to tell.

John tied Wilkie to the back of the carriage while Andrew helped Ruth into the back seat. John knew that even if he rushed, it would only save him a few minutes. Andrew was right, catching a soft spot in the road while driving fast will flip a carriage. It was not worth the risk especially since Ruth was with him. Besides, Bradley left almost ten days earlier, so whatever he planned to do was probably already done.

On the way back to town, it dawned on John that if Bradley had done something to provoke Captain Yardley, then he and Ruth could be in danger as they approached London. He felt confident that his appearance had changed enough that he wouldn't be readily recognized. Even so, he needed to remain calm and be careful not to draw attention to himself or carelessly allow someone to follow him home. If they could make it to the Murray residence unnoticed, then John felt they would be safe.

During John's visit with his brother-in-law, an in-depth discussion about John's trials had yielded speculation that Captain Yardley had not connected him with the Murrays. John reasoned that if an association had been made, then Yardley's men would have ransacked the Murray's home before beating Bradley. Bradley had even said as much two weeks earlier at Andrew's office. He had indicated that the Murrays were not entangled in Captain Yardley's web of treachery. If that was true, then John needed to get to the Murray's home undetected to preserve their sanctuary.

John wanted to let Ruth know his thoughts concerning the potential danger. Just as they approached the edge of London, he slowed the carriage to a stop and then turned to speak. "Ruth, if Bradley did retaliate in some way, then we could be in harm's way. I'm going to take the back way to your home so I can avoid Fleet Street. I'm also going to take some extra turns to make certain no one is following us."

Just as John got back underway, a police officer turned his horse around to follow them. John was determined not to panic, confident that he would not be recognized. The police officer sped up to catch them and then rode next to them for a few moments. John nodded and the police officer passed on. After the close call, John made several extra turns and even stopped for ten minutes pretending to tend to Wilkie. Satisfied that no one was trailing them, he made his way to Ruth's home.

Nothing on the property seemed to be disturbed, so he accompanied Ruth safely through the back door of her home. Once he felt that she was secure, John continued on to the livery to stall her horse and carriage.

In a snap decision, John chose to give a false name when he introduced himself to the stable hand who greeted him. Lying about his name was awkward, something he had never done before. Immediately, he felt he had made a mistake. John had originally intended to open an account so he could board his horse. Rather than open an account under an alias, he chose to just leave Ruth's carriage and say nothing else. He would have to find a way to undo his misstep at a later date.

Chapter Thirty-One
The Vigilante

John untied Wilkie and rode the two blocks over to Van Zandt's Printing Company. Unsure of what to expect, John ventured through the side door, which was a nonpublic entrance. Other than a few inquisitive glances, John was not questioned about being on the production floor. He hadn't planned to be so clandestine in his actions, but since he had reached London, he felt like he needed to be invisible. Starting with the zigzag carriage ride, then the alias and now he was slipping in a side door. Maybe he could get some fresh insight or wise counsel from Edward.

The manager's offices were attached to the offset printing workroom where John had entered through the shipping and receiving door. He spotted a large viewing window, overlooking the dimly lit shop floor, which revealed Edward was in his office.

John was uncomfortable knocking directly on Edward's shop door entrance, so he used the alternate door that led to the front half of the building where the reception area was located. John was surprised to see Mary behind the receptionist desk. "Mary! I am so glad to see you. I didn't know you worked here."

Mary gushed at the sight of John, who was completely rejuvenated. It took her a few moments to gather her words. "John, what a pleasant surprise... my... you look quite handsome." Trying to remain the gentile Victorian woman of demure composure was difficult. Regaining her poise, she responded to John's off-handed question. "Oh, I'm just filling in for Mrs. Baily, who is sick. May I help you?"

"I would like to see your father—I mean Mr. Van Zandt."

Thinking quickly, Mary seized the moment. "He just told me he's leaving for lunch. I believe he's going to the deli on Market Street. Perhaps you could join him."

"That sounds perfect."

"I'll go ask."

Mary stood to go and arrange the lunch appointment when Edward stepped through the back office doorway at a brisk pace. "Let's go Mary—John! I hardly recognized you. You want to join us for lunch?"

John looked at Mary, who was blushing, and then to Edward, who was wondering why the hesitation. "Of course, I'm delighted to join you." Mary was elated to have John join them for lunch even knowing that she would not have her father's attention as he and John talked.

John didn't move until he asked Edward the pivotal question, "How concerned do I need to be about being recognized?"

"The Market Street Deli is very low key; you'll be all right for now."

The Market Street Deli was located just a block and half away in the front half of a butcher shop. The side street entrance made the deli a nondescript eatery for locals. The trio talked as they walked, catching up on the latest happenings.

Edward ventured, "Does anyone know you're back in London?"

John put Edward's query aside for the moment; his first concern was for Bradley, "I've been worried for Bradley. Dr. Murray was concerned that he may try to extract some vengeance on his attackers." Unknown to John, Bradley had dominated the police blotter with his near murderous one-man vigilante escapades.

"I'm afraid, young man, that is old news. Bradley put those two gents in the hospital; they almost died. He then went after Captain Yardley and nearly killed him as well. As a gesture of goodwill, I went to see the captain a few times while he was recuperating. He lost an eye and his voice box was damaged; he can barely talk."

John was pale with shock. He knew Bradley well enough to know that he wouldn't just let his beating pass, but this degree of retribution was hard to believe. "Where is Bradley now?"

"I believe he is out of the country, possibly somewhere in Europe. There has been an ongoing manhunt since it all happened. Anyone who knows him is being questioned. Fortunately for everyone, Bradley removed the rotten element from the police department. Since Yardley and his men have been in the hospital, questioning by the police has been rather dignified. In fact, there has been a collective sigh of relief among those who knew the real state of affairs within the precinct. Even so, what Bradley did was wrong, and unfortunately, he'll have to pay for what he did, justified or not."

John was speechless for several moments before he could utter, "I had no idea he was going to start his own personal war. I was hoping that I could come back home and remain free to move about even if Bradley had stirred things up." After several more moments of reflection, he answered Edward's earlier question. "Edward, you asked me if I am known to be in town. As far as I am aware, no one has recognized me."

"Well, I'm certain you'll be wanted for questioning. However, you weren't mentioned by name when I was interviewed by the police concerning Bradley."

John wanted to divulge to Edward about his odd behavior at the Third Street Livery, "Also… just so you'll know… on an impulsive whim, I gave a false name to the stable hand where Ruth keeps her carriage. I think the reason I felt compelled to give an alias is that the police have not connected Bradley or me with the Murrays. I really didn't want anyone else being questioned because of my troubles with Romney or Captain Yardley."

Edward knew John was lagging in his thinking. "The world has moved on since Yardley is no longer Chief. For the moment, Bradley is the main focus for the new Police Chief, who is seeking him for his lawlessness. Yet, the rumor is that you may once again be in Romney's sights, but this time, the police won't be involved. John, I have been thinking about a plan to get you away from all of this. I have a ship that will be ready to leave port in a few days. What would you say about putting you on it as a crew member?"

John was perplexed with questions flooding his mind. His first question just gushed out, "You own a ship?"

"John, it's a very long story. However, the short of it is that when Romney sold off multiple ships a few years ago, Spurgeon's China Missions board elected to look into buying one. As a board member, I stepped in and purchased the best ship before it was taken by someone else. In the end, it has worked out beautifully."

John couldn't process the information fast enough. While John remained dumbstruck, Edward continued with answers to some of the obvious questions. "In the wake of your father's death, Romney began refusing to transport missionary provisions, books, Bibles and other needful supplies for the churches abroad, making one excuse after another. It made sense to have our own ship. One added benefit is that it has opened up more opportunities for mission work. John, I've prayed about this voyage, and I think you should consider going."

Edward's second offer to sail left John feeling a little dejected. Spending untold months at sea just didn't appeal to him at the moment. He had seen distinct glimpses of his future, and being aboard a ship wasn't part of the picture. Mary had been on his mind almost constantly for over two weeks, and to be separated from her just didn't make

> *"In the wake of your father's death, Romney began refusing to transport missionary supplies, ...making one excuse after another."*

sense either. Disheartened, he looked over to Mary with a sheepish grin. "I don't know. I'll have to think about it."

Edward could sense John's disillusionment. Feeling he was rudderless and needed steering in the right direction, Edward reached over to console John with a manly pat on the shoulder. Edward changed to a more upbeat tone, "John, would you consider coming over this evening. We have much to discuss. In fact, I'll take off early… perhaps you could come by at four o'clock." Mary perked up at the dinner invitation but remained quiet.

John did indeed need direction, so he acquiesced to Edward's fatherly prompting. Recovering from his mild frustration, John mused aloud, "As you can guess, I don't have any other business to attend to today. I could go with you and finally take a tour of your printing company. After you show me around, I'll just stay out of your way. Or better yet, you can put me to work sweeping. I don't mind… really."

Edward responded with a reassuring tone, "John, our time together is important to me so you won't be a distraction. In fact, I would like to include you in an experiment that may be of interest to you. I'll explain when we get back to the office."

Edward's personal affirmation that he extended to John began to change his outlook. In a more jovial upbeat tone, John voiced his appreciation, "Mr. Van Zandt, I'm at your service. Any help I can be to you is gratefully given. Thanks for helping me see things more clearly. And yes, I look forward to spending the evening with you and Mary. I do have one matter that concerns me. Ruth might get worried about me. I've never had a landlord, so I didn't think to let her know anything about my plans after I returned her carriage. Do you think she will be troubled if I don't show up until later tonight?"

"That's not a problem." Edward looked over at Mary, who had quietly listened to all of the male talk, and gave her a proud fatherly smile. "Mary can walk down and pay Ruth a visit—she'll be discreet."

Once back at the printing company, John was most intrigued by the calligraphy department. He had excelled in penmanship while at university, so he naturally had an interest in seeing the commercial side of handwritten documents.

If a printing project was not to be mass-produced, using the offset printing method, it was transcribed by hand. Various legal documents, letters, notices and even some books were still in need of handwritten transcription. Coincidently, the experiment that Edward wanted to undertake involved testing John's ability to write legibly enough to qualify as a transcriber—the writing had to be flawless. Edward was always on the lookout for writers who could make the grade. A good transcriber held the highest paid position in his company.

Chapter Thirty-Two
Captivating Love

It seemed that from one moment to the next John's life circumstances would change. Now a thirteen-month sea voyage was looming, upsetting any hope of normalcy. The two weeks spent with his sister gave him the impression his new life was going to be on an even keel. He had vivid imaginations going forward.

Mary had become so central to his thoughts that he included her in every aspect of his vision for the future. Yet, every time he settled on a pleasant storybook image, some new distraction would make it muddled and abstract. It was becoming difficult to get enthusiastic about any hopeful development because it would invariably turn out to be a mirage.

Edward, John and Mary gathered in the front room of the Van Zandt home. John was as uncomfortable as Mary was eager. Today was set to be the fulfillment of a promise made by Edward to revisit John's desire to court Mary. Victorian courtship was considered pre-engagement and not taken lightly by anyone. Up until now, their personal time together had been somewhat formal, as it should have been. Even so, John

> *Victorian courtship was considered pre engagement and not taken lightly by anyone.*

and Mary's courtship would be far outside the Victorian norm that was often more of a business proposition than preparations for a truly biblical marriage.

As the three were seated, the ambiance suggested a measure of closeness reserved for intimate family members. This type of comfortable intimacy was something John had never experienced in his entire life, partly because he had never known anyone on such a deeply personal level. It wasn't until the closing hours of his mother's life that John got a glimpse of familial love.

In his thoughts, Mary had become a part of who he was. Sure, he had dreamed of being this up close and personal with her, but now it was making him nervous. In the short time that he had known Mary, his interest in her had been conceptual, cocooned in rapture and bathed in hormones. Even so, the reality of today's topic was genuine, and the permanence of it was sobering.

Another certainty was pressing in and making John's breathing a labored affair—there was a finality to his decision to court Mary. This young woman will soon be his lifelong wife and companion if she chooses to say "yes" to his desire to enter into courtship with her. Seated in the parlor, Mary's answer to his heart-pounding emotionally charged query was about to be revealed.

John's palms were sweaty as the conversation was set to begin. Edward could sense John's apprehension, so he decided to talk about a few unrelated matters that needed to be discussed anyway. "I noticed you're riding a different horse. What happened?"

The diversion worked. John was immediately more at ease. "My horse was attacked by a wildcat while stalled at Dr. Murray's. He survived, but his injuries will keep him from running with any conviction, so I made a trade with Mr. Jenkins. My new horse is excellent… even came with a name, Wilkie."

Another matter that was uniquely tied to the question of entering courtship was John's immediate future, "John, I was very impressed with your writing skills today. Perhaps you would consider working for me in the transcription department. With a little training, I think you could become one of my best calligraphers."

John was a little puzzled at the job offer. "What about the commitment to working on the ship?"

"John, you have to understand that I'm not going to make you do anything. I extended an offer that had multiple merits... something I thought you should seriously consider... I still do."

Now that the pressure was off concerning the voyage, John could think more positively. He had not intended to broach the subject, but his thoughts of the future were so engrained with Mary in it, he spoke without hesitation. "What about Mary? I don't think I could bear to be absent from her." Even though his words of endearment were premature and might be considered improper, he was all right with them. They were spoken from the deepest recesses of his heart.

John's declarations of devotion enriched the temperament of the conversation. Edward knew that John had affections for Mary, but he also knew that a young man can get carried away with superficial feelings of love. Seeing that John's sentiments were deeply derived gave him an assurance of John's intentions.

Mary was also moved by John's authentic affections. Even so, heeding her Victorian guidance, it would be improper to emotionally respond to him directly, only a polite acknowledgment was suitable. Mary's mum, Elizabeth, died when she was just entering the age when such things as courtship were discussed. Nevertheless, Mary had diligently studied the guidebook her mum left her, entitled: *The Lady's Guide to Perfect Gentility.*

Even with the subject of courtship opened for discussion, Edward chose to steer the conversation. There was much to discuss before he spoke to John about courting Mary. "John, let's go outside and continue our conversation while Mary prepares the evening meal."

John took a quick look at Mary to study her expression, wanting to find some meaning. She could only give him a gentle smile of reassurance. John regained his composure to accept Edward's suggestion. "Yes, sir."

The early evening was ideal for being outdoors, especially for two men who were deliberately conspiring to change the world, but were innocently unaware of the magnitude of their future successes.

Edward and John walked silently out to the side yard where a fence divided the property. Both men leaned forward against the fence, resting on their elbows and standing shoulder to shoulder to talk—the way men do. There was an unspoken mood of seriousness about their pose that suggested the weightiness of the topic they were to discuss. "John, the gravity of what I want to talk to you about is not meant for the cowardly or the weak of heart." Edward paused, knowing what he was about to say was a key to John's future. "Not many men yearn to willingly give their life for a cause, yet that is exactly what God asks of us. When God calls us, and we say yes to Him, we are no longer our own; we belong to Him for His good pleasure. The scripture says that *we are bought with a price.* We are no longer subject to the whims and worldly pleasures that draw us away from the plans and purposes that He has destined for us."

John's brother-in-law, Paul Wheaton, had mentioned the same concept about being "dead to the things of this world." It was a topic he had intended to inquire of Edward, but he broached the subject without John having to ask. "Edward, this subject of dying yet living is confusing. In one way I understand, yet in another, I don't."

"John, there are many concepts in the Bible that cannot be fully known to you, unless they are revealed to you by God's Spirit. I encourage you to ask God to 'open up His Word' to you as you read it. Make it your prayer every time you read and study the Bible."

Edward looked toward John and waited for him to make eye contact before continuing. "The Bible tells us in Galatians 2:20 that *we are crucified with Christ.* The essence of the Christian faith is that we must consider ourselves as dead to our old way of living, but that's not the whole of it. We also identify with His resurrection. We are raised to a new life by the same power that raised Christ from the dead. This resurrection power is resident in us, giving us new life and the power to walk in victory over sin and death. But, John, if you do not reckon yourself dead, then God's provision for His power in your walk is not available to you. *You cannot have*

His resurrection power evident in your life unless you have died with Him. The Bible says you must reckon yourself as dead. *You cannot be raised unless you first die.* John, this is a major biblical concept called the Resurrection Principle. In God's Kingdom, the new Life He offers is always preceded by death. This is why so many people, who are otherwise known as Christians, live a compromised, unhappy and hypocritical life before others. It is *Christ living in you* that makes you able to live your faith before others in a genuine way."

John was intrigued by the significance of what Edward was trying to relay to him. "I understand the concept, but how does this principle relate in real life? How do I die... or how do I die to... as you said, my old way of living?"

"I'll give you two examples. First: before you gave your life to Christ, you were like a seed... say like an acorn. We all know that an acorn has the potential to be an oak tree. In the same way, you have within you all the potential to be who God made you to be. Here is the point I want to make: If the acorn is not put in the ground to die, it can never become what it was originally intended to be... *but in its death, it becomes the great oak tree it was designed to be.* My second example comes directly from scripture where the genuineness of being a true Christian is compared to being a soldier prepared for battle."

Edward had his Bible with him and opened it up to 2 Timothy 2:3-4. "John, this passage explains what I'm trying to convey to you. Verse three reads: *Thou therefore endure hardness, as a good soldier of Jesus Christ.* Then verse four says: *No man that warreth entangleth himself with the affairs of this life that he may please Him who hath chosen him to be a soldier.*

> It is fine for a true soldier to have captivating love for his wife. However, once on the battle field those sentiments are put away.

"John, I was deeply touched by your heartfelt sentiments that you expressed about Mary. It is fine for a true soldier to have captivating love for his wife. However, once on the battlefield, those sentiments are put away. You will have to make up your mind if God's will is your driving force and number one priority or the dictates of pleasing a wife. Every notable man of God has first gone through a crucible to shape him and form him to be unwavering in his devotion to God and His will for his life."

John remembered the mention of a crucible when Andrew prayed with him. "Edward, explain to me what you mean by a crucible."

Edward was pleased to see John's hunger for understanding. "You are asking all the right questions. There are many references in the Bible where God uses the analogy of a refiner's fire to purify His people. The imagery depicts the impurities, which exist in precious metals, such as gold and silver, being removed when the metal is subjected to the harshest heat. God will often place us in a harsh environment in an effort to purify us and cause the impurities to rise to the surface, so He can take them out of our lives—*He places us in a crucible to purify us so He can use us for His purposes.*

"The greatest men mentioned in the Bible encountered a crucible. Moses, Joseph, David, Jesus and Paul were all subjected to the severe hardships of a wilderness experience, also known as a crucible. The wilderness represents a time of separation and testing where utter dependence on God is worked into your life—it is where God begins to remake you into His image." Edward paused to give John a chance to comment.

"I never realized all that the Bible held for me. The understanding of its message is life changing. It makes me want to live in biblical times."

Edward smiled at John's musings. "It's too late for you to be included in the Bible; nevertheless, you can still be a man among men. You can be counted as worthy before your Lord and King. I personally believe that you, John F. Taylor, will be listed in the annals of history as one of the greatest men to live for the glory of God—consumed for His purposes."

John was overwhelmed by Edward's affirmations of faith in him, as well as his encouraging words. "The crucible makes much more sense to me, but I'm guessing that it will mean much more to a person who actually goes through it."

"John, I have personally talked with people who have gone through the worst imaginable pain and suffering who would not change a thing. The travail is often embraced because of the work that God was able to do in their lives in the midst of their anguish. I have often been told that: *...if given the* *opportunity to go back and avoid the 'crucible,' I wouldn't because it would mean missing God's purifying touch."*

John was nodding his head as he listened. He could envision his mother saying those very words. Mental connections were being made in John's mind as he contemplated all the things that Edward had spoken to him. "Do you see this voyage to the Orient as my crucible experience? Is that why you suggested that I go?"

"Not necessarily. Of the examples I mentioned earlier, only Jesus and Paul could foresee their wilderness. Even then, the scripture states that they were *led into it*, which, to me, means that there was a choice involved, as well as an understanding of its meaning. Moses, Joseph and David *weren't led but thrust* into their crucible, only to live it out day by day through God's mercy and grace with His end result in mind. The only question to ask is: *are you being led to go,* because I don't see that you are being thrust by God into it. If you are being led, then by all means you should go."

"You've given me a lot to think about, Edward, and I must say that you certainly know how to make things crystal clear. Thanks for your patience with me. I can see I've got a lot to learn."

"Not to take anything away from what I have said, but John, the crucible doesn't have to be life crushing and full of despair; quite the contrary. For instance, were all your exams at university painfully difficult? Preparation, attitude, submission and discipline all play a part in the outcome, so not all tests have to be arduous and painful. Not much is said about Paul's wilderness experience; however, the inference from scripture is that he was intensely discipled by the Holy Spirit during his time of separation. We don't know all that might have entailed. His torturous persecution came later, which in my opinion, does not fit the definition of a crucible experience. Remember that God does not forsake us in our trials. The whole purpose is to teach us to turn to Him and be dependent on Him."

"That makes sense to me, and that goes along with what you said about being faithful and yielded."

Edward had an important concept he needed to convey to John. "There is another aspect that I want you to consider concerning the voyage. This trip is a missionary journey for all who are aboard, even for those who are being paid to navigate the ship. Every port of call will be utilized to spread God's Word in some way or another. You will be paid as a crewmember, yet you will have a role to play as an evangelist when you are in port. Missionary organizations refer to this arrangement as a "tentmaker" ministry. The term comes from the Apostle Paul's method of supporting himself as he carried on in his apostolic missionary journeys. John, only God knows what calling He has for you. However, I sincerely believe that this trip will be a good place to discover what it is."

"I can see how you were led to encourage to consider this voyage. It makes much more sense to me."

After an extended pause, Edward moved on to the subject of Mary's courtship. "John, two weeks ago you approached me about your desire to court Mary. I have much to say about that, but first I think it would be most appropriate that I complete

Elizabeth's story and the circumstances surrounding how she died. I had previously mentioned that I wanted you to hear the full explanation from me. I tell you this so you will know the truth, as well as to make the point that we all make mistakes. I told you of my mistakes and the devastation that I brought upon Elizabeth and Mary those many years ago. I wanted to complete the narrative but felt I should wait for a more appropriate time. Now is the proper moment to finish the story."

Edward collected his thoughts and then began his poignant account. "John, Elizabeth died in a tragic carriage accident. She was being escorted by an acquaintance who was taking her back to your parents' estate late one evening. Since Elizabeth and I were in the process of trying to reunite our marriage, all of those who knew about our reconciliation were overwhelmed with shock. It was a terrible time. I asked God many times, why… why now? There were occasions when I thought I wouldn't recover from my grief."

Edward was taken with emotion as he relived the heartbreak of his past. After taking a few moments to regain his composure, he continued, "Then one day, in the midst of my pain, I realized that Mary needed me and that I had once again abandoned her, depriving her for a second time. I had to come to my senses for her sake." Edward paused before finishing the story. "One important point I want to make is that Elizabeth was not involved in any impropriety. Those closest to the tragic event assured me that the man she was with was only a friend who volunteered to assist her home."

John could sense the great loss that Edward had suffered, knowing how it must have affected him and Mary. "Edward, that was tragic. I know that your story must have been difficult to share with me, so thank you for telling me."

Both men stood erect from leaning against the cross fence. A new pose was needed as a break from the weighty and emotionally charged topics. As they were taking their long pause, Mary left out the back door to make her evening rounds—her nightly ritual of helping the neighbors. In a wordless gaze of admiration, the pair watched as Mary gracefully walked down the lane with an angelic presence.

It was another several minutes before either felt the need to say anything. Men have the amazing ability to stand side-by-side and let the time pass if need be.

Chapter Thirty-Three

Mary's Answer

Edward knew the time had come. "John, I guess it's about time that we discuss your relationship with Mary. First, I want to tell you that Mary and I have had long discussions about you and her future. You have seen how reserved Mary is, yet you also know that she has a mind of her own. Her wish is to address you personally regarding your desire to court her. She has explained to me several concerns, so she wants to hear directly from you."

John was ready to talk about Mary. As she left to help the neighbors, he was reminded how he had become enamored with her. He was no longer nervous. "Her respectful independence is one of the qualities that I'm drawn to. I am grateful for how you have raised your daughter, sir."

"Thank you, John. That means a lot to me." Edward was ready to present the details of the courtship. "For us to continue we must thoroughly discuss several topics. Since Mary's mum is not here to guide her through her courtship, especially as her chaperone, we need to come to an understanding."

John spoke up almost too quickly, wanting to reassure Edward about his commitment to be proper in honoring his dictates. "Sir, as I stated earlier, I'll respect whatever you say."

"That's good, John. Mary and I have methodically studied her etiquette handbook on proper courtship, so I am relying on her to show proper behavior. These are the practices on which we agree. While you are here in the evenings, I will act as Mary's chaperone in the absence of her mum. When you are away from home, at a social function, then Mrs. Murray has agreed to step in as Mary's chaperone. Now, from a father's perspective, an understanding you should already have, I expect an engagement announcement within two months as a gesture of your intentions." Edward paused to allow John to agree.

John took a few moments to reflect the terms of his courtship. "I think that is fair. I completely understand your concerns."

It suddenly occurred to John that he had nothing to offer Mary as a means of support: no estate, no inheritance, no accumulated wealth, not even an occupation other than an apprenticeship offered by her father. In a humbled state of contrition, John conceded, "Mr. Van Zandt, you know the state I'm in. I have nothing. Mary deserves better."

"John, no one understands you better than Mary and me; we know everything about you. You are a solid young man with a great future ahead of you."

"Thank you, sir. Your unwavering confidence in me has helped sustain me."

"John, we're not finished. I am sorry for the untimeliness of the request I'm about to make. Nevertheless, I need to know by tomorrow morning, if you intend to sail on the voyage to the Orient. As you already know, that decision will affect the terms of your courtship with Mary. Additionally, I need to make preparations with the captain of the ship if you are going on the voyage."

John was feeling the weight of two momentous decisions that were upon him. Even so, Edward's steady hand was deftly guiding him with the precision of a Thames river pilot. "Since we've been discussing the voyage, I've been thinking about the advantages of going... I think you're right—that I should go. It will allow me time to get on my feet."

"John, I want you to do more than think about it. I would like for you to hear from God. In fact, I wouldn't want you to go *unless* you heard from Him."

"I'm not entirely sure how to do that."

"John, this is how I have experienced hearing from God. You have your Bible, so make a point to ask Him to guide you as you read. Ask Him to make His will known to you. Read awhile and talk to Him awhile. Take the rest of the evening and use our guesthouse. Spend the whole night if you need to. In the morning, come and tell me what you heard."

In a revelatory tone, John remarked, "So that's how you hear from God?"

Edward clarified further, "God will always direct us according to His written Word. Since you don't know much scripture, you'll have to depend on Him to direct your reading and to show you His intentions as you read. John, it is a two-way conversation. He will be speaking to you from the pages of His Word—*so listen as you read.*"

"I will do it. I'll go to God for His answer."

Edward's many years of close relationship with God enabled him to understand that God sees from a much larger perspective. Edward's part was to listen and obey, trusting that God would honor his obedience as he counseled and directed John. Even so, Edward was still mortal and couldn't have known how important his careful instruction would be for John's future. *Yet there was an understanding* based on his complete trust that God was using him as he mentored John.

"John, there is one more significant requirement that I have as it relates to your intentions to court Mary. I don't mean to be unyielding in this matter, but I have my reasons. I am confident you will understand if you think about it. John, if God calls you to be a tentmaker on this voyage, I will require an announcement of engagement to Mary before you leave. I know this is a lot to ask, since you would be leaving in two days. Even so, if that is your decision, I will arrange a small gathering to allow you to formally announce your intentions of engagement. When you return from the Orient, I ask that you restate your intentions to continue your courtship until a date for your wedding can be set."

John knew the proper conventions of courtship, and he recognized the extra care Edward was being forced to take under very unusual circumstances. He was glad that Mary had such a wise and protective father.

The day John discovered his mother's wedding ring, just weeks earlier, he never imagined that a proposal of marriage to his future wife would come so soon. "Edward, as you know, I have my mum's wedding ring. Do you think Mary will be willing to accept it as an engagement ring?"

Edward considered John's question sincerely as he paused to phrase his words carefully, "John, a ring is an expressed sentiment of love; a matter of the heart. You know that Mary was very close to your mum, especially during the last years of her life. So, yes, I think she would be honored to have your mum's ring as a token of your engagement."

"Edward, I would like to speak with Mary, possibly after the evening meal."

"I'm confident that will be all right with Mary. If you prefer, I'm sure we can all sit down and have your discussion before she sets the table."

"That would be just as well, thank you."

"She'll be back in about an hour. That will give us time to tend to the animals in the meantime."

Today, it was a basket of turnips that Mary carried, gathered from the widow's garden. When John saw her coming down the lane, returning from the neighbors, he excused himself from his chores and ran to assist her with the basket. His impulsive act of chivalry innocently set up an unplanned private moment with Mary, much to their mutual delight. Edward stopped working to lean on his broom handle, taking in the heartwarming scene of his daughter's joyful interaction with John.

Gathered in the kitchen, Edward broached John's request, "Mary, John has a few things he would like to say to you. Would now be a good time?"

"I was hoping we could talk; right now is good."

Rather than sit at the kitchen table, which would have been improper for the formal topic at hand, the three made their way to the front room. As the men yielded to Mary to lead them from the kitchen, she stepped very close to John, brushing him with her dress. It was then he noticed that she was still wearing her nice clothes, which she had earlier worn to her father's office, and not her normal, more mundane work attire. In an effort to look pleasing for John, Mary had worn her best dress while cooking, digging in the neighbor's garden and doing the widow's laundry. John was duly taken by her desire to charm him.

John had a lump in his throat as he searched for the words to begin. He looked over at Edward for assurance, but Edward just tilted his head over toward Mary as if to signal that she was the one John needed to address. It would be fair to say that John was smitten—words were eluding him. Slowly, he began to speak, "Mary, as you know, I have asked your father for his permission to court you. However, I have learned something today that might change your mind about me. If what I say offends you, I beg your forgiveness now." John was holding his hat clutched with both hands in his lap. The tension of the moment was causing him to grip the brim so hard he was bending it. He just knew that Mary would reject his wishes to court her. "Mary, I'm not certain you'll understand what I am about to say, but... what I learned today is that... you can't be the most important person in my life—God has to be first."

Mary's eyes welled up with tears as John spoke from his heart. She gently nodded, displaying her understanding. John and Mary sat for several moments gazing into each other's eyes, searching for a mutual comprehension of what he had just said to her.

John knew that his truthfulness about putting God first might mean an end to his dreams and aspirations with Mary. With his newfound faith, he decided to trust God by honoring Him. Edward had told him that the seed itself is not what we hope for—the promise is *in* the seed. Like the seed, if he didn't allow his dreams and aspirations to die, his life with Mary could never reach its fullest potential... *but in its death it* becomes what God designed it to be—God will resurrect what is dedicated to Him.

From the deepest recesses of his heart, John spoke with new faith, "God, and His call on my life, has to be my most important aspiration. But Mary… please hear my heart… I perceive that by putting Him first is the only way that I will truly be the best husband, friend and companion that God could have for you. If you reject me for my insistence on putting God first, I will understand."

Mary's eyes were no longer moistened; they were flooded with tears of joy. The seed that John faithfully put to death was in the throes of resurrection. After several moments of reveling in her gladness, Mary spoke to John from her heart, "John, you have answered my most earnest prayers. The one thing I needed to hear from you was that it is in Him that you will give your whole heart. *God must be first—I could not have answered 'yes' if you felt any other way." Mary was unable to remain genteel as she gushed, "Yes, John, the answer is yes."*

Sometime during the night, John had his answer from God. He would be leaving on his voyage in less than forty-eight hours. By necessity, the engagement celebration would take place that evening.

By 9:00 a.m., the morning of the engagement party, John and Edward had already traveled by carriage to his office to arrange for an express messenger to deliver three impromptu announcement invitations to the Wheaton's, Dr. Murray and Mr. Jenkins. Once the dispatch was sent, John and Edward then proceeded the short distance to personally invite Ruth Murray, who jumped at the chance to fill-in as Mary's chaperone. Bradley, was the only other remaining attendee who was coveted, but no one knew his whereabouts.

While visiting with Ruth at the Murray's in-town residence, John retrieved his hidden bank bag, securing possession of his mother's wedding ring. He also wanted to discuss how the voyage would affect the cottage rental, but felt it should wait until after the engagement party where Andrew's wisdom and business acumen was needed.

Since Edward already had a planned meeting with Charles Spurgeon for late morning, Edward decided to include John in the meeting and look for an opportunity to invite Mr. Spurgeon to join in John and Mary's engagement party. There was no way to know if Mr. Spurgeon could attend because of his recent arrival back from his European sabbatical. So with John accompanying him, the two men made the crosstown trip to engage the notable Charles Spurgeon. After a lengthy visit with Mr. Spurgeon, covering numerous details relating to the voyage of the clipper ship, *Anastasis*, Edward's evening invitation was accepted.

On their return trip through London, the two men stopped by the printing company to make one last messenger dispatch. Edward took several minutes to compose a detailed letter addressed to the captain of the *Anastasis*. Edward's letter confirmed John's status as an apprentice level employee— "*...job description to be determined by the captain post embarkation.*"

For all who attended the engagement celebration, it was an esteemed and cherished occasion; all that anyone could have hoped for. The gathering was described as a simple yet elegant affair, but most importantly, it was a reverent occasion where God was honored and His presence was welcomed.

Chapter Thirty-Four
The Tentmaker

Early Wednesday, the morning after his engagement party, John was ready. The little he needed for the voyage, he already had—tentmaker he would be. John went by the ship to drop off his gear and to introduce himself to the captain.

John's initial interview with Captain Philippe went well. The *Anastasis* was set to get underway early the next morning to coincide with the lunar high tide. Navigating the Thames would take almost three hours, so the ship would leave the pier at precisely 5:30 a.m., Thursday morning.

John then spent the rest of Wednesday, his final day, at the Van Zandt Printing Company. Over the last month, his admiration for Edward Van Zandt as his mentor, counselor and future father-in-law had reached larger-than-life proportions, and today was no exception.

John had not yet witnessed in detail the numerous printing projects that were underway at Edward's printing company. As the men went from department to department, John found himself in awe of all that was being accomplished. One of the most impressive ventures was the printing of Bibles in Mandarin, a common dialect throughout the Far East. The Bibles were already crated with the last of them being carted to the *Anastasis* for eventual delivery to Hong Kong. Once ashore, the Bibles would be transported inland to the Spurgeon headquarters. They would then be dispersed to the entire region, including parts of the Philippines and Malaysia. In another smaller room, Charles Spurgeon's weekly sermons were being printed and made ready for distribution.

Edward also wanted to show John a particular project that he had been working on for months. "John, come with me. I want you to see a book that the London Missionary Society is having printed with us." Edward led John out to the main workshop floor where he had previously entered via the side door. Standing next to a stack of wooden crates, Edward took a book off a nearby worktable. "This book was written by Dr. David Livingstone, who has been home on furlough from his missionary outpost in Africa. We'll be taking these twenty-five crates on the *Anastasis*, to Cape Town, S.A. The distribution and sale of his books is one means to fund Dr. Livingstone's work."

"How well do you know Dr. Livingstone?"

"I know him mostly through our connection with the London Missionary Society. As you know, he has spent most of his adult life in the mission field. However, since he has been in London these last months, we have become well acquainted, as we have worked closely on the printing of his book. However, I also knew of him during my university days while studying medicine in my first year at Oxford. I attended one of his lectures when He spoke of the need for medical missionaries to China. His talk was very inspiring, even for me in my unsaved state. You have to remember that back then I was still rebellious and unrepentant."

Suddenly, Edward stopped relating his story about David Livingstone as a poignant thought came to him. With measured and thoughtful words, Edward spoke as he made an obvious connection that God had orchestrated in his life. "John, looking back, I just realized that David's lecture influenced me just as much as my debates with Andrew. Just think, if I had missed his lecture… it's possible that I might not be standing here talking to you about his book… I could still be estranged from my daughter… I might not own the *Anastasis*… and I certainly wouldn't be a member of the London Missionary Society. There is no telling the course my life might have taken if David had not been there to lecture us." Edward concluded his heartwarming revelation with moistened eyes as he considered the wonder of God's overwhelming goodness in directing his steps.

After reviewing several more printing projects that were underway at Van Zandt Printing, Edward suggested they leave the office early. That would allow John to spend some time with Mary on his last evening before departing on his thirteen-month voyage to the Orient.

John, Edward and Mary spent the remainder of the afternoon and evening hours talking with times of fun and laughter, as well as praying. It was a night that he would always remember. Farewells were exchanged early, as John would be up by 3:00 a.m. and well on his way to the pier by four o'clock, walking the nearly three miles to the ship.

John was awakened earlier than expected as he heard the livestock being disturbed and restless. He got up and partially dressed to check on the ruckus. Just as John got his lantern trimmed, a dark figure bolted through the guesthouse door and charged him. The intruder wrestled John to the floor, placing his hand over John's mouth until he was persuaded to stay quiet.

> *Just as John got his lantern trimmed, a dark figure bolted through the guest house door and charged him.*

Once Bradley convinced John to keep quiet, he helped his friend to his feet. Bradley was on a mission. "John, the word is out on the streets that there is a reward for you. There will be an attempt to capture you before you board the ship this morning. Yardley has hired a group of men to ambush you before you get to the pier. I just came from their hiding place. I have a plan to get you on that ship. If we take the long way around, we can miss them by three blocks, unless they move in closer to the ship before we get there. We need to leave right now."

"Give me a few minutes to put my boots on and grab my coat… that's all I need."

Under the cover of darkness, John and Bradley set out on foot going east instead of south, allowing them to circle around and then come back toward the ship. In military terms, it would be the equivalent of flanking the opponent. Bradley's idea was brilliant except that another group of rival deck hands were poised to capture John as well.

As the hunted prey neared the ship, every effort was made to hide in the shadows as they moved quickly and quietly. Yardley's men had indeed moved in closer, gathered under a large gas streetlamp near the pier entrance. The men were casually posing as dockworkers, waiting for John to appear.

The two gangs of men spotted John and Bradley about the same time, creating a mad rush to see who would snatch the quarry and ultimately the reward. The clash was raucous with grunts and moans, pulling and grabbing, tearing and ripping, and then all at once it was over. John was being dragged away at running speed toward the ship by seven crewmembers of the *Anastasis*.

Bradley had been instrumental in taking down three of Yardley's men so that Captain Philippe's crew could rip John away. However, it was not good for Bradley. With their prize whisked away, the real brutes were eager to exact some pain on Bradley. He fought bravely to escape, but in the end, he was overcome and taken captive.

The thugs hoped that Yardley might offer them a reward, thinking that their night wouldn't be a total loss. He had offered as much on several occasions when ranting about Bradley. In an odd turn of events, Yardley was going to have a trophy after all.

As Bradley was being dragged away, he got a brief glimpse of John being carried safely onto the ship. Bradley, who was the strong, loyal, faithful friend and fearless avenger, wept tears for his best friend even as he was being taken to his own likely death.

Meanwhile, the *Anastasis* crew pulled John up the gangplank and onboard the ship. He had suffered a mild concussion in the brawl and was unable to make sense of what had just transpired. Even so, he was making incoherent pleas to the crewmembers to help save Bradley. Captain Philippe quickly made the decision to dispatch a foot runner to carry a message to Edward Van Zandt. Time was of the essence; the ship had to leave with the high tide.

Edward was left standing on his front porch just before 5:00 a.m., as the crewmember was gone in an instant. Captain Philippe's note was too brief. *Bradley in trouble—needs help— have not notified police. —Captain Philippe.* Edward was made to speculate on what had been left unsaid in the note. He needed more information if he was going to act quickly on Bradley's behalf. Edward had no other choice than to try to make it to the ship before it pulled away from the pier. Even the smallest detail could mean the difference in finding and saving Bradley. Anyone who knew the facts would know that Bradley was facing a life or death struggle with his captors, having several motives to do him in.

The dawn was breaking, giving Edward precious light to see while he quickly worked to saddle his horse. There would be little traffic at this hour, so he hoped to make it to the ship in less than ten minutes. Edward arrived at the *Anastasis* to find John recovered enough to talk intelligibly. John recounted the story that Bradley had told him about the thugs that Yardley had hired to ambush him. In the few minutes he spent with John, Edward had what he needed.

Police involvement at this point was not an option. For Edward, finding Bradley was the highest priority; contacting the police would have to wait. Once he found Bradley, he could then assess how to proceed from there. Since Yardley was at the center of this brutal abduction, Edward's gut feeling was that Bradley had not been taken far, at least not yet. The most logical strategy was to find Yardley—find Yardley and he would find Bradley.

Chapter Thirty-Five

The Execution

Early on in his career, Captain Yardley was ambitious and aggressive, but the power he achieved corrupted him. In the end, he became the incarnation of evil, grabbing and taking what he wanted. And so it was with Antoinette. She was only one of the casualties he left in his wake. Unknowingly, she was lured into his web of treachery, and in the end, she was ensnared and held against her will. She literally fought for her life, but eventually lost her battle to be free from her vile captor.

Antoinette was Bradley's childhood friend who had mistakenly become mixed up with Captain Yardley. Her death could never be linked directly to Yardley, but those on the inside whispered its truth. However, the public cover up shattered her family and infuriated Bradley. So, his month old rampage against Yardley and his men was more than vengeful retaliation for his recent beating. It was only the tipping point that gave him the justification he needed to remove a scourge from his beloved hometown of London.

In the days immediately following Bradley's storm, Edward gathered together some readily available information concerning Yardley's corrupted precinct. While Yardley and his men were still in the hospital, Edward met with the mayor to turn over his findings. He wanted to make sure that Bradley received fair treatment. The meeting with the mayor was short-lived because it was clearly evident how Captain Yardley had veered horribly out of control.

The mayor immediately ordered a precinct-wide investigation. Most of the office workers within the police precinct cooperated with the mayor's probe, yielding substantial evidence of corruption and malfeasance. Even while Captain Yardley, Eben Boles and Detective O'Hare were still in critical condition, charges were filed for multiple crimes against society, as well as the most serious charge of murder.

In the meantime, Romney Longfellow had to make his move on John Taylor. He had no choice. It might be his last opportunity to recover the "Papers of Relinquishment" that he had signed under duress, trying to save his life's work.

As an astute businessman, Edward Van Zandt stepped in and offered to save the company as a silent and unnamed partner, as long as reorganization guidelines were agreed on and met. However, once the crushing financial pressures were removed, Romney immediately regretted giving his silent partner a fifty-one percent stake in China Tea Trading Company at fire-sale prices.

Now, Romney was once again desperate to find John, who he thought could lead him to the relinquishment documents. If he couldn't destroy the papers, then Romney planned on doing John in. There were only two people who knew that *the relinquishment was to John Taylor, bypassing Edward.*

The news spread fast among the dockworkers about John's intention to sail with the clipper ship, *Anastasis*. Romney immediately reinstated a bounty for John's capture, increasing the reward substantially.

Yardley was the last of three men to be discharged from the hospital because of the nature of his injuries. Once out of the hospital, all three felons were arraigned and then released on bond. While awaiting trial, informants quickly brought Yardley the news of Romney's new bounty. Jobless and cash-strapped, Yardley and his former detectives conspired to seize John before he boarded the ship.

Beyond the reward, revenge was also a part of Yardley's motivation to capture John. Using irrational reasoning, Yardley held John ultimately responsible for his career loss, as well as the injuries he received from Bradley. Apprehending John would mean cash along with the possibility of catching Bradley.

Months earlier, his convoluted plot to capture John did not end well. The result of his treachery led to losing his sight in one eye, as well as a crushed voice box. However, the new plan was much more direct and simple. John would be unsuspecting as he approached the pier in the predawn hours, making him an easy target for abduction. Yardley hired a group of corrupt dockworkers to be in place to do the dirty work. Once captured, John was to be taken to Yardley's illicit warehouse by 6:00 a.m.

London's once highly regarded ex-police captain was still conducting criminal activities from a secret location within blocks of the precinct headquarters. The warehouse concealed various shipments of contraband that were being stockpiled by the nefarious two-faced ex-public servant.

Yardley still lived in his lavish fifth-floor penthouse that was perched atop the Riverview Suites building. It was too dangerous to allow the rough-and-tumble dockworkers to bring John to his suite, so John would be taken to his nearby warehouse for interrogation.

Yardley had no way of knowing that the kidnapping had gone awry. When the henchmen dropped the bruised and beaten body at Yardley's feet, he didn't recognize it to be Bradley. Bradley's disfigured face, as well as his blood-soaked clothing and matted hair further concealed the fact that John was safe on board the ship and out of harm's way. It wasn't until Bradley spit a mouthful of blood on Yardley's boots and pant leg did all hell break loose, revealing the hostage's identity. The resulting beating left Bradley near death.

Initially, Yardley was furious that he was not going to reap a financial reward for capturing John. After a fit of odd sounding curses and threats, he calmed down. He then slowly became resigned to the possibilities of having Bradley instead. With a strained raspy voice, the haggard ex-police captain ordered the prisoner gagged and further bound.

Bradley was left lying on the warehouse floor while Yardley went to have his usual sumptuous breakfast at the Bonaparte Café. As with most vile felons, Yardley was completely disconnected from his iniquitous actions. As he sat quietly having his eggs benedict and coffee, Bradley was struggling for each breath. In another strangely bizarre detachment, the splatters of blood on Yardley's boots and pant leg did not keep him from enjoying his breakfast.

The Bonaparte Café offered street-side dining that Yardley particularly relished when the weather permitted. While enjoying the crisp morning air, Yardley would occasionally stop to reconnect with his death-shrouded scheming. He would smile to himself when he would think of a particularly innovative manner of how he would extract retribution.

His best idea came while reading an article in the London Times that revisited an outlawed mode of settling disputes— dueling with pistols. Yardley lit up as he envisioned a redeeming scenario where he faced-off with Bradley in a duel to restore his honor. His self-deception was incomprehensible.

Yardley was not in a hurry—the die had been cast. He just needed to make some simple arrangements to finalize his plans to mete out his newly minted scheme of twisted justice, acting as Bradley's judge, jury and executioner. He already had the flintlock pistols. Granted they weren't dueling pistols, but that was hardly relevant. All he needed was a place to stage the duel and someone to share his moment of exoneration. His depraved mind needed company and who better to share in the proceedings than Boles and O'Hare, who could also help him with his plan.

Meanwhile, Edward hurriedly left the ship and rode his horse toward the part of town where he had most often seen Yardley. Knowing that he stayed fairly close to his old precinct offices led Edward to believe that he apparently lived close by as well. Making circles around the adjacent blocks, Edward rode past shops, offices and cafes for almost an hour trying to spot him.

It paid off. He saw Yardley getting up from a sidewalk table at the exclusive Bonaparte Café. With a measure of edginess, Edward dismounted and tied up his horse so he could follow Yardley on foot.

Yardley's gait was so casual that it was hard to imagine that he was plotting someone's murder. Nonetheless, Edward trailed him to a boarding house where the unemployed Boles and O'Hare shared a flat. After beating on the door several times, Yardley finally had to bang on a window to wake the men. It was at that moment that something went off in Yardley to make his persona match his evil intentions. He was no longer disconnected from his hostilities.

Once Yardley was inside, Edward made his way to the doorway just in time to hear him screaming at the groggy scalawags. "Get your clothes on and meet me at the warehouse… and don't keep me waiting!" Before he stepped back outside, Yardley quipped with a swaggering tone, "Bradley's challenged me to a duel. Bring your pistols, you might want to have them on you."

Yardley left the boarding house in a more hurried and agitated stride that revealed his crippling injuries. Arriving at the Riverview Suites building, he labored to negotiate the unforgiving flights of stairs to retrieve his pair of flintlock pistols. The ex-captain then plodded toward the warehouse oblivious to his menacing visage—a mad man toting two loaded pistols, one in each hand.

Witnessing Yardley's deranged state of mind, Edward had seen enough to surmise that he had no time to waste. He could see that he would be unable to secure a pistol of his own to stand in Bradley's defense. Edward had always believed in diplomacy as a first resort, but now it would be his only weapon.

With Edward following close behind, Yardley slipped inside the warehouse through oversized double doors left slightly open. Edward chose to remain outside, knowing that Boles and O'Hare would soon show up. However, it quickly became apparent that the two men had already arrived as he heard loud arguing, "I said load him into the wagon."

Boles responded defiantly. "I don't work for you anymore, and besides I don't like what you're up to. This man can't possibly have a chance in a duel with you. You have completely lost your mind and I'm not with you in this. I'm leaving!" Just then, Edward heard a loud report. Peering through the partially open door revealed that Yardley had shot Boles in the back as he turned to leave.

"O'Hare, if you know what's good for you, I suggest you get Bradley into the wagon." There were several minutes of grunts and groans as the still weakened O'Hare struggled with Bradley's dead weight. Thinking Bradley was lifeless, O'Hare mistakenly untied Bradley's feet, hoping it would help him in his efforts. Once untied, Bradley was free to fight off the attempt to load him into the flatbed wagon, infuriating Yardley.

With a fiendish taunt, revealing his insanity, Yardley yelled out as if to address a gathered audience—an imaginary crowd gathered to witness the restoration of his honor. "Bradley, I can see by your actions that you would rather challenge me here than in a more suitable countryside setting."

Bradley was hopelessly slumped on his knees from the numerous attempts to load him on the wagon when he found the strength to raise his head to speak directly to Yardley's sneering mockery. "You're nothing more than a murderer… you'll rot in hell for killing my Antoinette."

With the most despicable tone imaginable, Yardley gloated, "*Your Antoinette*… well, well. That tramp wasn't even fit for a bordello."

The cruel and slanderous words loosed the beast within. As the adrenaline surged, Bradley screamed out his angst. Against all possibilities, Bradley managed to right himself and make a desperate yet valiant attempt to charge Yardley. Astonishingly, he was successful in upending Yardley. However, with his hands still tied to his waist, Bradley was unable to break his own fall and landed face first on the hard warehouse floor. Unable to catch his breath, the severely weakened Bradley started choking while gasping for air.

Edward had no choice. If he was going to intervene, it would have to be now. While Yardley was still trying to upright himself, Edward rushed for Boles' pistol that lay next to his lifeless body.

Call it latent loyalty. Whatever it was, O'Hare gave up his chance to be free of Yardley's madness. When he realized that Edward was going after Boles' pistol, O'Hare pulled out his own weapon and shouted, "Stand back Van Zandt! I warned you about sticking your nose where it doesn't belong. Now get over there with your friend while he takes his last breaths."

Undaunted by the pistol-waving thug, Edward went to Bradley's aid, positioning him to help him breathe.

Yardley wanted his mock duel. Drunk with rage, he yelled,

Undaunted by the pistol-waving thug, Edward went to Bradley's aid, positioning him to help him breathe.

"Edward, get him breathing and on his feet—he's not going to die and deny me my due revenge." Yardley, stumbled slightly forward as if he was becoming unsteady, then grumbled, "Look at me. Look what he's done to me."

Edward complied, but it wasn't to satisfy Yardley's wishes for retribution. While Yardley was ranting, Edward had been whispering his plans to Bradley, preparing him to make a run for it. Once upright, Edward needed to try to buy some time to allow Bradley a chance to gain his footing.

With Yardley indeed looking pale and unsteady, perhaps this was the time to negotiate. In a firm and commanding tone, Edward tried to reason with Yardley, "Bradley and I are going to walk out of here and give you a chance to think about this when you're not under so much duress."

At first, the diplomatic effort seemed to be working. Yardley let them take several steps backward as he stood with a dazed look on his face. With mounting hope, Edward made a subtle effort to turn Bradley around and walk out of the warehouse.

Without warning, two shots were fired into the backs of the retreating men. O'Hare was the first to fire followed by Yardley. Suddenly, an earsplitting explosion of gunfire came from the direction of the large warehouse doors. Seven muskets sent screaming lead balls to pummel the murderous duo.

The ship's crew had arrived only moments before O'Hare and Yardley fired the shots that struck down their unarmed hostages. The moment Edward and Bradley were fired upon, Captain Philippe gave the order to return fire.

Edward had been hit in the shoulder and was not in mortal danger. Even so, he was severely weakened and in pain. He beckoned Captain Philippe to come to him. With halted speech, Edward began giving urgent instructions, "I'll be fine... just get me on my feet. Take Bradley.... if he doesn't make it... bury him at sea... he's military... he would want that."

"Sir, we won't be able to get under sail until the next high tide."

Edward was straining under a sudden jolt of pain, "Just leave when you can. Do what you can for Bradley in the meantime."

One of the sailors, speaking in his native Portuguese, informed the captain that Bradley was dead. "Mr. Van Zandt, I'm sorry to inform you that Bradley is deceased."

"Go! Go! Get him on the wagon and get out of here. Don't let anyone see you take him on the ship. If any dockworkers approach you, you'll need to have something to tell them. Once he is on board, come back with the wagon and take me to Dr. Murray. In the meantime have one of your men help me to my office… it's five blocks over."

Chapter Thirty-Six
Testing of God's Will

John was still in the ship's sickbay when Bradley's wrapped body was brought into its cramped quarters. John was distraught even though he had already prepared himself for the worst.

Listening to the sailor's overwrought conversation, being spoken in Portuguese, John could guess what was happening as he heard *Edwardo* mentioned several times. He was determined to go with the two men assigned to retrieve Edward—he wasn't going to be denied.

John hid in the back of the flatbed wagon the best he could. As far as he knew, he was still in as much danger as ever since it was obvious the ship had not left. The return trip was fast and raucous. It was all John could do to hang on as they made the jaunt in record time. The sailors knew the way to the printing company from the many trips they had made, carting crates of Bibles and other missionary related provisions.

While waiting for the wagon to return, Edward had mentally calculated how he would instruct the crewmen. However, since John came with them, he could use an easier plan. They would not be going directly to Dr. Murray's as he initially decided. Once the sailors helped Edward into the wagon, he proceeded to instruct the men with directions to his own home.

Then Edward turned to John, "I've got to get this lead ball out of my back as soon as possible, but first I'm taking you to my home before we head over to Andrew's place. As soon as I get you home, let Mary know what is going on. Then ready my carriage, fill the water trough and throw out some extra feed for the animals. Mary should be ready by then. Bring her out to Andrew's office—she can take care of me from there."

Edward was forced to stop talking. The wagon hit a hole and brutally jolted both men. Edward winced and then continued through his pain, "You and the crew will head straight back to the ship and have Captain Philippe draft a letter explaining what took place at the warehouse. Have these men take the wagon back to Yardley's warehouse and leave the message with the wagon.

John was unnerved. "I'm not leaving you like this. You have said all along that this voyage is optional… it was up to me whether I went or not."

Edward knew this was a test of John's resolve to be faithful. "Well, you told me that you prayed about it and that God told you to go; did He or didn't He?"

"Yes, I told you He did… very clearly."

"Then… if that's truly the case, all of this upheaval is nothing more than a commotion to make you question His voice. John, you can count on that happening every time you try to move on God's promptings…every time, John—depend on it."

"Alright… alright, Mary and I shouldn't be more than fifteen minutes behind you. See you there."

"One more thing… this is important… it is possible for the

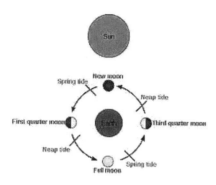

ship to leave at 1810 hours tonight. The captain and I discussed this last week. We are in the second lunar quarter so we will have the effects of a spring tide. If all the other conditions for sailing are in order, I suspect you'll be on your way later today. Be on that ship!"

"Yes, sir."

"And John, you don't have to worry about Mary, she's strong."

Several reports had reached the new police chief about a squad of naval personnel carrying out a military action in an in-town warehouse. The new chief, Captain Birdwell, was a former naval officer, so he was naturally curious about such an odd report, leading him to check out the rumors personally. After verifying the three bodies at the warehouse, he followed the trail of eyewitness accounts to the *Anastasis*.

It was 1430 hours by the time John and the crewmen made the countryside trip from Dr. Murray's. A small crowd had gathered around the gangplank with a few police officers standing guard. Chief Birdwell was questioning Captain

Philippe aboard the ship when John returned. With the ongoing interview that was taking place, there would be no need for the captain to compose a letter describing the actions taken at the warehouse. The crewmen, who had earlier commandeered the wagon, left it with the police and boarded the ship. After hearing Captain Philippe's account on how the killings came about, the only concern for the newly appointed police chief was the apparent use of overwhelming force.

Once Captain Philippe reminded Chief Birdwell of the laws governing a police action by a duly commissioned naval officer, the matter was closed. Nonetheless, the ship was ordered to remain docked until Chief Birdwell could make his report—just in case any more questions were raised.

Bradley had not been mentioned. Captain Philippe was not in a position to comment on Bradley's weeks-past vigilantism or his involvement in the predawn events of the day. Right or wrong Captain Philippe felt compelled to leave things as they were.

Captain Philippe addressed the police chief in a formal military fashion remaining respectful of his authority. "I respectfully request permission to be underway by 1810 hours due to the present expected tidal conditions."

"I'm aware of your need to be underway. If I have no further questions, I'll send one of my officers by 1800 hours to release you."

"If I may, sir?"

"Yes, what is it?"

"Could you send your authorization to shove off in written form with your signature? I'm a stickler for details, sir."

"I don't have a problem with your request. Godspeed, Captain Philippe."

"Thank you, sir."

The two officers saluted to end their formal interview.

Chapter Thirty-Seven
Ship Shape

Once Chief Birdwell went ashore, Captain Philippe summoned John to his quarters. "John, come in and sit down please. We have a few minutes to discuss some important matters. I fully expect to shove off at 1810 hours, so I'll need to make this meeting brief. Edward and I have spent several hours discussing your internship on my ship."

In a fast paced, military style presentation, Captain Philippe went through a litany of points that he wanted John to know. "First, you need to know that I am a disciplinarian and I run a tight ship. My men are second to none because I expect nothing less than their best. I'm expecting you to fall in line with their example. Edward tells me you are an exceptional young man, and he has high hopes for you. I'm going to see to it that you do your best.

Second, I am the captain, and I have complete authority in all matters. Legally, I have the final say in every aspect of living or dying aboard this ship."

Without the slightest hesitation, the captain continued his talk at a rapid tempo. "John, concerning your duties; you will not have any slack time on this voyage. Your duties will encompass every waking minute. Once you complete one task, you will be expected to begin another assignment, and so on. In addition, you will be available around the clock.

Your main duty is to maintain the ship's log, which will require you to be at the bridge every hour on the hour to document the helmsman's observations. Additionally, you will need to be at every assembly to record the for-the-record comments. Lastly, you will also need to make entries of my personal observations and comments that affect the operation of the ship. This means that you could be summoned at any time to record my commentaries.

Good communication is essential for any ship to run efficiently, so another assignment, which is related to the first, is to learn the Portuguese language as quickly as possible. John, hear me, this is not an option. I will test you and drill you weekly, expecting no less than rapid progress—the men will help you."

John was quietly stunned as the captain continued, "Your official apprenticeship that you will learn is that of a sail maker. Much of the hands-on work for this effort will occur while docked where most repairs are made. Even so, I want you to learn as much as you can while at sea so you can be of use when in port."

The captain paused to ascertain John's attitude before continuing. The captain knew that his enumeration of duties was not as demanding as it sounded. "That's not all, John. Edward Van Zandt has responsibilities for you as well. He has provided the last two years of Charles Spurgeon's sermons for you to study and then read to the men during the weekly church service. His instructions specify that he wants you to be knowledgeable about the sermons you will read to the men and have ready answers to their questions afterward. That means emphatically studying the scripture references so you can grasp the meaning of Spurgeon's sermons."

John was overwhelmed by the expectations that were being required of him. The truth is that he had never hardily applied himself to any task other than a few hours behind a shovel and a broom. "Captain Philippe, I want to make certain I retain what you have outlined thus far. May I restate your requisites back to you?"

"That would be expected. Yes, please do so."

John mentally went over the list in his mind before speaking. "You have complete authority. I'm to be available to you during the whole twenty-four-hour period. I'm responsible for the ship's log and every entry of official comment required for documentation. I am expected to quickly learn the Portuguese language. I am to learn the sail maker trade, as well as thoroughly study the scriptures, so that I properly conduct a Sunday service using Charles Spurgeon's sermons. Is that the sum of my duties?"

Captain Philippe replied with a curt, unrelenting expectation. "Yes, and as you become proficient at these tasks, I have others that you will be given."

"May I ask a question that is off topic?"

"Yes, but make it quick. We need to finish."

John was interested in the missionary aspect that Edward had mentioned, one reason John felt compelled to join the voyage. "Edward mentioned that when we are in ports of call that the crew members would operate in some evangelistic capacity."

"This is true. However, every port has a different need. For instance, when we reach Nigeria, we will off-load medical supplies and other provisions for various missionary endeavors taking place in the surrounding countryside. The work is backbreaking, but we do it from a servant's heart. Is that evangelism? As workers in the field, that Jesus proclaimed as ready unto harvest, yes, of course."

The Captain continued his crisp professional discourse, "In Cape Town, S.A., we will deliver twenty crates of Charles Spurgeon's sermons that will be distributed by the local churches. Many congregations read his sermons over the ensuing months. Laypeople also take them to the bush villages and read them as well. Cape Town is also where we will pick up supplies for ourselves, as well as much needed provisions for the ports of call in India. All of our ports of call will have the Good News ministered in some way.

> *In Cape Town S.A. we will deliver twenty crates of Charles Spurgeon's sermons that will be distributed by the local churches.*

One last thing, before we conclude our first meeting. We have sixteen passengers on this leg of the voyage, so until further notice, do not speak to any passenger unless someone asks for assistance. Typically, I do not repeat myself, but I want to make certain you understand. Do not initiate a conversation with any of our passengers until I give you permission. Have I made myself clear?"

Chapter Thirty-Eight
Corroborating Testimony

True to his word, Chief Birdwell sent his dispatch to the *Anastasis,* but it was not the 'all clear' message that Captain Philippe had expected. "Sir, Chief Birdwell requests your presence at his office to confirm an eyewitness account. We have corroborating testimony that needs to be verified before the chief can release your vessel."

"Officer, that will be near impossible. We need to clear the dock in forty minutes."

"The chief is aware of your departure plans and promises it won't take long if you cooperate. I have a carriage waiting, sir."

After quickly shouting orders to the helmsman and first mate, the captain hurried to the waiting carriage to be whisked off to the precinct headquarters. As promised, the official meeting was brought to order without delay. "Captain Philippe, I was near completion of my inquiry, as we discussed this afternoon when I received a report that shed new light on this matter."

"What is it you need from me, sir?"

"Please repeat your version of what happened this morning, so we may compare your testimony to that of our eyewitness, for the record. I have a stenographer here to record your statements. May we begin?"

"It's quite straightforward really. Knowing that we were only minutes from setting sail, Edward Van Zandt came to the ship at about 0500 hours and requested to see John Taylor, who had just been brought aboard under great duress. Apparently, he was the victim of a murderous conspiracy. Mr. Van Zandt needed information so that he could initiate a search for the perpetrators. After Mr. Van Zandt left the ship, John Taylor convinced me that Mr. Van Zandt was in mortal danger. I mustered my crew and gave orders to prepare for a military action. Within fifteen minutes, we were on the ground and in pursuit of Mr. Van Zandt. We arrived at the warehouse moments before two shots were fired, which cut down Mr. Van Zandt. The shooters were still armed when they turned and leveled their weapons at my men as we entered the building. I gave orders to fire when ready, which resulted in an immediate and simultaneous volley consisting of seven rounds. With the threat to my men neutralized, I turned my attention to Mr. Van Zandt. He had been severely wounded and requested to be taken to his house to attend to his family, and then assisted to his doctor. That about sums it up."

"Are you clear in your mind that is how the events of this morning unfolded? As I mentioned, we have an eyewitness. Please understand, I just want to make certain for the record."

"Chief Birdwell, you may enter my testimony into your record."

Chief Birdwell dismissed all the attendees who were present at the meeting, as well as the stenographer. He wanted to finish the meeting with a private conversation as he had unofficial business to conduct with Captain Philippe.

With a more personal and empathetic tone, the chief spoke with concern, "You'll be free to go in a few minutes. Here is my written authorization that you requested. You may shove off at your discretion. I have a man standing by to escort you back to your ship. Just so you will know, there was a first victim who was shot before you arrived who only received a minor wound. Mr. Boles choose to lay still and feign his death. Consequently, he heard every word that was spoken during the altercation at the warehouse. He was able to recount the exact chain of events as they occurred. I don't see any difficulties with your testimony that I can't resolve.

Secondly, you need to know that I went to cadet school with Bradley Spears. As cadets, we visited his parents several times when we took leave together. I got to know his family quite well; they even called me their second son." Despite Chief Birdwell's tough military conditioning, he needed to pause to hold back his emotions as Bradley came to the forefront of his thoughts. There was an unspoken understanding between the two men as the chief continued, "If the unfortunate situation were ever to present itself, I know that Bradley's parents would appreciate a military burial at sea with full honors. Is that something you could agree to?"

Chapter Thirty-Nine
Ports of Call

The Nineteenth Century British Empire

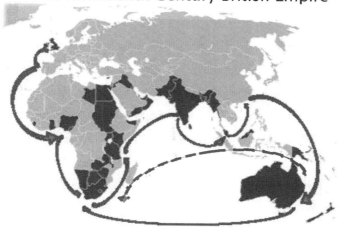

Anastasis Sailing to the Orient
Summer 1865–Fall 1866

Ports of Call: Lisbon, Portugal; Lagos, Nigeria; Cape Town, S.A.; Zanzibar, Tanzania;   Bombay, India; Singapore, Malaysia; Hong Kong, China; Sydney, Australia; Cape Town, S.A.; Lagos, Nigeria; London, England

The *Anastasis* left its moorings at the approximated high spring tide, which allowed the crew to navigate the River Thames out into open waters by nightfall. The timing had been crucial, leaving precious little daylight to clear the last shoal markers that signaled open sea navigation.

The first critical undertaking was to conduct a fitting memorial for Bradley and perform the ceremonial burial of his body at sea. Captain Philippe called his immediate crew together to plan a sunrise interment service that would include a prayer, an honor guard, a eulogy and a seven-gun salute. The final tribute would be the playing of taps at the time Bradley was released into the sea.

At daybreak, one hundred miles out to sea, Bradley Spears' solemn burial was indeed an honorable homage to a courageous and noble man who loved deeply and sacrificially. John delivered Bradley's eulogy reminding everyone of his dying devotion and loyal friendship. He then gave a moving testimony, detailing how Bradley had given his life to save him. John quoted a verse that he had just recently discovered while studying the scriptures: *Greater love hath no man than this that a man lay down his life for his friends.* Bradley's courage and loyalty would continue to be a driving inspiration that John would emulate the remainder of his life.

True to his word, Captain Philippe kept John moving and not one minute was wasted. John prevailed with his duties, studying while eating and refusing to speak English when around the crew. John's other responsibilities, which included making entries in the ship's log, transcribing the captain's remarks, teaching and apprenticing made the days go quickly.

With less than three weeks at sea, the *Anastasis* arrived at its first port of call, Lisbon, Portugal. Ironically, this port was home base for many of the crew, so the ship would remain in port for three days, allowing the crew to be with family. For several of the men, it was the end of a thirteen-month voyage. They would remain ashore as their replacements returned for the new tour. John was only allowed a half-day leave because he had to stay aboard with the sailmaker crew to help make repairs.

The captain was not heartless in his rigorous requirements. He fully intended his strict regimen to condition John, who had never experienced the rigors of hard duty. A military recruit is seasoned through excruciatingly difficult training; not for the sake of harsh treatment, but to save the lad when he faces the brutal reality of combat.

Dr. David Livingstone

Once again at sea, during routine transcription duty, Captain Philippe told John to put his pen down. He had some off-the-record comments to make. "John, Dr. David Livingstone is aboard the ship as a passenger. I want you to spend some time with him."

"With no disrespect intended sir, even considering how great an honor that would be, I don't see how I could possibly arrange to do that."

"John, did you forget that I'm the captain, and I can arrange anything? I will temporarily suspend your duties of keeping the captain's log. Meet me in my quarters for the evening meal, and I will introduce you to Dr. Livingstone. John, just so you will know, Edward knew that David Livingstone would be on board the ship. They are close friends, as well as fellow members of the London Missionary Society."

Captain Philippe wanted to make a personal comment for John to heed, "Tonight, please listen and learn. Dr. Livingstone is a very humble and understated man who does not enjoy bringing attention to himself. Please give him a chance to express what is on his heart. His words will demonstrate his intense love for all people on every continent. Dr. Livingstone is a gift to mankind—allow him to speak into your life."

A I AM ALPHA AND OMEGA, THE BEGINNING AND THE END, THE FIRST AND THE LAST **Ω**

Nigeria was an important port of call for the *Anastasis*. Unfortunately, various European countries were involved in military interventions, endeavoring to control the region and its profitable slave trade, so entering the Gold Coast region was always unnerving for the crew. Any ship, no matter its flag, could expect to be boarded by any one of the European rivals. Nonetheless, a naval flag bearing the Cross of Christ would most often allow missionary ships, as well as legitimate vessels of mercy to come and go without undo threats.

The *Anastasis* would be in Port Lagos for ten days to off-load medical supplies and oversee distribution to various missionary groups. This effort was spearheaded by Dr. Livingstone with the help of the *Anastasis* crew who would assist him. He would also facilitate a medical clinic while in port—an ongoing enterprise when supplies and doctors were available. He had a special burden for the African Gold Coast because this was the epicenter for the international slave trade. He had personally witnessed the barbaric treachery inflicted upon the native population by savage tribes engaged in profiteering from the slave trade.

Port Lagos was also the destination for two male voyagers who would be staying ashore as this was their desired destination from London. One of the disembarking passengers was a missionary returning from furlough. The other was a businessman who was searching for locally produced goods for his business to export. One new passenger boarded for a passage to India.

Once the crew finalized the local missionary outreach, a commercial shipment was taken aboard, bound for delivery to Cape Town, S.A. An immediate sailing schedule was then set, as soon as foodstuffs and other necessary provisions were loaded.

Back on the high seas, Captain Philippe called his crew leaders to a meeting in the galley. "Alright, men, as you know we are entering the shipping lanes that provide us with a high likelihood of a pirate attack. Until we reach Cape Town, we need to be vigilant for the sake of our mission and of course for our passengers' welfare.

> *"Alright, men, as you know we are entering the shipping lanes that provide us with a high likelihood of a pirate attack."*

Our first priority is to increase our watch. I want two men in the lookout, as well as one man on the bow at all times. Additionally, I want every crewmember scanning the horizon. When possible, I will enlist the passengers to assist as well.

We will spend the next two days going through and practicing evasive maneuvers just in case we are spotted and approached by a vessel with dishonorable intentions. We all know that the *Anastasis* can outrun any ship on the high seas. Nevertheless, it is always best if we have sufficient time to plan an escape, so an early sighting is crucial. Our weakness, of course, is that we are unarmed other than our muskets. If, by the way, we are forced to use them, we will go into our usual drill of five firing while five are loading. Does anyone have a question?"

John was a little wide-eyed with the matter-of-fact, business as usual, tone of Captain Philippe's briefing. He had to ask the obvious question, "Sir, what would be my duties if we sight a hostile ship?"

Not intending to dismiss John's naïve question, Captain Philippe answered, "John, you will be rotated through the various lookout stations for the next six weeks. You will have to do your best to keep up with your other responsibilities as well, just like the rest of us."

Fortunately, John had reached the point where he was meeting his duties and obligations, but having his responsibilities doubled seemed overwhelming, if not impossible. "I'll do my best, sir."

"John, I need to have a private discussion with you after we dismiss our meeting." Turning his attention back to the crewmen, Captain Philippe continued with his instructions, "Most of us have been here before, so these drills are nothing new. As usual, we need to work on our communication, as well as the execution of our avoidance maneuvers. We must avoid two main angles of attack; the *broadside* and the *breach*. Again, our best defense is an early warning. Because of our speed, the only way a ship can assault us is to approach us from the bow."

Captain Philippe suddenly felt like he needed to finish quickly. Before he proceeded, he sent his first mate topside to check with the helmsman. Moments later, he heard loud shouts and orders being screamed, followed by a shout down the galley stairwell. "SIR, WE HAVE A COMBATANT NEARING ON THE PORT SIDE... CLOSING IN AT LESS THAN ONE HALF MILE!"

"All hands on deck!"

Captain Philippe quickly ordered a hard starboard tack. Fortunately, the danger was soon over as the *Anastasis* was sailing with the southbound currents while their attackers were navigating against the flow. Immediately, the distance began to increase between the two ships, preventing the possibility of a confrontation.

On its eventual return trip to London, the *Anastasis* would take a northbound course well outside the southbound currents, which followed the coastline. This would prevent an encounter with the pirate ships that prowled the shipping lanes.

Captain Philippe was agitated. "That was too close. We must not let that happen again. Another few minutes and we could have been breached. There is too much at stake. We'll have to do better next time."

Despite the entire crew and passengers being on high alert, the remaining passage to Cape Town was uneventful. There was a collective feeling of relief as the *Anastasis* entered the South African port.

A somewhat arbitrary time frame of two weeks was always scheduled while in Cape Town. The ongoing weather conditions off the Cape were the critical factors in determining the ship's length of stay. Once the vital business at hand was completed, a favorable weather report was needed by an incoming ship captain, which could often take days or weeks. An incoming ship that had just completed navigating the treacherous waters around the tip of the continent could send the *Anastasis* underway within hours.

Five of the original sixteen passengers disembarked at Cape Town. Numerous crates of cargo were off-loaded, including the twenty crates of Spurgeon's sermons. Once the usual provisions were taken aboard, two new passengers needed to be located and given instructions to be available for an immediate pending departure. As always, several canvas bags of letters and parcels were exchanged with postal agents.

David Livingstone was once again feeling at home in this beloved land where he had spent a considerable amount of his life and yet had given up so much. In one of the most difficult trials of his life, his wife, Mary, died of malaria while with him in the jungles. Interestingly, if history had not twisted on itself,

David's hardships and toils, as well as his heavenly rewards would have been wrought in China—an unusual story in itself.

Even though Dr. Livingstone's final destination was Zanzibar on the east coast of Africa, little was seen of him while the *Anastasis* remained docked in Cape Town. He had numerous connections throughout the city, and he wanted to make as many of them as possible.

Dr. Livingstone's liberal absence, as important as his personal obligations were, left Captain Philippe in a management crisis. Since he needed to leave port at a moment's notice, all passengers and crew must be ready to sail at all times. Navigating the notoriously rough seas off the Cape has always been one of the most threatening stretches of the entire voyage, known for sinking numerous ships. The benefit of favorable weather was crucial, if not imperative, so he made the difficult decision to leave without David Livingstone if forced to do so.

Fortunately, Captain Philippe did not have to make that difficult decision. Reminiscent of Noah's timely departure, as if divinely called, David Livingstone showed up the morning Captain Philippe received his much sought after weather dispatch. Within two hours of Dr. Livingstone's mystical appearance, the *Anastasis* pulled away from its moorings and headed into the unbridled wind and waves off the Cape of South Africa.

Even though the ship and crew took a terrible beating from the ferocious and mean-spirited seas, the meticulously maintained *Anastasis,* as well as its skilled crew, were up to the task.

Incredibly, it was not until the ship began heading north along the east coast of Africa that John was able to have his second opportunity to spend meaningful time with Dr. Livingston. The constant watch-vigil for pirates along the west coast, as well as the extra duty required in the rough seas around the Cape, kept John working twenty hours a day. Over the next weeks, Captain Philippe allowed John ample time to listen and learn from one of the greatest missionaries of his era.

One warm evening, the two men met on the port side of the ship to view the distant coastline while sailing toward to Dr. Livingstone's final destination. David, in his low-key way of talking, opened with a bit of trivia. "Did you know the Cape of Good Hope was once called the Cape of Storms? Why they changed its name is a mystery to me—the roughest seas in the world, except the horn of South America, which, thank God, I've never had to endure."

John was content just to listen. However, he also wanted to be a good conversationalist, so he took an opportunity to ask an obvious question of interest. "What are your plans for your return to Tanzania?"

The hard life and difficult years spent in the often-deadly jungles of Africa had taken the edge off the once zealous missionary. Although his tone was matured with a hint of reservation, Livingstone spoke with new enthusiasm and hope. "I intend to finally find the source of the Nile. While in Zanzibar, I will put together a team of assistants, as well as the necessary carriers. We will then head south by riverboat, following the coastline to the mouth of the Ruvuma River, following it inland. This has been my great hope, to find an efficient means of reaching the interior of this vast continent with the Gospel of Christ."

Timidly, John probed, "I hope you don't mind my asking, but why did you give up on your earlier missionary work?"

David had answered that question countless times. Even so, he didn't mind answering John's query. "My young John Taylor, I had the zeal of ten evangelists when I first came to Africa. I was consumed with preaching in the mission field. I gave the best years of my life to it. I later found that I was more suited for and possessed the gifts of ruggedness and solitude, requirements necessary of an explorer; they were in me. I believe that God, in His wisdom, showed me that I should be the one to open up the African interior for others more suited to preach His Gospel. I want to throw the doors wide open for missionaries who follow after me."

John felt very privileged to be speaking with such a great man of accomplishment who held such lofty aspirations. "I was just recently Saved, so I don't know as much as I should about your work. Before we set sail, Edward Van Zandt showed me your new book at his printing office. It looked interesting."

"Did he give you a copy?"

"No, things were happening very fast that day. We didn't have much time to think about it."

"I'll have a book for you when we meet tomorrow."

John wanted to reach deeper for David's wisdom wrought from his experiences. "Edward tells me that he sees me as an evangelist. What are your thoughts on being an effective evangelist."

"I will tell you what I know from my experience and what I have seen in others. My first observation is that you must have an unquenchable burning desire for all lost souls and all races of mankind. You have to know that God loves the natives of the jungle just as much as He loves you or me. Second, the only way you can get that unquenchable desire is to ask God for it... plead with Him for it... and be willing to give your life for it—*you have to want that desire, to see others saved, more than life itself.* Would God trust His multitudes of precious souls to anyone who desired less?"

John understood with his natural ears what Dr. Livingstone was saying, but his heart did not comprehend the depth of its true meaning. "Help me understand. What you are saying has powerful implications, but how can any man do what you say must be done. *Plead with God... so that I may be willing to give my life for a total stranger?* It's not natural. It's seems to me an impossible concept."

"I am certain, if you have been around Edward for very long, you have heard him speak of giving up your life so Christ can live through you—dying to self, so the resurrection power of Christ can raise you up to do things that no human can do in their own strength. Does that sound familiar?"

"Yes, sir, it does, very familiar."

"John, Acts 17:28 tells us that *...for in Him we live, and move, and have our being....* Jesus Christ, is the only One who can love a wretched man or woman enough to give His life to save them. When we are in total surrender to Him, He will give us His gift of unconditional love for others. What is impossible with man, God can accomplish if we yield ourselves to Him and let Him live through us."

"So, I can just pray and ask God to give me His love for others?"

"It can be that simple if your heart is pure and yielded—for God looks on the heart and not necessarily what comes across our lips. Most men that I know, myself included, have to wrestle with God, not to talk Him into His blessings, but to wrestle ourselves out of a polluted heart and an impure motive. Once God knows He can trust you, He will write His desires on your heart as a gift—these are the treasures of His Kingdom.

"John, God's treasures are eternal and holy. The scriptures plainly state that He will have no part with darkness. He will wait for you to really mean business, choosing to be set apart. The unquenchable burning desire in one's heart for the lost is very near and dear to God's heart."

John was getting it. He just needed to search his heart and begin his quest to acquire God's love for the lost—to see people through God's eyes and love those who don't know Him. "I know what I need to do; thank you. You have been a great help."

"One last thing, John. He will test you from time to time to let you know that faithfulness is His measure for promotion, as well as a prerequisite for greater responsibility. Jesus said: *Those who are faithful in small things will be given charge over much."*

"Yes, sir, I'll remember that. Do you mind meeting out here tomorrow if the captain will allow it?"

"John, I look forward to it... I'll have your book tomorrow."

The *Anastasis* made its Zanzibar port of call, leaving Dr. David Livingston to make his mark on history. While in port for only twenty-four hours, provisions were loaded, and four new passengers boarded for passage to Bombay, India, as well as two travelers whose final destination was Hong Kong, China.

Bombay, India was one of the busiest ports in the world with massive amounts of goods received from and shipped to the corners of four continents. The harbor in Bombay was so congested, the last few miles of travel to the pier would often take days of uncivilized navigation just to dock, a chaotic free-for-all of sorts. However, once the various passengers and cargo were loaded and unloaded, the trip out to sea was much less arduous. The *Anastasis* was soon underway to Singapore, the dominant port city of Malaysia.

Singapore was known as the melting pot of the Middle East and the Far East, and was of special interest to Captain Philippe. He had chosen this picturesque and burgeoning city as his home. Consequently, the stay at this port of call would be the longest of the voyage, lasting three weeks. The men were given rotating shore leave with duties aboard ship carried on by the men who remained. In the meantime, Captain Philippe spent the majority of his time with his family, making bi-weekly visits to the ship to check on the crew.

Chapter Forty
The Evangelist

The *Anastasis* set sail for the next port of call with its largest contingent of passengers aboard, all bound for Hong Kong, the apex of the ship's thirteen-month voyage. Hong Kong was the busiest port in the Pacific and a major reason the *Anastasis* was in the employment of Spurgeon's China Mission.

Navigating the harbor river was in some ways reminiscent of piloting the River Thames in London. As the ship made its way upriver toward the business district, a months-long change was evident in John. He had taken David Livingstone's exhortation to heart, desperately praying that God would give him a burning passion for lost souls. His anticipation was ripe as the ship pulled up to its moorings for a weeklong stay.

Ten thousand Bibles were in the ship's cargo holds destined for the major population centers where the common Mandarin dialect was dominant. Since Spurgeon's China Mission's main headquarters was located five miles inland from the downtown district of Hong Kong, portage had to be arranged for the movement of one hundred small wooden crates of Bibles.

One of the passengers who boarded in Cape Town, S.A., was twenty-six-year-old Jack McDevitt, a missionary associated with the London Missionary Society, who was assigned to work with Spurgeon's efforts in China. He would be in charge of facilitating the Spurgeon's China Mission objectives, as well as the orderly and proper dissemination of the Mandarin Bibles. Great effort and cost were invested, so care was taken to make sure the Bibles did not fall into the wrong hands and possibly destroyed.

Α I AM ALPHA AND OMEGA, THE BEGINNING AND THE END, THE FIRST AND THE LAST. Ω

During the time John Taylor was having his regular evening talks with David Livingstone, he was introduced to Jack McDevitt, who had come aboard the ship in Cape Town. Once Livingstone disembarked in Zanzibar, John's evening talks continued unabated with his new friend, Jack. About the same age, the two men quickly became very close as co-laborers with a common zeal for the mission field—a passion set ablaze in John's heart by David Livingstone.

As a young man in his teens, Jack McDevitt felt a call on his life to the mission field. Shortly after Jack's salvation, he and his father were in church, where they heard a message describing the great need in China for missionaries. On the way home from church that day, Jack sought his father's counsel about allowing him to go to China as a missionary. His family was deeply spiritual, so they prayed about Jack's growing desire to see if God would give direction.

While waiting to hear God for a clear direction, Jack's family pulled together and saved enough money for him to begin attending Anderson College in Glasgow, England. His whole focus in college was to go to China as a missionary. Learning the Mandarin language was the most difficult task required of him, as he excelled in his other studies. While in his senior year, Jack applied to the London Missionary Society (L.M.S).

By the time Jack completed his studies, he was fluent in China's most common dialect, placing him as the foremost candidate for selection to be sent to China to represent L.M.S. Jack was accepted with the full support of the London Missionary Society in the spring of 1865.

Interestingly, just months before Jack's acceptance, representatives from Charles Spurgeon's China Mission met with L.M.S. to form a joint venture for a major outreach into mainland China and the region. Jack would be their man to spearhead the effort. He was sent to Cape Town, South Africa, for six months of intensive training led by an L.M.S. affiliate with extensive experience in preparing missionaries bound for China. At the end of his training, Jack was to board an incoming clipper ship named the *Anastasis* that was due to make its Cape Town port of call in late November.

Jack was immediately drawn to John Taylor, who preached the Sunday sermons aboard the *Anastasis*. He noticed in John an exceptional ability to understand the spiritual applications of scripture verses that most people might see as vague or ambiguous. In the almost three months of traveling aboard the ship, while listening to John preach, Jack had numerous scriptures opened up to him with certain clarity.

> *Jack noticed in John an exceptional ability to understand the spiritual applications of scripture verses that most people might see as vague or ambiguous*

By the time the *Anastasis* entered the Hong Kong harbor, John Taylor and Jack McDevitt were close brothers-in-Christ, akin to the biblical account of Jonathan and David's bond of loyalty. As the ship slowly and quietly slipped along the ever-narrowing river channel toward the Hong Kong docks, Jack invited John to join him ashore to meet his indigenous L.M.S. associates. "John, I have given this a lot of thought. I would like you to join me ashore as I meet the local L.M.S. staff for the first time. Once I arrange transport for the Bibles, we can go to the Spurgeon's headquarters where I will introduce myself and lay out the plans for the joint venture with L.M.S."

John knew he had obligations that would keep him busy for several hours once the ship docked. "I will have to arrange my absence with the captain, and that can't take place until we are securely docked. He's very busy until then."

"Fair enough. I'll go ashore to make arrangements for overland delivery of the Bibles and then return to pick you up before I head over to the L.M.S. offices."

John quickly calculated the time needed to secure the ship. "Let's plan on a two-hour timeframe for meeting back at the gangway. I'll know then if I can go with you."

The two-hour arrangement to reunite back at the ship went perfectly. John was ready and waiting. While gone, Jack had more time to think. He had a new twist to his earlier idea of meeting with his staff. "John, I have a great idea. Once we meet the L.M.S. staff, we will all go over to the Spurgeon Headquarters and meet as a united group. Once I finish discussing the joint effort, I would like for you speak to the assembled staff—bring us a Word from the Lord—something that might launch our endeavor to reach the region with the Gospel. Of course, I can certainly translate into Mandarin as needed."

John immediately knew the topic of his talk. He would give the same exhortation that he received from David Livingstone about asking God for a deeper desire for lost souls. "I would be happy to talk with the group; I'm ready right now."

Following Edward Van Zandt's directions, relayed to him by Captain Philippe, John had been faithful to diligently study the scriptural basis and underpinnings for Spurgeon's sermons. After months of preaching to the ship's crew and passengers, John began to develop his own style of delivering the revelation given to him as he studied. Week after week, he became more aware of God's power to open up the revelatory significance of what he was reading. Soon he was only using Spurgeon's sermons as a starting point for his own deep plunge into God's Word.

John and Jack arrived at the headquarters where most of the two organizations' workers knew each other from previous overlapping projects. The group warmly and enthusiastically received the newest joint outreach between L.M.S. and Spurgeon's China Missions.

Standing with his feet firmly planted in the vast mission field of China, John's spirit was ignited with a burning desire to see every kindred, tongue and nation reached for God's Kingdom. The impassioned assertions that David Livingstone had expressed to John months ago were spoken with such clarity that many in attendance began to weep. God had touched their hearts. After an extended time of intentional worship, borne out of a revelation of God's desire for His lost people, many repented, for their hearts had grown cold.

Afterward, the workers approached Jack with a plea to invite their families and friends to hear John speak. Jack had no choice but to ask John to preach the next afternoon and evening. The following day, a crowd of thirty gathered at three o'clock anxious to hear the powerful teaching that John brought to the people. Each night the crowd doubled. On the evening before John was scheduled to leave the country, over five hundred souls had gathered to hear him speak.

The next morning the *Anastasis* crew was especially busy, tending to the last details of preparing the ship for sea. The expected departure was around 1530 hours in the mid-afternoon, according to the estimate of high tide. Jack was on the pier to send off his new best friend, knowing it may be years before they would see each other again, if ever. Jack spoke his gratitude to John for his intense desire to preach God's uncompromising Word with such powerful revelation. "John, do you realize that God's gift to you, the ability to unwrap and reveal the truth of His Word, was the subject of Jesus' affirmation to Peter in Matthew 16:19? Jesus proclaimed to Peter that it was the unveiling of God's Word, by the Holy Spirit, that would be the foundation upon which He would build His church. Jesus told Peter:

...upon this rock (the revealed understanding of who I am) I will build my church... And I will give unto thee the keys of the kingdom of heaven...

John, I believe, according to scripture, God has entrusted you with the *keys of the kingdom of heaven.* You have been a tremendous blessing to me and I am eternally grateful for you. God has given you a special calling... go with Godspeed, my friend."

After Jack had finished his last words of encouragement, John turned to walk up the gangplank to the ship's main deck. To everyone's surprise, the harbor authorities, including ten armed troops, closed in from three directions. Speaking in Cantonese, the uniformed officers were yelling, waving their weapons and motioning for the *Anastasis* crew to lie prone on the ship's deck. Captain Philippe came running down the gangway, but was unable to communicate, as he knew little Cantonese. As he stepped in to intervene, the lead Harbor Patrol Officer fired his weapon just over the heads of all who remained standing.

Captain Philippe refused to be intimidated as he once again attempted to address the lead officer. By all governing laws, local, as well as international, Captain Philippe would be the superior officer and have jurisdiction, especially in a British

Colony. It didn't seem to matter in this case as the rifle-bearing troops closed in, tightening their circle to subdue John and Captain Philippe. In a gallant attempt, Captain Philippe tried to reason with the overly hostile forces only to receive a rifle butt to his face.

To be continued in Volume Three

The
Crucible
for John Francis Taylor

Other Books by David E. McFadden

—Volume One—

The Journals
of John Francis Taylor

The Premiere Edition of the
His Story Chronicles

www.DeeperLifeSeries.com

Being Transformed
from Glory to Glory

How to walk in God's Plan for Wholeness

A primer designed to help you grow in your Christian walk. Scriptures, anecdotes, diagrams and more are presented in simple terms to help you be transformed into the image of Christ.

www.DeeperLifeSeries.com

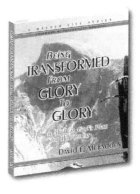

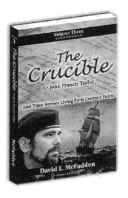

—Volume Three—

The Crucible
for John Francis Taylor

Grace Chloe Wheaton continues telling the story of her family legacy in Christ. John Taylor experiences the trials of life that tests his faith to make it rock solid.

Taylor – Wheaton Heritage
1923- 1965

Continued from front inside cover

1924	Chloe Wheaton born – Papa Wheaton's second-born daughter
1927	Charles Lindbergh flies "Spirit of St. Louis" – John Jr. decides he will someday be a pilot and fly aero- planes.
1929	John Francis Wheaton dies (John Jr.'s grandpa).
1932	The great harvest miracle brings renewal in Clearwater Springs. Chloe goes to the circus.
1933	The miracle of Christmas – *The Angel and Anna.* Chloe dies from diphtheria.
1940	John Wheaton Jr. marries Elizabeth.
1941	John Wheaton Jr. enlists in the air force. Elizabeth stays stateside in San Diego.
1942	Papa Wheaton dies.
1945	Paiyan's family escapes big island - 3 weeks later arrive at new home on deserted and uncharted island
1946 pilot.	John Wheaton Jr. re-enlists and becomes a career Accidental tractor-drop over Pacific.
1947	John Wheaton Jr. decommissioned – wife leaves him.
1948	John Wheaton Jr. reassigned to Europe and becomes interested in and uncovers his family lineage.
1950	John Jr.'s wife, Elizabeth, repents and becomes radically saved, but does not seek out her husband.
1951	Elizabeth moves to Seattle from San Diego.
1956	John Jr. contacted by Joey about uncharted island with cornfields. Request temporary reassignment to survey the island.
1957	Discovers Paiyan to be great-uncle.
1961	Retires from military to become full-time missionary to the Pacific islands near Paiyan's island
1962	John Jr. visits the church in Seattle, Washington to raise funds for missionary work. He reacquaints with Elizabeth and renews marriage vows. She joins John on the mission field.
1963	Grace Chloe Wheaton born
1965	Francis "Paul" Wheaton born.
⇩	
1987	Grace and Paiyan discover Sir John's journals and begin writing the *His Story* chronicles

The *His Story* chronicle begins here in the premiere edition: *The Journals*

Made in the USA
San Bernardino, CA
13 March 2016